The Anomie of the Earth

The Anomie of the Earth Philosophy, Politics, and Autonomy in Europe and the Americas

FEDERICO LUISETTI, JOHN PICKLES & WILSON KAISER, EDS.

FOREWORD BY Walter D. Mignolo   AFTERWORD BY Sandro Mezzadra

Duke University Press   Durham and London   2015

Library of Congress Cataloging-in-Publication Data
The anomie of the earth : philosophy, politics, and autonomy in Europe and the Americas /
Federico Luisetti, John Pickles, and Wilson Kaiser, eds. ; foreword by Walter Mignolo.
Afterword by Sandro Mezzadra.
pages cm
Includes bibliographical references and index.
ISBN 978-0-8223-5921-0 (hardcover : alk. paper)
ISBN 978-0-8223-5893-0 (pbk. : alk. paper)
1. Geopolitics—Europe. 2. Geopolitics—America. 3. Political anthropology—Europe.
4. Political anthropology—America. I. Luisetti, Federico, 1969–
II. Pickles, John, 1952– III. Kaiser, Wilson, 1978–
JC319.A566 2015
306.2094–dc23
2014045004
ISBN 978-0-8223-7545-6 (e-book)

Cover art: Leyla Cárdenas, *Recollection 69–10*, 2012. Peeled paint, pins. © Leyla Cárdenas,
courtesy of Galería Casas Riegner.

Anomie, Resurgences, and De-Noming

WALTER D. MIGNOLO

NOMOS (*noun*)

1. a law, convention, or custom governing human conduct
2. (Greek mythology) the daemon of laws and ordinance

    —*Collins English Dictionary* (2011)

NOMIC

Customary; ordinary;—applied to the usual English spelling, in distinction from strictly phonetic methods.

—*Webster's Revised Unabridged Dictionary* (1913)

ANOMIE OR ANOMY (*n.*)

1. Social instability caused by erosion of standards and values.
2. Alienation and purposelessness experienced by a person or a class as a result of a lack of standards, values, or ideals: *"We must now brace ourselves for disquisitions on peer pressure, adolescent anomie and rage"* (Charles Krauthammer).

    —*American Heritage Dictionary of the English Language* (2000)

RESURGENCE (*n.*)

1. A continuing after interruption; a renewal.
2. A restoration to use, acceptance, activity, or vigor; a revival.

    —*The Free Dictionary online*

Global Linear Thinking and the Second Nomos of the Earth

This book is intended to confront Carl Schmitt's *nomos of the earth* and, as the editors put it in their introduction, "documents the antagonistic forms of autonomy that are moving away from the Western coordinates of the planetary nomos." This is indeed one of the crucial aspects of our time that will, no doubt, dominate the twenty-first century. My endorsement of the general and particular argument hereby put forward highlights the phenomena compressed in the expression "anomie and resurgences."

To properly understand the global dimension of this shift, of which of course the processes in Latin America documented here are paramount, it would be helpful to understand Schmitt's *trick*.[1] The nomos addressed in this book is indeed Schmitt's *second nomos*. Which means, obviously, that for him there was a *first nomos*. The first nomos was a plurality of them. Before 1500, following Schmitt's chronology but somehow adding to his conception of the first nomos, every socio-cultural-economic configuration (that today we name *civilization*)—ancient China, India, Persia, the Kingdoms of Africa, Mayas, Incas, and Aztecs—had its own nomos. Given the scope of this book, let's concentrate on the nomos of ancient civilizations, of what became known as "America," the fourth continent.

The emergence of the fourth continent, America, in the consciousness of European men of letters is a landmark of Schmitt's second nomos: "The *first nomos* of the earth was destroyed about 500 years ago, when the great oceans of the world were opened up. The earth was circumnavigated; America, a completely new, unknown, not even suspected continent was discovered."[2]

Notice the relevance for the issues at hand in this book: "America, a completely new, unknown, not even suspected continent was discovered." The statement is proverbial: America was not known to many people but for different reasons. Europeans had an idea of the world divided into Asia, Africa, and Europe. Mayas, Aztecs, and Incas did not know that America existed because it was invented as such around 1504. What they knew was Tawantinsuyu, Anahuac, and Yóok'ol kaab. At that point in history, what is today Europe was Western Christendom and it was part of the first nomos. The second nomos of the earth emerged, then, when a group of *indigenous* people of Western Christendom/Europe bumped into the land of *indigenous* people of Ayiti (the indigenous name of the Island that was renamed Dominica by the Spaniards and Saint Domingue by the French). Bottom line of this paragraph: at the moment of what Europeans call "the discovery of America" and more recently Latin American philosophers of history rebaptized "the invention of America," everyone on planet Earth was living under what Schmitt described as the first nomos.

So the second nomos inaugurates a planetary European narrative, a narrative that became hegemonic and was consolidated by Hegel's lesson in the philosophy of history delivered some time between 1822 and 1830. Schmitt is rehearsing such a narrative and connecting it with international law (jus publicum Europaeum). That is to say that the "discovery" that inaugurated the second nomos inaugurated at the same time the legal and symbolic European appropriation of the planet. The first nomos in Schmitt's narrative vanished, absorbed in the growing Eurocentric narrative:

> A *second nomos* of the earth arose from such discoveries of land and sea. The discoveries were not invited. They were made without visas issued by the discovered peoples. The discoverers were Europeans, who appropriated, divided and utilized the planet. Thus, the second *nomos* of the earth became Eurocentric. The newly discovered continent of America first was utilized in the form of colonies. The Asian landmasses could not be appropriated in the same way. The Eurocentric structure of *nomos* extended only partially, as open land-appropriation, and otherwise in the form of protectorates, leases, trade agreements and spheres of interest; in short, in more elastic form of utilization. Only in the 19th century did the land-appropriating European powers divide up Africa.[3]

Let's parse this sentence, in the old discourse analysis way. The first line is revealing: the second nomos is a European invention. The next two lines, good point: Schmitt, who was very insightful, realized that the second nomos came out of invasion. The following line reveals the same blindness as his uses of "discovery": land appropriation is also land dispossession. Schmitt is operating on the blind spot: what was not known to Europeans was supposed to be unknown to everybody else, including the people inhabiting the land Europeans did not know. Second, Schmitt is already a victim of the idea that what Europeans appropriated were empty lands. For that reason he doesn't see that dispossession, legalized-theological dispossession that started with the (in)famous *Requirement*.[4]

Then came Asia. Neither Russia nor China were dispossessed. They were disrupted but not colonized like India after Aztecs, Mayas, and Incas. After 1884 Africa was possessed by European states. All that is the work of the second nomos. But what happened to the first nomos? Schmitt is already into the magic effect of linear time and he thinks of the first nomos as one, not as many. It is obvious that the nomos of Incas and Aztecs, of Russians and Chinese, of Indians and Africans was not one. But by making them one, Schmitt operates on the already established idea of one linear time, the linear time of European history as narrated by Europeans.

Schmitt's trick consists in this: when the second nomos of the earth materialized what happened to the diversity of the first nomos? It became one, all the planet belonged to the *first only nomos* on top of which the second nomos mounted and continued the supposed unilinearity of the first nomos.

Because the multiplicity of *first nomoi* was never superseded by the second nomos today we are witnessing their resurgence all over the planet. What this book is bringing forward is the variegated resurgence in South America, particularly in the Andes (Bolivia and Ecuador), and the South of Mexico (the Zapatistas).

Resurgences of Plural First Nomoi of the Earth

The first nomoi of the earth were many. Schmitt's trick consisted in two moves. The first was to cast the plurality of cultures and civilizations in terms of nomos and to see them as precursors to his idea of the second nomos. For we shall be clear that there is no ontological first and second nomos. Both were the result of Schmitt's powerful fictional narrative. The second move consisted in converting the plurality of first nomoi into a singular one and to place it *before* the second nomos. But by so doing he reinforced that idea that emerged in the eighteenth century: the idea of the *primitives* that in the unilinear unfolding of history were the precursors of the *modern*. This powerful fiction is cracking in its foundations and the signs are already seen in the awakening and resurgence of the overwhelming majority of people who have been placed beyond the lines of the second nomos and its internal family feuds (e.g., Western Hemisphere, South of Europe). But let's stay within the boundaries of the Western Hemisphere.[5]

Often and increasingly Pueblos Originarios (ab-originals, natives, Indigenous people) are reported as heroes of resistance against corporations. *Avatar* became an emblem of it. A group of Shuar people, from the Ecuadorian Amazon, went to Quito, in three buses, to watch *Avatar*. It was reported after the movie that they all recognized that it is their story and their history.[6] However, seldom were any of their thinkers, intellectuals, scholars, and activists quoted. White intelligentsia still holds the privilege of controlling the word. Let's hear a couple of them, Native Americans to start with. It would be helpful to get the general picture to start with this two-minute video of Richard Twiss, Lakota American: "Richard Twiss: A Theology of Manifest Destiny."[7]

George Tinker, Native American theologian of liberation, tells an interesting story to start his brilliant argument under the title *Spirit and Resis-*

tance: Political Theology and American Indian Liberation.[8] The story is a sort of *Requerimiento* reframed. It took place in 1803, almost four hundred years after the original. The rhetoric of modernity has changed, and so the logic of coloniality. It was no longer God's design in the pens of Spaniards that guided the *Requerimiento* but God's design in the pens of Anglo-Americans that proclaimed Manifest Destiny in the name of nation-state:

> In 1803 the United States purchased the entirety of Osage land—from France. It had to do with something called the Louisiana Purchase and something having to do with some obscure European legal doctrine called "the right of discovery." What it ever had to do with Osage people, who were never privy to this doctrine or included in the negotiation leading to the purchase, is still a mystery. It was nevertheless a powerful intellectual idea, mere words that, in a sense, enabled Mr. Jefferson to double the size of his country overnight.[9]

Osage were never invited to participate in the negotiation. This is an "oversight" not just of the predators but of the defenders as well. Bartolomé de las Casas, who vehemently protested the *Requerimiento* and put all his energy in defense of "the Indians," never had the delicacy to invite "Indians" to help set up his arguments. In both cases, there was a business among white men (theologians defending just war and theologians defending the Indians and promoting conversion in the first case; and between French and American men in the second).

Tinker's narrative and argument is a consequence of the first internal scramble, among Western states, for the control of the second nomos of the earth: the Monroe Doctrine and the idea of the Western Hemisphere put a halt to the initial European imperial impulse of possession and dispossession. The Western Hemisphere placed an imaginary line in the Atlantic claiming the rights of Americans to the lands of the Western Hemisphere. Needless to say, "American" meant the United States of America. Explicit demand for auto-nomos of the Western Hemisphere established also a nonexplicit line demarcating the North of the Western Hemisphere from the South (Central America, including Mexico, the Caribbean, and South America). A demarcation in the Americas that was already established in Europe: when France and England took over Spain and Portugal in planetary land and sea, and Germany took over the intellectual legacies of the Italian Renaissance, the "South of Europe" was a dominating symbolic construction that made possible the control of the second nomos of the earth. Thus, in the Americas, the struggle to recover the land is common to all (Pueblos Originarios/Native Americans/First Nations) but the arguments and the specific claims are tied up to the specific local histories of which particular European imperial state (e.g., Spain, Portugal, France, England, Holland) shaped the land's destiny. That struggle has a name today: resurgence.

De-Noming of the Earth: Resurgences and Border Thinking

We shall give Schmitt the credit he deserves, that of honestly mapping the second nomos of the earth and explaining how crucial was and is international law in establishing, transforming, and maintaining it. The Western Hemisphere was the first scramble among peers; the partition of Africa at the Berlin Conference of 1884 the second: all that was within the boundaries of re-noming and accommodating new players within the same family.

The book you have in your hands abounds in arguments that explain the re-noming: the appropriation and expropriation of land by international corporations with the cooperation of nation-states in South and Central America. Today, the politics of states re-noming moves in two directions. The purely financial and economic interests take precedence over any possible social consideration. This is the politics of the Alianza Pacifico (Chile, Peru, Colombia, and Mexico). The second is the social taking precedence over the economic. This is the politics of the Union of South American Nations (UNASUR) (Brazil, Venezuela, Ecuador, Bolivia, Argentina, Uruguay, Nicaragua). But we shall not be mistaken and confuse the two trajectories of re-noming with that of de-noming. De-noming is the general project of Indigenous political organizations. The difference is radical: while both Alianza Pacifico and UNASUR do not question the politics of economic growth and development, Indigenous projects go to the root of the second nomos of the earth: territoriality is a living space where life is regenerated (and not of course, reproduced, which is the concept that defines the economy of accumulation). In order to regenerate, the basic philosophical principle of any of the many first nomoi of the earth (that is, the nomos before the second nomos established regulations for appropriation, expropriation, and exploitation) was based on life regeneration.

De-noming names the processes of erasing the regulation of the second nomos. The task is long and difficult; difficult because the second nomos can neither be avoided nor erased. It has to be overcome. And overcoming needs knowledge and arguments. But not knowledge that unfolds from the very institutions that were created by actors and institutions that established and maintained the second nomos. Although such knowledge and arguments are important and help in understanding the deadly consequences of the second nomos, the deadly consequences cannot be overcome by means of the same principles that established them, even if such projects are defended by well-meant actors. Amartya Sen's *Development and Freedom* (1998) could be one such example.

De-noming demands the resurgence of knowledges and forms of life, and knowledges that emerge from forms of life who do not build themselves on the ideological principle of "change" and "progress," for "change" is the consequence of the unfolding of life. Nothing remains as is. However, the civilization that was built upon the foundations of the second nomos (e.g., Western civilization) capitalized in "newness" (e.g., the New World) and "change" (progress, development). The ideology is clear upon close inspection: if you "control" change and progress you control the destiny of a civilization, and you hide and repress the fact that "change" always happens whether you want it to or not.

De-noming and resurgences are ethical and political building-processes to supersede and delink from the tyranny of the second nomos. This vision is extremely clear already and also provides the energy, the joy, the enthusiasm, and the motivations of all Pueblos Originarios, Native Americans, First Nations, and Ab-Originals from the Americas to New Zealand and Australia, from Asia to Africa. However, since this book concentrates on the Americas (and the Caribbean) I close this foreword with the voice and insights of Leanne Simpson.

Dancing on Our Turtle's Back: Stories of Nishnaabeg Re-Creation, Resurgence and New Emergence,[10] addresses many of the issues in this book, particularly the contributions focusing on de-noming in the Andes and Southern Mexico/Guatemala. Difficult to resist the temptation of devoting four or five pages to underscore some of the crucial points Simpson is making. I will restrain myself to a few paragraphs, and then I will tell you shortly why these paragraphs.

The paragraphs are extracted from two chapters: "Nishnaabeg's Resurgence: Stories from Within," and "Theorizing Resurgence from within Nishnaabeg Thought" (34–35) and reads as follows:

1) Building diverse, nation-culture-based resurgences means significantly reinvesting in our own ways of being, regenerating our political

and intellectual traditions; articulating and living out legal systems, language learning, ceremonial and spiritual pursuits; creating and using our artistic and performance-based traditions. All of this requires—as individuals and collectives—to diagnose, interrogate and eviscerate the insidious nature of conquest, empire, and imperial thought in every aspect of our lives.[11]

2) Western theory, whether based in post-colonial, critical or even liberation strains of thought, has been exceptional in diagnosing, revealing and even interrogating colonialism. . . . Yet western theories of liberation have for the most part failed to resonate with the vast majority of Indigenous People, scholars or artists. In particular, western-based social movement theory has failed to recognize the broader contextualization of resistance within Indigenous thought, while also ignoring the contestation of colonialism as a starting point. . . . Indigenous thought has the ability to resonate with Indigenous Peoples of all ages. It maps a way out of colonial thinking by confirming Indigenous life-ways or alternative ways of being in the world.[12]

3) Cree scholar, poet and visual artist Neal McLeod has written extensively about the importance of storytelling, . . . Neal writes that the process of storytelling within Cree traditions requires storytellers to remember the ancient stories that made their ancestors "the people they were," and that this requires a remembering of language. He also emphasizes that storytellers have a responsibility to the future to imagine a social space that is just and where Cree narratives will flourish. Storytelling is at its core decolonizing, because it is a process of remembering, visioning and creating a just reality where Nishnaabeg live as both *Nishnaabeg* and *peoples*. Storytelling then becomes a lens through which we can envision our way out of cognitive imperialism, where we can create models and mirrors where none existed, and where we can experience the spaces of freedom and justice. Storytelling becomes a space where we can escape the gaze and the cage of the Empire, even if it is just for a few minutes.[13]

As far as the second nomos of the earth caged regions and people with the foundations of global lines and global linear thinking through its process, the second nomos was not only legal regulations and justification of boundaries and legitimization of economic expropriation and dispossession but, above and foremost, the creation of arrogant subjectivities and colonial subjects. Colonial subjects had to endure arrogance, and it was a long process until the global veil began to be removed. Leanne Simpson's quoted paragraphs give you an idea of what de-noming means and that it starts from the decoloniality of being. Decoloniality of being, like Freedom, cannot be *given* but has to be *taken*. And de-noming and decolonizing being is not a question of public policies and brilliant theories but is a question of reemerging form of knowledges and sensibilities, knowing and sensing. However, reemergences are not promises of "return" to the "authentic" and "primal" paradise before the second nomos arrived. Re-emergence means to deal with the second nomos out of the ruins and energies that the second nomos attempted to subdue, supersede, and destroy. But it couldn't. Today first nomoi of the earth, in their planetary diversity, are re-emerging in confrontation with the second nomos. Border thinking and doing is implied in re-emerging and resurging because of the sheer fact that de-noming processes have to walk over the ruins of the second nomos. Directly and indirectly, this book documents diverse processes of resurgence and re-existence.

NOTES

1. I unfolded this argument in chapters 2 and 3 of *The Darker Side of Western Modernity: Global Futures, Decolonial Options* (Durham, NC: Duke University Press, 2011).

2. Carl Schmitt, *The Nomos of the Earth in the International Law of the Jus Publicum Europaeum*. Trans. G. L. Ulmen (New York: Telos Press, 2003).

3. Schmitt, *Nomos*, 352.

4. See López de Palacios Rubios, Juan, *El Requerimiento*, 1513. Accessed Oct. 15, 2014. www.encyclopediavirginia.org/El_Requerimiento_by_Juan_Lopez_de_Palacios_Rubios_1513.

5. For more details on the idea of the Western Hemisphere in relation to this argument, see Walter D. Mignolo, "Coloniality at Large: The Western Hemisphere in the Colonial Horizon of Modernity," *New Centennial Review* (2001), http://muse.jhu.edu/journals/ncr/summary/v001/1.2mignolo.html.

6. See Alexander Zaitchik, "To get the gold, they will have to kill every one of us," *Salon*, February 10, 2013. Accessed October 15, 2014. www.salon.com/2013/02/10/to_get_the_gold_they_will_have_to_kill_every_one_of_us/.

7. Richard Twiss, "Richard Twiss: A Theology of Manifest Destiny," YouTube video, posted by Wicon International, March 7, 2008. Accessed October 15, 2014. www.youtube.com/watch?v=4mEkMy1KNWo.

8. George Tinker, *Spirit and Resistance: Political Theology and American Indian Liberation* (Minneapolis, MN: Fortress Press, 2004).

9. Tinker, *Spirit and Resistance*, ix.

10. Leanne Simpson, *Dancing on Our Turtle's Back: Stories of Nishnaabeg Re-creation, Resurgence and New Emergence* (Winnipeg: Arbeiter Ring, 2011).

11. Simpson, *Dancing on Our Turtle's Back*, 17–18.

12. Simpson, *Dancing on Our Turtle's Back*, 31–32.

13. Simpson, *Dancing on Our Turtle's Back*, 34–35, citing Neal McLeod, *Cree Narrative Memory: From Treaties to Contemporary Times* (Saskatoon, Canada: Purich, 2009).

Autonomy Political Theory/Political Anthropology

FEDERICO LUISETTI, JOHN PICKLES, & WILSON KAISER

The traditional Eurocentric order of international law is foundering today, as is the old *nomos* of the earth. —CARL SCHMITT, *The Nomos of the Earth* (1950)

This book puts in dialogue two of the most intriguing trends in social and political theory: Italian autonomism and Latin American decolonial thinking. In the United States, the emergence of the antiglobalization movement in the 1990s and the publication of Michael Hardt and Antonio Negri's *Empire* in 2000 had brought increasing attention to Italian autonomism—arguably one of the most innovative post–1968 radical movements and theoretical paradigms in the West. On the southern border, in the meantime, decolonial thinking, theorized by the likes of Aníbal Quijano and Walter Mignolo, was starting to yield its fruits, connecting its agenda with the indigenous movements that swept the political landscape in Mexico and Colombia, Ecuador, and Bolivia. This book brings together scholars working in the two fields in order to highlight the historical conversations and growing number of convergences between conceptions of autonomy emanating from both European social movements and decolonial movements in the Americas.

The book explores in particular the ways in which poststructuralist and neo-Marxist autonomist theories, which were originally articulated in the context of a critique of Western capitalist modes of production and labor, have in recent years been engaged and broadened by debates emerging from biopolitics and political anthropology in Europe, and from indigenous and postcolonial studies in the Americas. The main goal of this collection of essays is thus to address the notion of autonomy from the double perspective of antagonistic voices within mature capitalistic societies and postcolonial theorists who have questioned Western modernity's balance of individual autonomy (freedom) and the institutional order of the nation-state (the law).

Of central concern to many essays in the book is the geophilosophical concept of the nomos formulated by Carl Schmitt in *The Nomos of the Earth in the International Law of the Jus Publicum Europaeum* (1950).[1] The common meaning of *nomos* as "law" derives for Schmitt from a broader, "spatially conceived" dimension: *nomos* is "the Greek word for the first measurement from which all other measurements are derived, the word for the first taking of the land, for the first partition and division of space, for primitive partition and distribution."[2] The periodizing, phenomenological category of the nomos allows Schmitt to sketch out a topological description of the primitive law that founds the political order, providing a picture of the prepolitical, concrete spatial dynamics operating through mechanisms of land and sea appropriation. Since there is no law without land, the political space is always sustained by geohistorical practices of order and localization (*Ordnung-Ortung*), as demonstrated by the triple meaning of the verb *nemein*, from which *nomos* derives: to take/conquer, to partition/divide, and to cultivate/produce.[3] According to Fredric Jameson, Schmitt's *nomos* indicates, at the same time, an innovative "spatial analysis, which, combining juridical and geographical reference, transcends both"; a "phenomenological spatiality . . . as regressive as Heidegger's ontology"; and "a kind of equivalent of the function of the 'mode of production' for Marxism; that is, it names a structure of totality that has taken various historical forms."[4]

In *The Nomos of the Earth*, Schmitt concentrates on what he calls the "second *nomos*," on the spatial and political organization of the earth imposed by the sixteenth-century colonial conquest of the New World and sustained by the seventeenth-century development of the European territorial nation-state system. This nomos of modernity replaced the "essentially terrestrial" and localized nomos of antiquity and the medieval age, carving a Eurocentric global order, "based on a particular relation between the spatial order of firm land and the spatial order of free sea."[5] The second nomos, mainly structured through a colonial and Atlantic relation of power, is "a completely different spatial order" that "arose with the centralized, spatially self-contained, continental European state . . . : unlimited free space for overseas land-appropriation was open to all such states. The new legal titles characteristic of this new, state-centered international law . . . were *discovery* and *occupation*."[6] The political/spatial order of the nomos and its "amity line" presided also over what was considered the area of "civilization"—the legal dimension of European international law—separating it from what had to represent the "state of nature" of primitive people and savage lands, where no lawful truce was respected and predation ruled.

According to Schmitt, this Eurocentric nomos of the earth, this global arrangement of land-appropriation and industrialization, of civilized Europeans and brutal savages, of territorial states and sea power, lasted until World War I, when the United States took over the "maritime existence" of the British Empire and began to impose a "new nomos," prolonging the destiny of Western planetary hegemony into a nightmarish "total war."[7]

This volume critically engages Schmitt's propositions and documents the antagonistic forms of autonomy that are moving away from the Western coordinates of the planetary nomos,[8] such as the indigenous, postcolonial, and naturalistic perspectives that are reconceptualizing traditional notions of the political in the Americas and Europe. In their essays, Alvaro Reyes and Mara Kaufman, Gustavo Esteva, Catherine E. Walsh, Zac Zimmer, and Jodi A. Byrd illustrate dramatically the alternative forms of autonomy practiced and conceptualized by the Zapatistas in Chiapas and by Bolivia's and Ecuador's indigenous movements, by Andean thinkers turning the Western nomos "inside out" and by theorists of indigenous sovereignty challenging the foundations of mainstream political philosophy. Meanwhile, from a Euro-Atlantic perspective, Joost de Bloois, Gareth Williams, Benjamin Noys, Frans-Willem Korsten, and Silvia Federici propose a "transvaluation" of political and cultural values, aligned with postcolonial experiences and aimed at the deconstruction of the Western nomos of capitalist modernity and imagination of new commons. In our opinion, it is crucial to foster this conceptual dialogue and political alliance between contemporary movements of dewesternization and the resistance against capitalist labor and biopower coming from workerism and postautonomia: in both instances, a line of flight from the central institutions and commitments of Western modernity is calling into question century-old habits of thought and political action, proposing concepts and practices that bypass the lexicon of political modernity and academic cosmopolitanism.

The contributions collected in this book originate from such a geophilosophical interference, having been initially presented and discussed at a conference held in the South of North America, where South and North

American intellectuals and militants met with their European peers, experiencing the exciting forces and political tensions that still inhabit what used to be the route of the transatlantic slave trade and what is now a space crossed by digital cables, cargo vessels, and international flights.[9]

In framing the book title as *The Anomie of the Earth*, thus rephrasing Schmitt's *The Nomos of the Earth*, we draw attention to the chiasmus that anomie/earth and auto/nomy constitute. "Anomie" and "earth" represent in fact a semantic reversal of the term "autonomy," which derives from the Greek *autos* and *nomos*, indicating forms of self-governing rule: instead of the lawful nomos of the current nation-states, the anomie of the emerging politics of nature and commons; instead of the autos of the political subjects of rights of liberal democracies, an impersonal earth. The chiasmus linking autonomy and the current anomie of the earth thus signals the need to rethink ethical and political communities, as well as traditional notions of nature and society, outside the forms of subjective autonomy and colonial nomos that have hitherto dominated Western conceptions of the political.

Our assumption is that the current geopolitical shift—the biopolitical reconfiguration of power within capitalist societies, the progressive erosion of the centrality of the Euro-North Atlantic space, the autonomization of South American and Eastern blocs[10]—is not just a systemic rearrangement of global capitalism, guided by crisis-devices fully controlled by neoliberal practices and ideologies, but can be seen also as a mutation making room for alternative political and micropolitical practices and imaginaries, requiring different conceptual vocabularies and a shift in the understanding of autonomy. The actual antagonistic forms of autonomy and sovereignty are moving away from the Western nomos, thus reconceptualizing traditional notions of political autonomy in the Americas and Europe.

In this sense, although Schmitt maintains an uncompromisingly Eurocentric standpoint on the history and construction of a global planetary order, some of his intuitions might be useful for tracing a critical genealogy of modern legal and philosophical concepts. Two centuries before workerist Marxisms transfigured autonomy into a subversive battle cry, staging against capital the rebellious freedom of working-class subjectivities and of social labor, Immanuel Kant, in his *Critique of Practical Reason* (1788), set the theoretical and political standards for modern Western autonomy. The "autonomy of the will," the self-determination of the will and its subjective, "directly legislative" force, are for Kant the "formal supreme principle of pure practical reason" and also the foundation of all political and moral freedom. From the perspective of Schmitt's second nomos, the universalistic freedom of Kantian practical reason can be interpreted instead against the concrete geohistorical background of Atlantic sea power and European nation-states. The Kantian notion of autonomy, which structures most Eurocentric ontologies of modernity, appears exclusively within this framework of maritime domination and land appropriation, civilized legality and state of nature predation.

Radical intellectuals positioned in postcolonial studies, autonomous Marxism, Foucaultian biopolitics, or Deleuzian geophilosophy have been among the most aware of the exhaustion of the framework of Western political modernity and the need to introduce other interpretative categories, beyond the horizon of Schmitt's Eurocentric nomos. This book showcases several examples of this increasing awareness. Chapters focus on the critical potential of a minor "savage political anthropology" that questions the foundational "state of nature" of modern political philosophy (de Bloois), the Zapatistas' reshaping of political autonomy through a confrontation with the Mexican institutional left (Reyes and Kaufman), and the non-Western-centric forms of life and agency that are being experimented with by South America's *buen vivir* and indigenous movements (Esteva, Walsh). Others show the urgency and aporias of "indigenous sovereignty" (Byrd) or the communal potential of the "unenclosed" theorized by Andean thinkers (Zimmer), while some criticize the notion of hegemony that infuses much contemporary critical theory (Williams), unmasking the Hegelian foundation of the ontologies of life of insurrectional anarchism and neovitalisms (Noys). Finally, two chapters address the anticapitalist micropolitics of lifestyles (Korsten) and the resistance of the "autonomous powers" of life's reproduction to the fascination of capitalist technologies (Federici).

Since the notion of autonomy has been the crucial site of theoretical investigation and political militancy for the Italian workerist movement (*operaismo*) of the 1960s, and later for the postworkerist (*postoperaismo*) or autonomist movements (*autonomia*) of the 1970s and 1980s, several chapters of this book openly engage these workerist and postworkerist positions, taking issue with the ideas of Mario Tronti and Antonio Negri, Paolo Virno and Franco "Bifo" Berardi. Recalling the genealogy of Italian workerism, and its successive transformation into autonomia and then into a global anticapitalist discourse through the work of Hardt and Negri, might be useful, then, for grasping the political conjunctions, but also the historical divergences, between conceptions of autonomy of Euro-North

American descent and the contemporary postcolonial and indigenous autonomist movements.[11]

Operaismo, like the Socialism ou Barbarie group in France, developed around journals—*Quaderni rossi* and later *Classe operaia*—and outside of the direct influence of the Italian Communist Party and institutional trade unions. Operaismo's protagonists—Renato Panzieri, Mario Tronti, Sergio Bologna, and Antonio Negri among them—came from a variety of backgrounds: revolutionary syndicalism, anarchic socialism, militant Catholicism. They were united by a common refusal of the official Gramscian line of the Italian Communist Party, of the historicism and idealism associated with Antonio Gramsci's "philosophy of praxis," to which they opposed a return to Marx's texts, in particular the *Grundrisse*.[12] This genesis of Italian workerism explains its distance from the mostly Gramscian and humanist Marxism of the British New Left, of India's subaltern studies and Anglo-American cultural studies. Workerism followed instead the anti-Hegelian and antihistoricist lesson of Italian positivist philosopher Galvano della Volpe, eluding the appeal to the "workers' culture" and the Gramscian apparatus of the national-popular, hegemony, and passive revolution.[13] "Della Volpe took apart, piece by piece, the cultural line of the Italian Communists. . . . Marx *contra* Hegel, like Galileo against the Scholastics, or Aristotle against the Platonists. . . . What, then, is *operaismo*? . . . an attempted cultural revolution in the West."[14] This programmatic shift away from the national and progressive agenda of most European Communist parties is summed up by the slogan of the editorial of the first issue, in 1963, of *Classe operaia*: "first the workers, then capital," and translated into a method of attributing immediate political value to the struggles against work taking place in the large factories of the industrial north of Italy.

Tronti's epoch-making book *Operai e capitale* (1966), a key text for Italian workerism, theorized the political and epistemic localization of the workers' struggles, embracing the irreducible partiality of their subjectivities against the national-popular of Gramscian Marxism and the universalistic and progressive democratic strategy of the Italian Communist Party.[15] Workerism thus produced a map of "neocapitalism" by concentrating on workers' autonomous subjectivities and demands, promoting sociological "militant investigations" into the living conditions and apparently unpolitical behaviors of factory workers.

The context for the emergence of workerism is the late and rapid industrialization of Italy in the 1950s and 1960s, accompanied by a spreading conflict in the large Taylorist factories of the north, where peasants who had emigrated from southern Italy were subsumed into the processes of capitalist mass production. The *operaisti* saw these events as an opportunity for reviving the great workers' struggles of 1930s America and the unique possibility of challenging the national and progressive agenda of Italian communism and trade unionism.[16] More than a combat against an abstract capitalist system, at stake was thus the attempt to transform the political anthropology of a Western society, defeating "bourgeois populism" and implanting a "post-proletarian aristocracy of the people." Nurtured by the "culture of the crisis" and a "passionate love affair" with "nineteenth-century Central European thought," operaismo mobilized the high aristocratic culture of European negative thought and nihilism, even reinventing Nietzsche's critique of Western civilization and bourgeois culture as a leftist political tool for achieving new forms of life, outside the "ideology of the workers as a 'universal class,' saturated with Kantian ethics," of institutional communism.[17]

The widespread student movement of 1968 and the "hot autumn" of the massive industrial workers' mobilization of 1969 marked a rupture between early workerism and the postworkerist forms of autonomy of the 1970s. The result was Italy's long 1968, the violent decade of the "years of lead," of state-sponsored terrorism and antagonistic insurgencies, culminating with the 1977 revolutionary movements, the Red Brigade's assassination of Italy's prime minister, Aldo Moro, in 1978, the suppression of numerous workerist and postworkerist autonomous experiences in Italy, and the political exile in France of leading militants of autonomia such as Antonio Negri and Oreste Scalzone.

Groups such as Potere Operaio, Lotta Continua, and later Autonomia Operaia—a noncentralized archipelago of autonomist organizations and social movements—prolonged and reshaped early workerism well into the 1970s. The description of labor broadened to include categories of immaterial labor and social reproduction, abandoning the centrality of the industrial workers (the "mass workers" of operaismo) and embracing practices of mass illegality and sabotage, in order to intensify political antagonism and prepare an insurrectionary situation.[18]

The "social workers" of the "social factory"—unemployed and precarious workers, students, women, migrants—became the new subjects of "constituent power," and autonomia spread throughout Europe, creating a rich field of experimentation for new forms of political action and social organization.

These trans-European experiences were not coordinated around a single philosophical paradigm or political project but developed independently according to historically situated conditions. In France, for example, autonomism successfully intersected with poststructuralist theories in the work of intellectuals such as Michel Foucault, Félix Guattari, and Gilles Deleuze, adding a vitalist, biopolitical, and micropolitical toolbox to the originary Marxist lexicon of Italian workerism.

During the past two decades, theorists such as Franco "Bifo" Berardi, Silvia Federici, Andrea Fumagalli, Maurizio Lazzarato, Christian Marazzi, Sandro Mezzadra, Carlo Vercellone, and Paolo Virno have articulated new connections between Marxist categories, Spinozan materialism, and feminist, anthropological, semiotic, and economic motives, elaborating concepts such as "general intellect," "cognitive capitalism," and "exodus," and expanding the focus of autonomia to questions of life's reproduction and to technological and financial mechanisms of production and control. With the publication of Michael Hardt and Antonio Negri's *Empire* (2000), antagonism finds a new political subject in the "multitude," and world capitalism takes the shape of a global imperial biopolitical apparatus of domination. In postworkerist texts such as Hardt and Negri's *Multitude* (2004) and *Commonwealth* (2009), Federici's *Caliban and the Witch* (2004), and Sandro Mezzadra's *La condizione postcoloniale* (2008), the attention shifts across the Atlantic, testing the hermeneutical and political potential of autonomy on questions of globalization and decolonization. While forcing workerism to expand its previously European political matrix and rethink the efficacy and latitude of its theoretical categories, this development reconnects the experience of autonomia with some of its inspirational sources: the struggles for decolonization that, from Algeria to Palestine, from Nicaragua to Vietnam, were shaking the global order after World War II.

By observing autonomist Marxism through the lenses of postcolonial studies and political anthropologies; by moving along the path traced by the "provincialization of Europe" set forth by Dipesh Chakrabarty and subaltern studies; or by rehearsing the critique of capitalist development and mobilizing of indigenous knowledge exemplified by liberation theology, the contributors to this collective book are staging a productively disorienting conversation that reformulates the rich history of thought centered on autonomy from state politics, across the current struggles for commons, and against new waves of enclosures. Despite their different backgrounds and approaches, the authors of this book recognize the necessity to rethink the universalizing concepts of Eurocentric political theory. Their strategies do not always converge, but their latitude demonstrates the vitality of the current alternatives to the paradigm of the *homo economicus*.

A distinctive feature of this book is the desire to avoid any philosophical or political synthesis. What takes place across these pages is instead a complex and often conflictual interchange that projects an impressive picture of the fissures of the Western nomos. Around the battle cry of autonomy, a constellation of terms such as "forms-of-life" and "nature," "new commons" and "reenchantment," are dancing on the stage of thought, suggesting a variety of practices of decolonization and the experimentation of modes of resistance to capitalist accumulation. In order to preserve the embodiment of ideas within their sociogeographical and geopolitical contexts, and escape a disembodied theoretical hubris, this book has chosen the form of the counterpoint, not reducing but dramatizing the heterogeneous discursive strategies adopted by intellectuals rooted in such diverse milieux as Dutch academia, the insurgent social movements of Chiapas, Ecuador, and U.S. college campuses. Linked by several conceptual genealogies and a common anticapitalist horizon, the contributors have produced a collective transatlantic exchange, focused on the multiplicity of existing practices of radical autonomy from the apparatus of Western modernity.

This book argues that in this sociohistorical moment, a multiplicity of cross-currents are generating alternative geopolitics of knowledge, holding the promise of reconfiguring the modern Eurocentric episteme. For this reason, drawing the shifting conceptual contours of contemporary anticapitalist movements—from Afro-Colombian indigenous insurgencies to the Spanish *indignados'* protests, from the Zapatistas' *mandar-obedeciendo* autonomy to the Occupy Wall Street tactics in North America—requires us not only to recognize the mutual influences between decolonial and postworkerist practices, nurtured by processes of cross-fertilization and decades of contacts between militants, but also the existence of a pluricentric map of struggles for political autonomy and conceptual definitions. The essays here reflect this complexity, documenting for instance the primitivist and antimodern line of "savage" political anthropology (de Bloois), the decolonial legacy of the Austrian-born Catholic priest Ivan Illich's theories of "deschooling" and "conviviality" (Esteva), and the naturalistic potential of a body politics centered on the sphere of reproduction (Federici).

In order to trace the new lines of the "colonial difference" and the neverending actuality of primitive accumulation,[19] the book presents a series of reflections on the new nomos, highlighting the disorienting translations, the interchanges, and the irreducible divergences between autonomisms of different kinds. These include: Byrd's emphasis on "indigenous sovereignty" and its divergence from Reyes and Kaufman's illustration of the Zapatistas' "tendential unmaking of sovereignty" as well as their rejection of any critical potential of the discourse of "savagery"—a position shared by most postcolonial intellectuals—and one that stands in sharp contrast with de Bloois's mobilization of the Lévi-Strauss, Clastres, Deleuze-Guattari, Viveiros de Castro lineage of savage political anthropology.[20] Noys's critique of the alliance between poststructuralist neo-vitalisms and insurrectional anarchism targets the presuppositions of the "savage ontologies" of life maintained by many post-Deleuzian, post-Foucauldian, and postautonomist analyses dealing with desiring machines and constituent power. At the same time, Federici, a protagonist of Italian autonomist thinking, calls for a shift away from the technophilic and productivist imaginary of Eurocentric postworkerism, advocating a rethinking of technology and nature, the commons and bodily experience.

The exchanges between European and North/South American theorizations of autonomy and the new nomos are organized around three complementary areas of investigation—geographies, commons, and forms of life. Joost de Bloois's opening essay starts the work of bridging autonomism and decoloniality through the notion of "savage thought" and establishes very useful links between Negri's "alter-modernity" and Mignolo's "de-coloniality." Alvaro Reyes and Mara Kaufman look at Chiapas to glean from Zapatismo a refusal of the state (and therefore of the very notion of sovereignty) and a new conception of power (*Mandar obedeciendo*) that could in turn be redeployed in the "civilizational crisis of 'the West.'" In Part II, the idea of the commons starts taking a poststatist path, a position of autonomy from the state, with Gustavo Esteva's opening essay, and with Catherine E. Walsh's following one, which looks at the limits of the state even at its most progressive point of development—as in the constitutional attempts of Ecuador and Bolivia to include not only indigenous movements but also nature as subjects of state rights. This withering away of the state from the stage of autonomist and decolonial thought poses of course the question: on which community, precisely, should the "common" be based? The issue of indigeneity, already present in Walsh, then becomes the main topic for both Jody A. Byrd and Zac Zimmer. Their essays, surprisingly, question the very category of "indigeneity" from the perspective of a progressive politics. Their question is simple: how is it possible to imagine a common that does not close on any "indigenous" or "nativist" claim to ownership? It is from this question that Gareth Williams's quest for a "post-hegemonic forms of thought" begins, opening Part III. This is followed by Noys's trenchant critique of what he sees as the re-ontologization of the forms of life in debates about indigeneity and autonomy, Frans-Willem Korsten then goes back to one of autonomy's most central concerns—time—to engage in a very interesting, if at times a little too distant from properly decolonial concerns, discussion of "preciosity." Silvia Federici's last essay could in itself be an apt conclusion to the book, as it pulls together the various threads—buen vivir, nature, biopolitics, the state, technology—that were laid out in the preceding essay to propose the possibility of a "reenchantment of the world" as the very goal of autonomist and decolonial politics.

In his contribution (chapter 1), Joost de Bloois traces the genealogical line connecting European (and especially Italian) autonomist movements to the diverse struggles for, and debates about, autonomy in current decolonial movements in North and South America. De Bloois argues that the Italian movements of the 1970s understood their position as a point of transition between older Marxist-Leninist models of state-oriented politics and an emerging postautonomist political anthropology that resists the dominant liberal democratic Western consensus. Following theorists of operaismo and autonomia such as Franco Berardi and Mario Tronti, de Bloois asks whether the 1970s signaled the end of the modern emancipatory ideal and concurrent modes of struggle, precipitating the emergence of a new kind of political subject, one that demands the overcoming of the sociopolitical anthropology of the liberal democratic homo economicus. By drawing on Pierre Clastres's "savage ethnography," these approaches to autonomy have challenged the Hobbesian conception of a violent, prepolitical "state of nature," the Rousseauian myth of political consensus, and the Kantian ethic of a self-disciplinary citizenship. Whereas for Hobbes the savage is a negative limit-condition of permanent war, for Clastres the savage becomes the guarantor of the social, an affirmative subject that obstructs the advent of the repressive apparatus of the nation-state. In place of Hobbes's *bellum omnium contra omnes*, primitive sociality instantiates a constructive society-for-war in which power is shared within and among local communities in the process of negotiating shifting territories. As Antonio Negri has argued, this "savage" political praxis implies that postautonomia movements are in the process of shifting and deconstructing the founding Western political vocabulary articulated by Hobbes, Rousseau, and Kant, replacing it with a Spinozan model of *multitude*, with a "multiplicity of subjects" and their "constructive power."[21] Most significantly for de Bloois, the theorization of a society-for-war and its alliance with postliberal notions of multitude is currently most fully expressed in the burgeoning post-Leninist, local autonomist movements in North and South America. We are thus at the historically unique point of conjuncture where post-Marxist European political philosophy and non-Western decolonial autonomist movements are converging through their mutual engagement with new political conceptions of life and social being.

In chapter 2, Alvaro Reyes and Mara Kaufman engage with the birth of a new politics in Latin America. Pointing out that if the new millennium saw first the rise and consolidation of progressive governments throughout Latin America, it also saw the deactivation of large sectors of the social movements that had brought those governments into being. Out of this moment came a series of new events (the Zapatistas' "Other Campaign," the conflict between the administration of Evo Morales and the indigenous people of the Isiboro Sécure National Park and Indigenous Territory [TIPNIS] ecological reserve, the opposition mounted by the Confederation of Indigenous Peoples and Nationalities of Ecuador against the administration of Rafael Correa, to name just a few) that seem to place us on the edge of a new political horizon in the region. Reyes and Kaufman investigate these events and propose that what might appear today as temporally succeeding cycles of struggle (the first against orthodox neoliberalism and the latter against "progressive governments") is instead the expression of two distinct tendencies that have characterized these movements and organizations across various cycles of struggle. These latest revolts are evidence that for many of those involved in the cycles of struggles of the past three decades (most specifically the leading indigenous organizations of the region), the counter-hegemonic parties and projects that assumed state power in the early years of this century were never intended as a historical terminus. Rather, Reyes and Kaufman argue that they were viewed as but one tactic among many in a growing strategy for the creation of an entirely *other* politics whose very aim has always been the dismantlement of hegemony as such. That is, these new expressions of discontent cannot be understood without also understanding that while the past three decades in Latin America have reconfigured the domestic relations of force in each country and the geopolitical map of the region as a whole, they also represent an enormous shift in the conceptualization of the means, ends, and scope of what it means to do politics under the various localized expressions of global neoliberalism.

In chapter 3, Gustavo Esteva launches a manifesto for contemporary autonomous movements that speaks to and integrates the other essays in this collection. Covering a broad range of developments, from the Zapatistas and the 2011 Bolivian marches to the Occupy Movement in North America and the recent resistance efforts in Spain and Greece, Esteva looks to the "archipelago of conviviality" that is reformulating power in terms of social relations instead of expressions of domination. This *comunalidad* is composed of the emergent communal subject as the primary cell of ongoing global social movements, reconfiguring the Kantian trope of abstract citizenship into a model for concrete collective action, and abandoning the Hegelian premise that people cannot govern themselves. Both autonomous and integrated into a complex territoriality, these diverse, often divergent movements are integrated by a common concern for buen vivir, living well, a motif that expresses the pragmatic turn to a more proportional scale at the level of the everyday life and the rejection of the centralized Leninist-statist approaches that have characterized both the left and the right over the past century. In place of nouns bespeaking dominating institutions like "education," "health," and "food," the peoples' movements are replacing these industries with verbs that express lived communal action ("learning," "healing," "nourishing"), that recover personal and collective agency and enable autonomous paths of social transformation. With increasing food production in cities, the struggle to reclaim land, the revival of ancient learning traditions and their integration with contemporary technologies, the construction of centers of knowledge outside of private research, the reformulation of globalized discourses of hierarchy and privilege derived from industrial and biomedical regimes, and the development of systems of exchange outside the capitalist economy, Esteva sees the possibility of a new harmonious coexistence of differences, an already emerging world in which "many worlds can be embraced."

In her provocative engagement with South American decolonial movements (chapter 4), Catherine E. Walsh looks at two key events: Ecuador's 2008 Constitutional Assembly and the meeting in Ecuador on April 28–29, 2012, of the Latin American–Caribbean Network Grito de los Excluidos y Excluidas (Shouts of the Excluded). In a carefully developed reading of the political charters of these groups, she argues that the shouts (*gritos*) of social movements, organizations, and ancestral peoples of Abya-Yala ("the name, originally from the [Chibchan] Cuna language, that indigenous peoples give to the Americas") are important because they speak from the still colonial reality, conditions, and struggles of the global present. But the gritos also express the actions, propositions, and thought increasingly evident in the activism of the global south. In Abya-Yala the current conjuncture is not an undertaking based in government, academia, or sectors of the white-mestizo left, but instead is communicated in the persistent practices and struggles of indigenous and African-origin communities and social movements. These practices and struggles represent an insurgency of social, political, and existential forces that are producing non-Western-centric forms of life, nature, knowledge. By mobilizing ancestral philosophies and praxis with the goal of shaping national societies as a whole, these movements aim to engage with and unsettle coloniality's still persistent hold on the imagination and on the political. The force of this movement comes from the refounding, pluralizing, and reorienting of Carl Schmitt's Western nomos and its attendant practices of exploitation, domination, and control that prescribe the horizon of the decolonial struggle for social transformation. In contrast to this colonial nomos, the movements investigated by Walsh present newly emergent configurations of knowledge, subjectivity, and nature as central components in the reconfiguration of an increasingly polycentric world that not only addresses the economic cultural axis but also speaks to the appropriation of nature and the model of civilization itself.

In chapter 5, Jodi A. Byrd argues that in many of the movements described in the preceding essays, the ethos of possession continues to pervade strategies for resisting the Western nomos. The very notion of occupation overlooks the rights of indigenous peoples and the process of dispossession that subtends the movement to reclaim common spaces. Byrd writes: "Within the context of the Americas, freedom, equality, and liberty were hewn in a crucible of violence, subjugation, enslavement, extermination, and expropriation that made such promissory ideals intelligible, desirable, and enforceable. Savage, animal, and female were differentiated in order to cohere civilized, human, and male into the normative structures through which power, politics, and livability could be structured." Through this process of distinction and categorization, Byrd continues, "indigenous peoples and lands became recognizable as they were conscripted into Western law and territoriality and then disavowed from the space of actor into that space which is acted upon within the systems of colonial governmentality that continue to underwrite settler empires." By opening up a dialogue with the theories of savage anthropology and the legacy of Carl Schmitt developed in other chapters, Byrd questions the presuppositions at work in a politics that privileges indigeneity and decoloniality without locating such political practices in much broader power geometries. Given the coterminous rise of sovereignty as a political concept and the advent of settler colonialism in the New World, Byrd asks what it means to delineate something as potentially dangerous as indigenous sovereignty. How can (or does) the "indigenous" function to shape systems of subjectification and objectification—first as the appropriation of prior presences within a horizon of governance, and second as a recuperation of the "native" for a politics of redistribution, access, and justice?

Chapter 6, by Zac Zimmer, explores the thematic center of this book: Carl Schmitt's notorious apologia of Western geopolitics, *The Nomos of the Earth*. Focusing on Schmitt's claim that the fence precedes all social relations, Zimmer contrasts this notion with the emergent politics of the commons. Not only does the fence divide, it brings order and establishes law, providing the basis for the conceptual maneuvers underlying expropriation from our contemporary geopolitics to our subjectivizing biopolitical institutions. In his engagement with the communal potential of the unenclosed, Zimmer argues that the fence is not ontologically prior to community and identity but rather effaces the commons, in which a "savage" sociopolitics precedes the appropriation of power within the state. By focusing on Andean commoners from both the colonial and the contemporary period (including Inca Garcilaso de la Vega, José Carlos Mariátegui, José María Arguedas, Manuel Scorza, and Alberto Flores Galindo), Zimmer maintains that Schmitt's nomos is actually premised on the erasure of a nativist subjectivity predicated on the unenclosed commons. Schmitt's project of enclosure has never been and probably cannot be completed, because the subjectivity of the commoners that Zimmer locates in these Andean movements still makes up an essential part of the communal state of relations, or *socius*. The Andean vision of commonly shared land counters the European vision of the Americas as a blank slate with a logic of use and occupation. At the same time, Zimmer notes that this counterlogic, most often expressed in the idealization of a communal Incan golden age, also introduces a problem in the form of an idealized Andean homogeneity that is no longer tenable. Navigating between these two tensions (the Andean resistance to the

Western nomos and the problematic vision of a homogeneous precolonial Incan people), Zimmer explores the central problematic of autonomous politics, particularly when it situates its argument in the identity of particular communities, naturalizing their "being" and thereby potentially failing to develop a logic that is open to the complex spatial and historical deferment of identity.

In chapter 7, Gareth Williams examines the exhaustion of the conceptual apparatus contained by the ideologies of the nation-state and the imperial jus publicum Europaeum, focusing on what Carl Schmitt called the *katechon*, or the restraining force of the international system of law. In criticizing the notion of hegemony, Williams calls for a new analysis of globalization and a rethinking of the post-Westphalian world order and forms of resistance to capitalism. Williams's critical history of the territorialization of power and its relationship to modernity forges a path for imagining posthegemonic communities situated outside of the ideologies of the unitary nation-state.

Chapter 8, by Benjamin Noys, takes up recent theories of "Life" as revolutionary excess, probing the origins of the vitalist turn to a Foucauldian "savage ontology." According to Noys, both academic theorists and anarchist practitioners of vitalism share a common genesis in their rejection of the Hegelian synthesis and their valorization of the power of a Nietzschean vitalism. This radicalization of the discourse of life is not as straightforward as it seems; it risks misunderstanding the capitalist forms of relation that are grounded in a "savage ontology" that is supposed to be a unique source of cultural and intellectual resistance. If this is the case, Noys argues, the current deployment of vitalism is not so much a challenge to the fundamental tenets of capitalism as a new avenue for replicating the core of its ideology. Using the work of Mikhail Bakunin, Max Stirner, and Renzo Novatore to situate the development of our contemporary "savage ontology," Noys then turns to a consideration of Deleuze via Alain Badiou to demonstrate that the classical insurrectionalist models are being resurrected in French philosophy's retooling of a vitalist metaphysics. The resonance between traditional insurrectionist approaches and this new language is no accident, as we see clearly in texts like the Invisible Committee's *The Coming Insurrection* (2007), which codes insurrection in clear vitalist terms. Similarly, thinkers such as Antonio Negri argue that capital unleashes life as a productive force it cannot finally control. Instead, and in productive contrast to de Bloois and Korsten, Noys argues that "Life" plays a more ambiguous role. Turning back to Marx and Foucault, he observes that both of these foundational thinkers never posited life as exterior to power. Against the "Christian" discourse of reversal and salvation (in which the most extreme state of destitution is simultaneously the path to glory), Noys concludes by arguing that we need a more nuanced, strategic thinking that does not simply repeat the mantra of the "excess" of life.

Chapter 9, by Frans-Willem Korsten, begins by observing that capitalist crises have now entered into a persistent delirium. Here Korsten reads capitalism as a system in a perpetual state of panic and yet economically vigorous, both demented and operationally continuous. In the shadow of what Korsten sees as the Marxian analytical failure to grapple with this new capitalist delirium, he turns to a different, anthropological conception of economy in its relation to life in order to explore some of the successful responses that have been launched against the capitalist colonization of the everyday. Korsten sees the composition of dispersed social movements that fundamentally change the codes by which resistance can be understood to be exemplified in globally dispersed economic and social movements extending from Tiqqun and Precarias a la Deriva in Europe to the Colectivo Situaciones, and social geography movements in North and South America. Whereas Marxism read the working class as the universal subject whose interests were the interests of all, a conception of political subjectivity that led to the party state, Korsten argues that we can no longer speak about political structure through the lens of one privileged subject position. Instead, he interprets our current situation as one in which different groupuscules and movements embody heterogeneous, often incompatible *styles* of living. These different modes of "worlding" involve unique compositional strategies and different intensities of value, which nonetheless share a common feature, what he calls "pretiosity." If capitalism functions by means of what David Harvey defines as "accumulation through dispossession," then pretiosity expresses the anthropological turn toward what is outside the current economic system. In contrast to the historical vision pitting struggle against synthetic *Aufhebung*, we have a struggle between different forms of human beings, what Pierre Clastres describes as "primitive war." If considered as the current metamorphosis of class struggle, these dispersed movements, these always potentially diverse forms of pretiosity, are anchored in webs of relations that capitalism can never capitalize.

In the final chapter, Silvia Federici extends her work in *Caliban and the Witch* (2004) to the present, arguing that the mechanization of the West (and increasingly the world) has been premised on and preceded by the mechanization of the human body. Max Weber's claim that "the fate of our times is characterized above all by the disenchantment of the world" resonates even more today with the extension of rational control through technologies that are changing the human body and social communities on an unprecedented scale. Like Gustavo Esteva, Federici contends that the capitalist rationalization of reproduction reshapes our autonomous powers through the regimentation of production as it decollectivizes the reproductive activities that form the basis of autonomy. Reworking the Marxist hypothesis that industrialization generates revolutionary collectivities, she looks to reproductive social and agricultural work within the commons that resists capitalization by the market. In her view, practices that link bodies and environments, construct collective memories, and imaginatively generate new social futures continue to be our most powerful tools of resistance to disenchantment. Many of these interstitial practices and social spaces have continued to nurture life as a process of experimentation and an active redefinition of what it means to be a human being, permitting a "reenchantment of the world," a reimagining of the knowledge and human powers that have been repressed in the capitalist process of rationalization. By contrast, communities in industrialized countries are more vulnerable than ever to rationalization because communications technologies maximize the extraction of surplus labor while promising the age-old technotopia of reduced work burdens. These technologies continue to function within an economy of scarcity, however, because they are expressions of the capitalist relations of extraction and environmental degradation that they recreate. Technologies cannot dictate how we come together, nor are they generative of creative participation; rather, it has been the less technologically advanced regions that today are the milieu for political struggle. As earlier contributions to this collection discuss in detail, some of the most significant examples of autonomous movements come from the everyday struggles of indigenous communities precisely because, Federici argues, these movements are establishing new paradigms for the "commonwealth" from the fields, kitchens, and fishing villages in their struggle to disentangle their reproductive process from the hold of corporate power.

The conversations, convergences, and conflicts that resonate among the essays unpack two of the most intriguing trends in contemporary social and political theory: Italian autonomism and Latin American postcolonial conceptions of autonomy. While these hemispheric debates have their own specific origins and goals, bringing these essays together in this way illustrates first how the two seemingly independent trajectories of thinking and practicing autonomous politics have borrowed and translated concepts and practices from each other. Each of the authors strives for a geographically and geopolitically grounded reading of the emergent forms of autonomy with which they are concerned. Whether this be a postcolonial critique of the nomos or its privileging of world space and *techne*, a feminist critique of disembodied thought, or an attempt to locate and ground new forms of life beyond the biopolitical formations of the state, each aims to understand autonomous movements in their diversity, to analyze them as embedded practices, and to create new forms of intellectual space for alternative political configurations of being, thinking, and living together in common. Each of the essays also responds to Carl Schmitt's *Nomos of the Earth*—the very text that attempted to give a single nomos to planetary relations between peoples. This sustained interaction with Schmitt highlights the common goal of both autonomism and decolonialism—creating a common platform from which global events can be theorized and understood. From that interaction this book assembles an anomic (rather than monolithic) staging of theory capable of understanding events that not only Schmitt's nomos but also orthodox Marxism seem incapable to comprehend anymore.

The emergence of the anti- and alterglobalization movements in the 1990s, the increasing attention given to Italian autonomism in the 2000s, and the interaction of decolonial thinking with the indigenous movements that are currently transforming the political landscapes of southern Mexico, Ecuador, Colombia, and Bolivia, thus emerge as salient markers for concrete political transformation today. In this sense, the essays are not only about autonomy per se but about the commonalities faced by different forms of life in the present conjuncture, forms of life experiencing changing forms of conquest, new forms of accumulation by dispossession, and struggling to reframe the meaning of insurrection after occupation.

In the name of the heterogeneous trajectories of contemporary political thought, we have allowed disagreements—between decolonialism and autonomism, but also within each of the two camps—to stand. Rather than attempting convergences where there can be none, some essays stand firm in questioning decoloniality, autonomy, or both. Indeed, in his afterword Sandro Mezzadra stresses the necessity of provincializing both autonomist and decolonial political thought. Like him, we are wary of the reification of any social subject and the privileging of any site of struggle. We hope that the essays open up conversations, rather than close them down around any notions of a privileged subject of history or a benevolent "native informant". Our goal throughout is to deontologize, not reontologize, the multiple spaces and subjects of transformation; to see struggles over place, the commons, and forms of life as thoroughly relational. In this sense, our effort has been to allow difference to play itself, recognizing the multiplicity of ways of living life, organizing the social, and struggling for autonomy.

NOTES

1. Carl Schmitt, *The Nomos of the Earth in the International Law of the Jus Publicum Europaeum*, trans. G. L. Ulmen (New York: Telos, 2003); the quotation in the epigraph to this chapter is from p. 39.

2. Schmitt, *Nomos*, 31–32.

3. See Carlo Galli, *Political Spaces and Global War*, trans. Elisabeth Fay (Minneapolis: University of Minnesota Press, 2010); and "World Orders: Confronting Carl Schmitt's Theory of the Nomos," ed. William Rasch, special issue, *South Atlantic Quarterly* 104, no. 2 (Spring 2005).

4. Fredric Jameson, Notes on the "Nomos," *South Atlantic Quarterly* 104, no. 2 (Spring 2005): 200.

5. Schmitt, *Nomos*, 49.

6. Schmitt, *Nomos*, 66.

7. For a decolonial engagement with Schmitt's "new *nomos*," see Walter D. Mignolo, *The Darker Side of Western Modernity: Global Futures, Decolonial Options* (Durham, NC: Duke University Press, 2011), 29–35.

8. Decolonial scholarship has mobilized concepts such as Aníbal Quijano's "coloniality of power," Enrique Dussel's "transmodernity," Walter Mignolo's "border thinking," and Arturo Escobar's "postdevelopment" in order to affirm forms of thought that are not beholden to the process of westernization of the nomos favored by Schmitt.

9. "The Anomie of the Earth," *Postautonomia*, University of North Carolina, Chapel Hill, May 3–5, 2012, http://postautonomia.org/.

10. See Mignolo, *Darker Side of Western Modernity*; Mahbubani Kishore, *The New Asian Hemisphere: The Irreversible Shift to the East* (New York: Public Affairs, 2008), and Andre Gunder Frank, *Re-Orient: Global Economy in the Asian Age* (Berkeley: University of California Press, 1995).

11. On the history of workerism, see Steve Wright, *Storming Heaven: Class Composition and Struggle in Italian Autonomist Marxism* (London: Pluto, 2002). For a critical discussion of postworkerism, see Alberto Toscano, "Chronicles of Insurrection: Tronti, Negri and the Subject of Antagonism," *Cosmos and History: Journal of Natural and Social Philosophy* 5, no. 1 (2009), 417–33.

12. See Paolo Capuzzo and Sandro Mezzadra, "Provincializing the Italian Reading of Gramsci," in Neelam Srivastava and Baidik Bhattacharya, eds., *The Postcolonial Gramsci*, New York: Routledge, 2011.

13. See Dario Gentili, *Italian Theory: Dall'operaismo alla biopolitica* (Bologna, Italy: Il Mulino, 2012), for a genealogy of Italian political thought centered on Tronti's workerism and the biopolitical debate. On this topic see also Andrea Righi, *Biopolitics and Social Change in Italy: From Gramsci to Pasolini to Negri* (New York: Palgrave Macmillan, 2011).

14. Mario Tronti, "Our Operaismo," *New Left Review* 73 (January-February 2012): 119–39.

15. "The working class, by following its own, partial interests, creates a general crisis in the relations of capital." Tronti, "Our Operaismo," 120.

16. "In fact the northern Italian workers' struggles of the early 1960s were closer to those of New Deal America than to those of the southern Italian farm workers in the 1950s. The Apulian laborer who became a mass worker in Turin was the symbol of the end of 'Italietta' history" Tronti. "Our Operaismo," 130.

17. Tronti, "Our Operaismo," 131.

18. See Antonio Negri, *Dall'operaio massa all'operaio sociale: Intervista sull'operaismo* (Verona: Ombre Corte, 2007).

19. See Sandro Mezzadra, "The Topicality of Prehistory: A New Reading of Marx's Analysis of So-called Primitive Accumulation," *Rethinking Marxism: A Journal of Economics, Culture & Society* 23, no. 3 (2011): 302–21.

20. Claude Lévi-Strauss, *The Savage Mind* (London: Weidenfeld and Nicolson, 1972); Gilles Deleuze and Félix Guattari, *A Thousand Plateaus* (London: Continuum, 2004); Pierre Clastres, *Society against the State: Essays in Political Anthropology* (New York: Zone Books, 1989); Eduardo Viveiros de Castro, *Métaphysiques Cannibales* (Paris: Presses Universitaires de France, 2009).

21. Antonio Negri, *The Savage Anomaly*, trans. Michael Hardt (Minneapolis: University of Minnesota Press, 1999), 8.

PART I Geographies of Autonomy

1

The Death of Vitruvian Man Anomaly, Anomie, Autonomy

JOOST DE BLOOIS

1492 to 1977: The Passage beyond Modernity

In his recent "Towards a Critique of Political Democracy," Mario Tronti argues that "there will be no genuine and effective critique of democracy without *a profound anthropological investigation*, a social anthropology but also an individual anthropology." For Tronti, "we witness the epochal encounter between *homo economicus* and *homo democraticus*. *The subject of the spirits of capitalism* is precisely the *animal democraticum*. The figure that has become dominant is the mass bourgeois, which is the real subject internal to the social relation." [1] In autonomist discourse this democratic animal gets different names, such as the Bloom in the work of Tiqqun, the virtuoso opportunist in the work of Paolo Virno, the entrepreneur on Prozac in the work of Franco "Bifo" Berardi. [2] These notions proceed from the conviction that it is vital that any alternative to what Tronti calls the "mass biopolitics" that goes under the name of democracy has to start from a far-reaching critique of the different incarnations of the anthropological subject. Therefore, I would like to argue that we might consider autonomist thought to constitute a *savage political anthropology*, in the sense that the French anthropologist Pierre Clastres speaks of a "savage ethnography": an ethnography that claims a certain primitivism that thinks with the savage against the Western political anthropology of the *zoon politikon*. Although such a savage political anthropology draws crucially, as I will show, on what I will call "the anthropological perspective," which is indebted to the anthropology of savage thought (*pensée sauvage*) that spans from Lévi-Strauss via Clastres to contemporary anthropologists such as Eduardo Viveiros de Castro, it does not so much refer to a specialized area of study as to an "underground current" of political philosophy, in the sense that Althusser speaks of "the underground current of the materialism of the encounter":[3] an obscured but no less operative tradition. To reconsider autonomist thinking as a savage political anthropology thus uncovers strange bedfellows with whom it shares a vocabulary as well as an ethos.

Crucially, such a savage political anthropology constitutes a vital *critique of modernity*, that is to say: of political modernity and its epistemological and subjective architecture.

Franco "Bifo" Berardi describes autonomist thought and activism precisely in terms of "passage" and "premonition." For Berardi, the year 1977 heralds the "passage beyond modernity." The acme of autonomist thought in Italy witnesses the closure of "the modern horizon": autonomism breaks away from the epistemology of modernity by no longer thinking emancipation in purely historical terms.[4] The notion of "history" constitutes the pivot of modernity's epistemology. Historical thinking provides modernity with its horizon of *humanitas* and intrinsically Western spatiotemporality. It was the centrality of "history," and its ensuing dialectics, that connected Marxism to the epistemology of modernity. In fact, *operaismo* constitutes a first instance of departure from it. The year 1977 therefore marks the "premonition of an *anthropological mutation* and the emergence of a new transformative subject."[5] For Berardi, this "anthropological mutation" is highly ambiguous. What he describes as "the implosion of the future," as the horizon of political, social, sexual emancipatory thought, *also* sees the emergence of the animal democraticum or "mass bourgeois" referred to by Tronti.[6] *This* anthropological figure constitutes the subject of a posthistorical humanitas that in fact fulfils the project of modernity by universalizing the subject of Western capitalism, the Vitruvian man of economic globalization. Berardi therefore insists on the need "to resume the thread of analysis of social composition and decomposition if we want to distinguish possible lines of processes of recomposition to come."[7]

One such possible afterlife of autonomist thought is, I argue, its alliance with *decolonial thinking*, as exemplified by the work of Walter Mignolo, Arturo Escobar, Rámon Grosfoguel, or Nelson Maldonado-Torres. Both (post)autonomism and decolonial thinking attempt to grasp the epistemological and political ramifications of the "passage beyond modernity" vis-à-vis new forms of autonomy. As Maldonado-Torres writes, the modern conception of autonomy presupposes a subject caught up in the master/slave dialectics of self-affirmation (of its humanitas) through the negating of others: "It is as if the production of the 'less than human' functioned as the anchor of a process of autonomy and self-assertion."[8] The idea of modernity has *coloniality* as its "constitutive and darker side."[9] The year 1492 thus constitutes the passage to modernity. Modernity's epistemology, and subsequent (political) anthropology, its hierarchy of potential subjects, is inextricably linked with the encounter and subsequent negation of Amerindian civilization and the ensuing Atlantic slave trade. Autonomy and emancipation are thus conditioned by an epistemology that is scaffolded by "the systematic differentiation between groups taken as the norm of the human and others seen as the exception to it."[10] The modern conception of autonomy supposes the prior conception of an "epistemic zero point" that is the privilege of those inhabiting it and who may claim their ensuing humanitas; it is from his "zero point" that, at the same time, those "who inhabit the *exteriority* (the outside invented in the process of defining the inside)" are created, precisely as the objects of observation or *anthropos*: the barbarian or the primitive.[11] Decolonial thinking proposes an "epistemic delinking" that, in a sense, stages a different encounter. It revaluates anthropos before humanitas, by taking indigenous practices and epistemologies, without unproblematically considering them as latter-day *robinsonnades*, as the anchor point of new forms of autonomous politics. Decolonial thinking therefore draws on what I coined earlier as the anthropological perspective. It is this perspective, along with the reappraisal of autonomy that it enables, that allows for a joint reading of contemporary decolonial and autonomist thinking. The potential of such an alliance is discussed, most notably, by Michael Hardt and Antonio Negri in *Commonwealth*.[12] However, I would like to argue against their attempt to incorporate decolonial thinking, as well as contemporary radical anthropology, in a somewhat overstretched autonomist notion of "the commons." Such a project, as we will see, remains still determined by dialectical figures of thought that are in fact radically challenged by decolonial thinking. On the contrary, I propose to reconsider autonomist thinking from the anthropological perspective, that is to say: in particular, outside of the exclusive bias of political economy. This will allow us to highlight autonomism's intrinsic proximity with decolonial thinking and its potential for reassessing "savage thought."[13] I therefore propose a reading of autonomist thinking as *savage political anthropology* that, crucially, gravitates toward the savage, unmodern element in autonomist thinking and that recurrently stages a different encounter between the (political) epistemology of modernity and its outside (as is shown, for example, in the work of Negri and Virno and of Byrd [chapter 6 here]). In particular, this alternative staging of the foundational encounter of modernity, and its impinging master/slave dialectic, allow for a radical departure from the Hobbesian imperatives that dominate modern political thought.

A New Nomos of the Earth?
Altermodernity, Decoloniality, Autonomy

"Modernity is always two," write Michael Hardt and Toni Negri in *Commonwealth*.[14] Modernity is not so much a result of diachronic thinking as it is at the very origin of the conception of historical linearity. Therefore, "modernity" is a profoundly speculative affair: its concept emerges as both origin and end of historical reason. Modernity constitutes the very heart of a complex historical-teleological thinking that thinks history from its point of arrival, the very point where it locates itself. This point of arrival is thus spatiogeographical as much as it is temporal. Its proper name is Europe.[15] The constitutive "two" of modernity referred to by Hardt and Negri consists of the couple colonizer/colonized, or master/slave. "Coloniality . . . is constitutive of modernity—there is no modernity without coloniality," Mignolo writes in turn.[16] The year 1492 testifies of the advent of a new nomos of the earth that, at its core, consists of a double-bind: it is shored up by the idea of a "universal history" that, paradoxically, has as its condition of possibility its particular geographical location: Europe. Modernity simultaneously invents "history" (as an entity) and cuts through it like a knife. It divides into those with and those without history; those within the salutatory realm of history and those whose salvation will depend on their compliance in being maneuvered within it. Europe—and its twenty-first-century avatar "the West," still firmly rooted in the autonarrative of its intrinsic modernity—thus becomes the "civilization destined to lead and save the rest of the world," most notably from "barbarism and primitivism."[17] What is thus put into place has been amply theorized over the past decades by Latin American theorists as "the colonial matrix of power."[18] As Rámon Grosfoguel argues, this matrix cannot be reduced to its economic component. It consists of a "broad entangled 'package'" that includes, vitally, a vision of history, but also, on equal and intimately related terms, an epistemology, a cosmology, a spirituality, and visions of race and sexuality, as well as the economic rationale we call "capitalism."[19] The new nomos of the earth is nothing less than the violent attempt to universalize this complex "package" of epistemic hierarchies. Vitruvian man has the conquistador as his shadow.

"Modernity is always two," Hardt and Negri write, adding that, more precisely, "modernity lies between the two."[20] Cautious not to replicate modernity's autonarrative, they argue that "resistances to colonial domination, are not outside modernity but rather entirely internal to it, that is, within the power relation." Being intimately entwined with the colonial matrix of power, modernity hinges upon the inside/outside binary of a history of salvation and its subsequent epistemological, cosmological, or racial imaginaries. According to Hardt and Negri, modernity is therefore coextensive with the emergence of "the forces of antimodernity," ultimately resulting into what they call "altermodernity."[21] Consequently, modernity is to be understood neither as the unilateral narrative of conquest nor as the interminable Adornian dialectic between modernity and its "monsters" of myth and barbarism, leaving any foreseeable resolution of this dialectic at the price of the eruption of modernity's opposite, a new kind of barbarism.[22] The latter dialectic, by either dragging the colonized back into modernity's uniform interiority or banishing it to its antehistoric outside, in fact replicates that most pervasive diagonal of the colonial matrix of power, the inside/outside binary. For Hardt and Negri the veiled logic of modernity is that of the dynamics between encounter and foreclosure: the encounter with Amerindian and Caribbean civilizations has led to the foreclosure of "the innumerable resistances within and against modernity which constitute the primary element of danger for its dominant self-conception. Despite all the furious energy expended to cast out the 'antimodern' other, resistance remains within."[23] Walter Mignolo similarly dismisses a dialectical reading of modernity as the tacit endorsement of Eurocentrism, arguing that the nomos of the indigenous cultures of Latin America was "negated and discarded, not incorporated." The latter defiance of dialectical inclusion is vital here, since it accounts for the fact that "today we see that the 'first *nomos* of the earth' was not 'destroyed.' Because they were not destroyed they are reemerging in the twenty-first century in different guises: as religious and ancestral identities rearticulated in response to and confrontation with Western global designs (globalism rather than globalization). This is not, of course, to propose a return to the past but, precisely, to open up the roads toward global futures."[24]

For Mignolo, as well as for Hardt and Negri, the vicious circle of modernity, redefined here as the colonial matrix of power, can be broken only by recognizing how "the monstrousness and savagery of the native" that is called upon to legitimate European rule in the name of salutary modernity also holds the "positive, productive monsters of antimodernity, the monsters of liberation, [that] always exceed the domination of modernity and point toward an alternative."[25] This alternative will be conceptualized as "altermodernity" by Hardt and Negri and "de-coloniality" by Mignolo and others: "de-colonial thinking is, then, thinking that de-links and opens . . . to the possibilities hidden (*colonized and discredited, such as the traditional, barbarian, primitive, mystic, etc.*) by the modern rationality."[26] That is to say that, for Mignolo, the institution of the colonial matrix of power, with which modernity is coextensive, is also the moment when decolonial thinking materializes.[27] Decoloniality is therefore engrained in coloniality, not in a dialectical logic of opposites, but rather: it is akin to the mutual becoming of molar and molecular segmentations in Deleuze and Guattari, the latter continuously undermining the alignment of the former.[28] In decoloniality and altermodernity, the stakes are simultaneously epistemological and practical, cultural and political. Both ground epistemology on the terrain of struggle, as Hardt and Negri write.[29] By "delinking" indigenous, antimodern, or unmodern epistemologies from the modern nomos, both altermodernity and decoloniality make way for a rationality different from, and even diametrically opposed to, the modern power matrix. Perhaps the founding act of this alternative rationality is to overcome the binary thinking/doing. As Mignolo states, decolonial thinking means engaging in "decolonial options."[30]

The alternative to modernity consists, precisely, of a "truth constructed from below," grounded in practice, or rather: a multiplicity of practices.[31] Such practices, vitally, include those "colonised and discredited, such as the traditional, barbarian, primitive and mystic," referred to by Mignolo, or what Hardt and Negri call "the savage power of monsters."[32] It is crucial here to note that such notions as "savage" of "primitive" are not necessarily essentializing notions. They neither obtain their meaning exclusively, and negatively, as exteriority in relation to the modern matrix, nor do they result solely, and positively, from phantasmagorias of the nonconstructed world of the pure given or the "narcissistic paradise" of an "immanent humanity," as Eduardo Viveiros de Castro calls it.[33] Discarding the savage and mythic either as modernity's projected antipode or as Rousseauist reverie might in fact entail, once more, equating liberation or autonomy and modernity.[34] For Hardt and Negri, "when we reduce all figures of antimodernity to a tame dialectical play of opposite identities, we miss the liberatory possibilities of their monstrous imaginings."[35] At least in part, the passage from anti- to altermodernity operates through the revaluation of those epistemologies, cosmologies, and practices that, having been branded "savage," were the prime objects of modernity's foreclosure.

Crucially, I would like to argue, this revaluation proceeds from an *anthropological perspective*—and more precisely of what we might call the anthropology of savage thought (pensée sauvage), as it originates in Lévi-Strauss and is taken up and rewritten by, in particular, Pierre Clastres, and the work of contemporary anthropologists such as Eduardo Viveiros de Castro or Todd Ochoa.[36] Decolonial and altermodern thinking intimately link with the anthropology of savage thought. As Lévi-Strauss famously writes, "the savage mind totalizes," but in a manner that is radically opposed to the (historical, economic, or racial) totalities of modernity: it displays an "intransigent refusal . . . to allow anything human (or even living) to remain alien to it";[37] its "thirst for objective knowledge"[38] does not result in objectifying what is exterior to it but rather presents us with a totality that consists of *imagines mundi*, which, like a "room of mirrors," help to understand the world as much as they resemble the world.[39] Savage thought simultaneously constructs a world and relates to that world.[40] In this sense, savage thought offers a perspective with which to probe modern epistemology, if not to imagine its beyond. As Hardt and Negri rightly argue, contemporary anthropologists such as Viveiros de Castro do not simply advocate an "unmodern Amerindian ontology," a kind of modern-day, albeit inverted, robinsonnade providing the antidote to modernity's ontology by replacing it with another. Rather, they use the anthropological perspective to "critique modern epistemology and push it toward an altermodern rationality."[41] For Viveiros de Castro, "Lévi-Strauss' profound idea of a savage thought has to be understood as the extrapolation of a different image of thought, rather than a different image of the savage."[42]

The anthropology of savage thought ultimately allows for what we might call a *savage anthropology*, a counteranalysis to the all-too-familiar humanitas/anthropos divide. What Viveiros de Castro calls "Amerindian perspectivism" not only constitutes an object for the modern rationality of the discipline of anthropology but, crucially, constitutes a different kind of anthropology, a new "theoretical image of theory."[43] By asking "what is a point of view *for* the indigenous?," "the classified become classifiers," equipped with an epistemology that defies anthropology's modern presuppositions (and binaries such as object/subject, human/nonhuman, life/death, knowing/doing).[44] Anthropology thus becomes akin to Lévi-Strauss's room of mirrors: the indigenous ontologies, epistemologies, and cosmologies that constitute its object force it to probe the modern, objectivist *episteme*. In particular, this reworking of the objectivist *episteme* challenges the alleged incompatibility between knowing and doing that, de facto, has obfuscated anthropology's complicity with the very real practices of the modern matrix of power (with all its epistemic, cosmological, racial, and sexual diagonals). Anthropology thus becomes "the anthropology of the concept."[45] For Viveiros de Castro this continuous mirroring of perspectives turns anthropology into the "theory of a permanent decolonization. A permanent decolonization of thought."[46] This savage anthropology thus puts *politics* at stake: it refutes the epistemic genealogy of Western political subjectivity, from the zoon politikon to Hobbes's *homo homini lupus* to the Schmittian enemy. Instead it offers insight into what Deleuze and Guattari call the "supple segmentarity" of primitive social/political organization: "a polyvocal *code* based on lineages and their varying situations and relations, and an itinerant *territoriality* based on local, overlapping divisions, form a fabric of relatively supple segmentarity."[47] What opens up here is a *savage political anthropology* in the Clastrian vein: a political anthropology that allows for a chiastic reading of decolonial and autonomist theory through the prism of the savage and primitive. Such an explicit perspective of the savage and the primitive, in the epistemic sense that runs from Lévi-Strauss to Viveiros de Castro, accounts for a more fruitful encounter between decolonial and autonomist thinking than is sketched by Hardt and Negri, whereby political anthropology, precisely, constitutes the hyphen between decoloniality and autonomy. In *Commonwealth* the juxtaposition between the decolonial and indigenous perspectivism of contemporary anthropology—with its decidedly nonmodern "multiple ontologies" and "multiplicity of beings constantly open to alterity"[48]—ultimately remains part of the surprisingly traditional dialectical schema of altermodernity's overcoming of the opposition of modernity and antimodernity. Instead, I would like to emphasize the joined project of decolonial and autonomist thinking, their mutual attempt to break through modernity's epistemological horizon and to create an alternative political anthropology that recognizes a multiplicity of anthropological subjects in opposition to the humanitas—an *affirmative* exteriority of the anthropos that is no longer the prerequisite for its negation. It is by reading autonomist thinking as savage political anthropology that autonomism's latent (epistemic and political) decoloniality can be put to the forefront.

Anomaly, Anomie, Autonomy: Negri's Spinozan Anthropology

In what can perhaps be described best as his first major postoperaist work, *The Savage Anomaly*, Toni Negri offers a political anthropology of what he calls "the Dutch anomaly." The anomaly here refers to the meteoric economic rise of the Dutch Republic that spans the mid-seventeenth century and, correlatively, Dutch colonial expansion into the Indonesian archipelago and the Caribbean. This geopolitical golden age coincides with the flowering of cultural and intellectual life in the newly constituted Dutch Republic and witnesses iconic figures such as Rembrandt, Huygens, and Spinoza. Negri speaks of "a prosaic but very powerful society, which makes poetry without knowing it, because it has the force to do so."[49] What Negri refers to as the Dutch anomaly points to a situation that is not only historically speaking exceptional but, consequently, for Negri, *holds the promise of a different political anthropology*. According to Negri, the Dutch anomaly, notably, indicates the exceptional status of the Dutch Republic in a historical context of monarchism and absolute statism, and thus the possibility of an emerging autonomous, self-affirming, and multiple political subject. The anomaly consists of the possibility of what Hardt and Negri will later call an "altermodern" political subject that appears at the very moment of consolidation of the colonial matrix of power. The Dutch anomaly therefore indicates the *constitutive crisis of political modernity*. The Hobbesian rationale of the state intends to ward off this crisis, and with it the advent of the *multitudo* that is nonetheless, as Spinoza will demonstrate according to Negri, intrinsically part of modernity. Hobbesian absolutism becomes all the more vital in the context of coloniality, since its stakes concern both Europe and its Outside: the state, foreclosing the very possibility of subjective multiplicities, becomes the absolute guarantor of the humanitas/anthropos divide, and thus the absolute measure for maintaining the inside/outside of modernity.

The constitutive crisis of political modernity, and its unremitting repression, therefore takes place simultaneously on two scenes: Europe and the colonial world. However, Negri underlines the profound ambivalence of the Dutch exception: the prosaic world of the new-born Dutch republican bourgeoisie is, in reality, made possible by what Negri calls "the savage adventure of accumulation on the seas."[50] The Dutch anomaly, for Negri, refers first and foremost to "this *disproportion* between the constructive and appropriative dimensions" of the bourgeois-capitalist revolution of modernity.[51] It is this dissymmetry between the ideology of the right measure and colonialist savagery that, according to Negri, signals "the *crisis* of the utopia of the bourgeois origins, the crisis of the founding myth of the market—the essential point in the history of Modern philosophy."[52] Again, the anomaly here is not merely a curiosity but in fact marks the constitutive and enduring crisis of the modern capitalist world. "The crisis destroys the utopia in its bourgeois historical determinateness," Negri writes; it "dissolves its contingent superficiality, and opens it instead to the determination of human and collective production."[53]

For Negri, Spinozism operates thoroughly from within this anomaly by "renew[ing] concepts that the entire century is moving against." Spinozism, Negri argues, *incorporates* the constitutive disproportion, "the immeasurable measure" as he calls it, of Dutch modernity, but by twisting it completely.[54] As the colonial divide of the world allows for the unimaginable accumulation and geographical transfer of riches on a global scale, Spinoza stages a different encounter, a different epistemic endorsement of Europe's expansion into the indigenous habitus. Rather than implying that Spinozism simply bears the hallmark of the advent of modern capitalism, as exemplified in Dutch colonialist imperialism, Negri conceives of Spinozism as an alternative imagining of the encounter with the New World: not as capitalist savage accumulation, and its reasoning in the humanitas/anthropos divide, but as the endorsement of multiplicity—a different kind of savagery. The Spinozan multitudo, Negri states, "opens up to the sense of the multiplicity of subjects and [their] constructive power. . . . It arrives, in fact, at the point of situating the theoretical and ethical problem on the threshold of the comprehension of the radical immeasurability of the development in progress."[55] The "savage element" in Spinoza, as Negri explicitly calls it, traverses the fables of the right measure and Hobbesian organicism.[56] Spinozism thus heralds the death of Vitruvian man: it offers an anthropology counter to that of European modernity in the sense that, so to speak, its world no longer mirrors its subject (as is the case with the Vitruvian subject of modernity, dividing those who inhabit the world into humanitas/anthropos), but its subject mirrors its world. By incorporating "the radical immeasurability of the development in progress," the Spinozan multitudo "is articulated on the density and the multiplicity of affirmations."[57] In *The*

Savage Anomaly Negri underlines this reciprocity between a (political) subject than can only be conceptualized in its irreducible multiplicity, as multitudo, and a world that "exalts its very own absoluteness only by recognizing itself in its very own givenness [and] collective, constitutive, material practice."[58] As I argued earlier, the "Dutch anomaly" is hence two-sided (anomalous in its two-sidedness): on the one hand Dutch republicanism tears wide open the constitutive crisis of modernity by affirming the constitutive power of the multitude; on the other hand, simultaneously embodying the acme of modernity in its bourgeois rationale, it remains inextricably linked with the colonial matrix of power.[59] For Negri the proper name of this anomaly is Spinoza. The constitutive crisis that Negri identifies in Spinoza, the crisis in Vitruvian measurability, functions as a kind of "historical a priori" for what we have coined savage political anthropology.[60] Spinoza's anthropology is savage precisely in so far as it refuses the state as the measure and guarantor of modernity's many divides. As Negri argues, even if Spinoza flirts with the Hobbesian realism of the description of natural society, he remains "the first anti-Hobbes that the history of Western political thought presents."[61] Negri's Spinoza ironically counters the dialectic between modernity and antimodernity that is prevalent in *Commonwealth*, foreshadowing its overcoming in altermodern resistances. It is precisely the emphasis on "the savage element" in Spinoza that allows Negri to rethink operaismo's class or social composition as multitudo; that is to say, by reconnecting with, and to an extent by recognizing, the autonomist project of a political anthropology of the savage subject.[62]

Toward a Savage Political Anthropology

As I have argued in the introduction to this chapter, reconsidering autonomist thinking as savage political anthropology uncovers strange and even stranger bedfellows with whom it shares an ethos as well as a vocabulary. It is in their decided anti-Hobbesianism that, for example, Toni Negri and Paolo Virno encounter the anarchist anthropology of Pierre Clastres. For Clastres, primitive society is characterized by the *refusal* of the state. Crucially, primitive society is not defined by a *lack* of the state. According to Clastres, the absence of the state is not a sign of immaturity: on the contrary, the positive, formal characteristic of primitive society is nothings less than the rejection of the state.[63] In Clastres, the state is minimally defined as the separate domain of the exercise of power: the refusal of the state is the refusal of social division, in favor of social multiplicity. Clastres thus proposes a *political anthropology* since, for him, the very being of primitive society is political: the "social machine" of primitive society, as·he calls it, is a machine against the state.[64] The crucial question of this peculiar political anthropology therefore is: how does primitive society operate to short-circuit the passage to the state?[65] For Clastres, this is not so much a *historical* question, since he rejects evolutionary anthropology for its complicity with the logic of political modernity. Rather, it is the question of a *historical a priori*. Clastres's predilection for early modern political philosophy, Hobbes and Étienne de la Boétie in particular, is concerned with this historical a priori of the passage to the state. In "Les sauvages sont-ils heureux?" (Are Savages Happy?), Clastres argues that primitive societies want to preserve their being as *absolutely political* by preventing the passage to the state, by maintaining forms of enduring social scission.[66] What constitutes primitive society is in a sense the obstinate refusal of the institutionalized "unhappiness" of the state, Clastres writes in close parallel to the Spinozan savage anthropology Negri proposes. What is at stake in Clastres is "to demonstrate that primitive society poses a problem to political philosophy because it is the *political form* that contests radically the Western model."[67] The political here is extracted from the very organization of social life.[68] The paradox of savage politics, Clastres argues in *Society against the State*, is that it exists even where, or perhaps better still: especially where political institutions are absent. Politics exists in absentia.[69] In this sense, Clastres's political anthropology is a refusal of the fable of the zoon politikon and of the subsequent logic of the social contract, of historical reason, of the humanitas/anthropos divide and so on. To the zoon politikon, Clastres opposes the idea of a *savage sociality*. Situating himself within Lévi-Strauss's appraisal of savage thought, Clastres explicitly refers to the subject of his political anthropology as *savage*, without any pejorative evolutionary connotation, but as *anomaly* in relation to the zoon politikon. Whereas for Hobbes the savage is he who remains outside the social, since the absence of the state makes the institution of the social impossible, in Clastres, on the contrary, the savage becomes *the guarantor of the social* precisely because he or she obstructs the advent of state. The savage literally wages war on the state.[70] For Clastres, the social being of primitive societies is a being-for-war that constitutes their very sociality.[71] It is his *savage sociality* (that is negatively translated in Hobbes's infamous dictum *bellum omnium contra omnes*) that haunts European political philosophy since the encounter with Amerindian civilization, in so far as it represents the subversion of Hobbesian political anthropology.[72] Clastres's anthropological perspective reveals that the historical a priori for the zoon politikon is in fact the appearance of the state.[73] The *savage*, as the subject of this political anthropology, is the effect of the functioning of the social machine (that is always already a *political* war machine) rather than a kind of interim animality.[74] Again, for Clastres, "primitive societies are societies without the State, not because the State is lacking provisionally, because *within them the state is impossible*."[75] In fact, there is no lack that the state could fill, since society is entirely directed against the division of power: the political-as-sociality is directed against the political-as-coercion. In this light, Clastres writes, "primitive societies are societies of *the refusal of labor*." It is the advent of the state, as the separate domain of the exercise of power that produces the economy. Obviously, Clastres thus turns the most basic of Marxist intuitions upside down.[76]

In his incisive study of the autonomist movement in the 1970s, Marcello Tari emphasizes autonomism's explicit claims to a similar kind of *primitivism*. The savage is explicitly claimed as a political subject, most tellingly perhaps in the figure of the "Metropolitan Indian." Intellectually, Tari argues, autonomism functions as a "savage theorization":[77] it offers a savage political anthropology of collective ways of being as "war machines against the state" and of the new subjects that constitute it.[78] For Tari, "Autonomia" constituted the most far-reaching of ruptures with what he calls "the phantasm of *civil society*."[79] Against civil society as a separate sphere constituted under the aegis of the state, autonomism claimed not the foreclosure of the sphere but the abundance of the *area*. According to Tari, autonomism as area entails "to be autonomous even within autonomy,"[80] to go forth and multiply, so to speak, to posit multiplicity as the guarantor of politics. That is to say, of a politics redefined as the organization of collective being against its alienation in the state, as the "ecology of voluntary associations," as David Graeber calls it.[81] In this sense, the *area* of autonomy exists as a *primitive society* as defined by Clastres, as it draws on the constitutive crisis that precedes the zoon politikon. With Tari, we might say that autonomism thus turns scission (*separazione*) against the divisions instituted by the epistemology of state-centered modernity. As Tari argues, autonomist thinking retains communism as a "minimal program," communism as ethos or "common ethical disposition," or even as "offensive ways of living," rather than "the qualification of a subject."[82]

Tari's analysis of autonomism's savage political anthropology echoes the reading of the autonomist legacy by the French collective Tiqqun, for whom autonomy represents the possibility of what they call a "subjectless revolt," a revolt not of the zoon politikon but *of the social* against the atrophy of the world of labor and the state.[83] Tiqqun thus refuses the statist containment of primitive war (of "civil war" as they call it) and expresses a fondness of the wars of religion. They celebrate sects and schisms as entirely *ethical*, that is to say, as communes rooted in forms-of-life, as shared penchants or shared tastes for forms of (collective) being. In Tiqqun, this genealogy of the state explicitly harks back to Pierre Clastres's onto-anthropological claim of "primitive" civil war as humankind's original resistance to stasis. In Tiqqun, Clastres's original fable is transposed to the primal scene of Western politics, that of Hobbes's *Leviathan*. Hence, the explicit claims to *sectarianism*. What lies at the heart of sectarianism is a "discordant ethics," the construction of a new collective ethos as a permanent force directed against stasis and entropy, as the offensive endorsement of permanently being-in-crisis. In Tiqqun we again find the immediate nexus between the onto-anthropological and the political. Again, discordance has to be assumed as the "original fact" of sociogenesis.[84] This ties in with recent work by Paolo Virno, who redefines the subject of the multitude as "that problematic, or better yet, unstable and dangerous animal whose life is characterized by negation, by the modality of the possible, by regression to the infinite."[85] For Virno this dangerous political animal is foremost a *linguistic animal*: "negation and the modality of the possible" are the work of language; *they are the effects of our mode of existence as speaking bodies*. Therefore, for Virno, "the multitude is a *historico-natural category*." If the advent of the multitude marks the crisis of the modern, central state, this is precisely because it demonstrates the "impossibility of separating political rules from species-specific regularity . . . *the crisis derives from the impossibility of leaving the natural state*."[86] The crisis of the modern state over and again harks back to a constitutive crisis (that Virno even refers to in terms of *historico-natural*) of politics and the political subject itself that is in the closest proximity with Clastres's and Tiqqun's primitivism and decolonial thinking. Interestingly, and this is perhaps a postautonomous vein to be explored, Virno has recourse to *ritual* in order to outline a modus operandi for these new means of autonomy. Virno writes: "Ritual fulfils a therapeutic function not because it erects a barrier *against* the crisis of presence, but because on the contrary, *it goes back over each stage of the crisis*. . . . Ritual praxis upholds extreme danger, widens uncertainty and chaos . . . it therefore constitutes a *symbolic repetition of anthropogenesis*."[87] This ritualistic-linguistic *katechon*, as Virno calls it, restrains but does not remove uncertainty; it lives off the very instability it wards off: it is "the institution that best adapts itself to the state of exception, when this state, far from being yet a prerogative of the sovereign, indicates rather the action and discourse of the multitude."[88]

The savage political anthropology that can be reconstructed from these examples precisely shows that contemporary autonomist thought[89] offers an investigation into modes of social being, that as such are to be politicized, that transgress the arena of Western political philosophy and practice. It addresses the possibility of a new nomos, beyond the universalizing project of Western modernity, its Vitruvian epistemological and subjective architecture. The urge "to resume the thread of analysis of social composition and decomposition if we want to distinguish possible lines of processes of recomposition to come," as Berardi stated, can be met by linking autonomist thought with decolonial thinking, a project that passes through the revaluation of autonomist thought as political anthropology. It is the anthropological perspective that remains vital to both autonomist and decolonial thinking, and that reveals their shared diagnosis of the constitutive encounter of (political) modernity, between Vitruvian man and the peripheral anthropos. It is the anthropological perspective that emphasizes the need to restage this encounter in a world that, once more, faces the scenario of modernity's constitutive crisis: the emergence of a polycentric world faces reduction through the universalizing reason of modern capitalism. The waning of the West's hegemony does not mechanically imply the end of modernity, perhaps merely its spatial dislocation. As Walter Mignolo writes, the pace of our present day is perhaps foremost set by the tension between dewesternization and rewesternization. The actualization of a new nomos asks for the epistemological and political ramifications of the "passage beyond modernity" to be the stake of an infinite variety of specifically located practices. ("I am where I think and do," as Mignolo states.)[90] The reconceptualization of autonomy thus becomes not the act of a self-affirming humanitas, whose proclamation of independence implies the passivity and unfreedom of those whom it concurrently excludes, but as the repeated affirmation of multiple subjects, who are "multiple" not merely in the sense of "plural" but also in the sense of their openness to alterity. The anthropological perspective demonstrates that, in a context foremost characterized by polycentricity, the "savage" becomes a resource for thinking and practicing a politics engrained in the multiple ontologies of such anthropological subjects: whether it is through notions and practices such as ritual, animism, or metamorphosis. Such a savage political anthropology heralds the death of Vitruvian man. It shows how the anomic subject, from the anomaly for political philosophy, might come to function as the condition for autonomy.

NOTES

1. Tronti, in Chiesa and Toscano, *The Italian Difference*, 102–3, my emphasis.

2. See Tiqqun, *Tout a failli, vive le communisme!* Virno, *Multitude: Between Innovation and Negation*; Berardi, *Precarious Rhapsody*.

3. See Althusser, *Philosophy of the Encounter: Later Writings, 1978–1987*.

4. Berardi, *Precarious Rhapsody*, 14.

5. Berardi, *Precarious Rhapsody*, 15.

6. Berardi, *Precarious Rhapsody*, 30.

7. Berardi, *Precarious Rhapsody*, 31.

8. Maldonado-Torres, *Against War*, 238.

9. Mignolo, *The Darker Side of Western Modernity*, 2.

10. Maldonado-Torres, *Against War*, 238.

11. Mignolo *The Darker Side of Western Modernity*, 83.

12. Hardt and Negri, *Commonwealth*, 67–118.

13. The epistemological as well as political potential of such a reassessment of "savage thought" is equally central to the work of Federico Luisetti. In his work, Luisetti explores the convergence between radical European epistemologies, in particular those attempting to rethink the (Vitruvian) humanitas (Nietzsche, Deleuze and Guattari, Clastres) and contemporary decolonial thinking. It is this convergence in a "savage decolonialism" that inscribes European philosophies, ethnographies and (Latin) American decolonial theory in a now newly articulated "savage paradigm." This essay owes much to Luisetti's work: any overlaps are in fact programmatic and hopefully co-constitutive of such a paradigm. See for example Luisetti, "Savage Decolonialist" and *Una Vita*.

14. Hardt and Negri, *Commonwealth*, 67.

15. As Walter D. Mignolo argues in *The Darker Side of the Renaissance*: "Western expansion and colonization, in the sixteenth century, coincided with a radical transformation of the concept of time that impinged on the concept of history and created the necessary condition to place different conceptual frameworks somewhere in a temporal scale that had its point of arrival in the present, sixteenth century Christian European civilization" (327).

16. Hardt and Negri, *Commonwealth*, 2.

17. Hardt and Negri, *Commonwealth*, 28.

18. See, in particular, the work of Aníbal Quijano, Walter Mignolo, and Arturo Escobar.

19. Grosfoguel, "Transmodernity, Border Thinking, and Global Coloniality."

20. Hardt and Negri, *Commonwealth*, 68.

21. Hardt and Negri, *Commonwealth*, 67.

22. Hardt and Negri, *Commonwealth*, 96.

23. Hardt and Negri, *Commonwealth*, 69.

24. Mignolo, *The Darker Side of Western Modernity*, 30.

25. Hardt and Negri, *Commonwealth*, 97.

26. Mignolo, "Epistemic Disobedience and the De-colonial Option: A Manifesto," e-text, my emphasis.

27. Mignolo, *Darker Side of Western Modernity*, xxiv.

28. Deleuze and Guattari, *Thousand Plateaus*, 234.

29. Hardt and Negri, *Commonwealth*, 121.

30. Mignolo, *Darker Side of Western Modernity*, 10; "'I am where I do and think,'" xvi.

31. Hardt and Negri, *Commonwealth*, 121.

32. Hardt and Negri, *Commonwealth*, 98.

33. Viveiros de Castro, *Métaphysiques Cannibales*, 28; my translation.

34. As Walter Mignolo writes, "even progressive intellectuals support capitalism by critiquing the outmoded, traditional, romantic, Arcadian potentials of indigenous spirituality. After all, we know that since 1492 indigenous people all around the world have been thought of as barbarians; and furthermore, in the eighteenth century they became primitives. Many people still think so today." *Darker Side of Western Modernity*, 64.

35. Hardt and Negri, *Commonwealth*, 99.

36. See for example Viveiros de Castro, *From the Enemy's Point of View*; Viveiros de Castro, *Métaphysiques Cannibales*; and Ochao, *Society of the Dead*.

37. Lévi-Strauss, *Savage Mind*, 245.

38. Lévi-Strauss, *Savage Mind*, 2.

39. Lévi-Strauss, *Savage Mind*, 263.

40. "It builds mental structures which facilitates an understanding of the world in as much as they resemble it. In this sense savage thought can be defined as analogical thought." Lévi-Strauss, *Savage Mind*, 263.

41. Hardt and Negri, *Commonwealth*, 124.

42. Viveiros de Castro, *Métaphysiques Cannibales*, 46; my translation.

43. Viveiros de Castro, *Métaphysiques Cannibales*, 43–44.

44. Viveiros de Castro, *Métaphysiques Cannibales*, 44, 51.

45. Viveiros de Castro, *Métaphysiques Cannibales*, 46.

46. Viveiros de Castro, quoted in Melitopoulos and Lazzarato, "Assemblages."

47. Deleuze and Guattari, *A Thousand Plateaus*, 231.

48. Hardt and Negri, *Commonwealth*, 123–24.

49. Negri, *Savage Anomaly*, 5.

50. Negri, *Savage Anomaly*, 6.

51. Negri, *Savage Anomaly*, 6–7.

52. Negri, *Savage Anomaly*, 8–9.

53. Negri, *Savage Anomaly*, 9.

54. Negri, *Savage Anomaly*, 122.

55. Negri, *Savage Anomaly*, 8.

56. Negri, *Savage Anomaly*, 15.

57. Negri, *Savage Anomaly*, 222.

58. Negri, *Savage Anomaly*, 217.

59. We might even argue that it in fact absolutizes the colonial matrix of power by secularizing it.

60. For the notion of "historical a priori," see Agamben, *Signature of All Things*.

61. Negri, *Savage Anomaly*, 112.

62. Perhaps we might even say that it is this emphasis on the savage element that provides Negri with his key notion: the multitude.

63. Clastres, *La Sociétié contre l'État*, 161; Clastres, quoted in Abensour, *Pierre Clastres*, 13, 25.

64. Clastres, quoted in Abensour, *Pierre Clastres*, 17; my translation. This is perhaps best exemplified by the role of the chief in primitive society, according to Clastres: instead of being the locus of power, the chief is a vital part of the social machine *against* the state, the chief occupies the place from which the destruction of the state remains possible: *the chief is granted prestige, but not power*: the chief has obligations toward society, but not the other way around, and his prestige can be revoked at any moment (28–30).

65. Clastres, quoted in Abensour, *Pierre Clastres*, 14.

66. Clastres, quoted in Abensour, *Pierre Clastres*, 0.

67. González Broquen, quoted in Abensour, *Pierre Clastres*, 223; my translation.

68. González Broquen, quoted in Abensour, *Pierre Clastres*, 224.

69. Clastres, *La Sociétié contre l'État*, 20–21; my translation.

70. The pivot of Deleuze and Guattari's critique of Clastres consists of the assumption of the mutual exclusion of primitive society and state segmentarity: "He [Clastres] tended to make primitive societies hypostases, self-sufficient entities. . . . He made their formal exteriority into a real independence. Thus he remained an evolutionist, posited a state of nature. Only this state of nature was, according to him, a fully social reality instead of a pure concept, and the evolution was a sudden mutation instead of a development. For on the one hand, the State rises up in a single stroke, fully formed; on the other, the counter-State societies use very specific mechanisms to ward it off, to prevent it from arising. . . . We will never leave the evolution hypothesis behind by creating a break between the two terms, that is, by endowing bands with self-sufficiency and the State with an emergence all the more miraculous and monstrous." Deleuze and Guattari, *A Thousand Plateaus*, 396.

71. Clastres, *Recherches d'anthropologie politique*, 173–74.

72. Blechman, quoted in Abensour, *Pierre Clastres*, 289.

73. Clastres, *La Sociétié contre l'État*, 171.

74. Clastres, *La Sociétié contre l'État*, 118.

75. Clastres, *La Sociétié contre l'État*, 179.

76. Clastres, *La Sociétié contre l'État*, 167–69.

77. Tari, *Autonomie! Italie, les années 70*, 40.

78. Tari, *Autonomie! Italie, les années 70*, 29.

79. Tari, *Autonomie! Italie, les années 70*, 53.

80. Tari, *Autonomie! Italie, les années 70*, 47.

81. Graeber, *Fragments of an Anarchist Anthropology*, 73.

82. Tari, *Autonomie! Italie, les années 70*, 28. In autonomist discourse, according to Tari, "working class" only remains "the name of the hostile separation in relation to the society of capital, the powerful evocation of the possibility of extinction of the state" (48).

83. Tiqqun, *Tout a failli, vive le communisme!*, 73.

84. Tiqqun, *Tout a failli, vive le communisme!*, 31.

85. Virno, *Multitude: Between Innovation and Negation*, 18.

86. Virno, *Multitude: Between Innovation and Negation*, 37.

87. Virno, *Multitude: Between Innovation and Negation*, 52.

88. Virno, *Multitude: Between Innovation and Negation*, 62.

89. Notwithstanding, and against, the analyses of post-Fordist political economy with which it is mostly associated.

90. Mignolo, *Darker Side of Western Modernity*, xvi.

2

Sovereignty, Indigeneity, Territory Zapatista Autonomy & the New Practices of Decolonization ALVARO REYES AND MARA KAUFMAN

Since the morning of January 1, 1994, when the almost exclusively indigenous Zapatista Army for National Liberation (Ejército Zapatista de Liberación Nacional [EZLN]) took over seven municipalities in the southeastern state of Chiapas, Mexico, and declared war on the Mexican government, thousands of pages have been written placing the Zapatista movement at the very center of indigenous movements in Latin America and of anticapitalist projects around the world. Following those early days, a long series of attempted negotiations and government betrayals led the Zapatistas to sever ties with the entirety of the Mexican political class, including the institutional left, embodied in the Partido de La Revolución Democratica and its 2006 presidential candidate, Andrés Manuel López Obrador. This radical break by the Zapatistas was interpreted by many as a sign of revolutionary purism, the consequence of which, according to these commentators, was their increasing marginalization and consequent political irrelevance. Since this article initially appeared, in 2011, the chorus of "progressive" opinion that deems the EZLN a spent and irrelevant social force in Mexico and the world has only grown. As Uruguayan social theorist Raúl Zibechi has noted, anyone who during these years spent time with Mexico's intellectual urban left had the disconcerting experience of being presented with the thesis that "the Zapatistas no longer exist."[1] For us, as longtime participants in Zapatista-related activities, this thesis conflicted with what we felt was the lasting singularity of Zapatista innovation and with our own eyewitness experience of the continuing growth of the Zapatista project. As the saying goes, we were forced to confront the thesis that "the Zapatistas no longer exist" with our lying eyes. As the initial article we published in 2011 is witness to, in defiance of that chorus of "progressive" opinion, we chose to believe our lying eyes.

Readers, however, do not have to take our word regarding the continued vitality of the Zapatista movement; the EZLN itself has given a resounding response to doubts regarding their existence with a march on December 21, 2012 (what some believed would be the "end of the world" according to the Mayan calendar) by some fifty thousand EZLN bases of support through five cities in Chiapas, some of the same cities taken in the 1994 uprising.[2] This time, however, in their biggest public manifestation ever, the Zapatistas marched in absolute silence, unarmed, in perfect disciplined order that made it impossible to break their ranks, in effect "taking" those cities again. In each town square a makeshift stage had been constructed, up and over which the Zapatistas marched in silent waves, raising their left fists in the air as they crossed, without pausing or turning a masked face. No one spoke from these stages and they were dismantled shortly after the march, but the EZLN communiqué released later that day declared: "Did you hear that? It is the sound of your world crumbling, it is the sound of our world resurging."[3] In addition to these marches, which themselves demonstrated a deep organizational capacity extending across the state of Chiapas, the EZLN asserted in a series of subsequent communiqués that during the time of their supposed "disappearance" they had in their own words "grown exponentially" and that the autonomous systems that we describe in this article are even further developed today than a mere three years ago at the initial writing of it. In addition, they issued an invitation to the "Zapatista Little School" for those interested to come to Zapatista territory and see the strength of the Zapatista project for themselves and begin building joint initiatives.[4]

How then are we to make sense of the existence of the thesis within "progressive" circles in Mexico (as well as some academic circles in the United States) that "the Zapatistas no longer exist?" Can we reduce such a thesis to pure malice on the part of the partisans of Mexico's electoral left (for example, the supporters of Andrés Manuel López Obrador in the presidential elections of 2006 and 2012)? Certainly this sector's animosity toward the Zapatistas has been abundant, but it would be a mistake to reduce the incomprehension of the Zapatista project to the electoral winds of Mexico's official political calendar. Rather, we feel that this recurring thesis is more productively viewed as an invitation to examine the permanent and ever deepening bifurcation of "the left" in the face of the quickly unfolding global conjuncture.

Schematically, we can say that on the one hand we have a "left" that insists on continuing to do politics as if it were possible to take the state (through electoral means) in order to implement social programs to alleviate the worst consequences of neoliberalism while simultaneously accepting the long-term imposition of capitalist accumulation. This has been more or less the path embarked upon by nearly every "progressive government" in South America's "turn toward the left" (with the result of deepening social and environmental contradictions across the continent associated with the "neo-extractive" industries upon which this path depends) and has undoubtedly served as the inspiration for the populist electoral aspirations of much of Mexico's "progressive" left.[5]

As of 2014, two things were clear with regard to this path that were not so apparent during the electoral victories of these "progressive governments." One, the "poverty alleviation" programs of these governments in South America have not only been the key brake on the momentum of the powerful political movements that appeared throughout the region in the last two decades of the twentieth century, they have also left wholly untouched the radically unequal distribution of income, the concentration of wealth (with the possible exception of Venezuela), the extreme concentration of land, and the monoculture of the commodity export economy dominant in the region.[6] And two, the crisis of capitalism, which since 2008 has once again been at the center of political discussion, is not a short-term cyclical crisis but increasingly appears to be a long-term structural crisis of capitalist accumulation accompanied by the consequent refunctionalization of what has been thought of as the entire "superstructural" edifice of capitalist modernity.[7] In other words, we are seeing a long-term *civilizational* crisis of "the West" to which "the state," "political parties," and "civil society" are hardly in any position to respond, given their existential debt to the very levels of aggregate capitalist growth that began with the era of conquest and primitive accumulation but that today seem a relic of the past. Despite this, much of Mexico's "progressive" left (as is true of much of "the left" around the world) continues to insist that the electoral realm and the attempted suppression of the worst consequences of neoliberalism must take political precedence over and above these realities, and thus they dive head first, seemingly unperturbed, into the next electoral cycle—at times even going so far as to blame lack of support from the Zapatistas for their ongoing debacles.

On the other hand something quite novel has taken place in Mexico. Over the course of eleven years, through their national campaign to change the Mexican constitution with regard to "Indigenous Rights and Culture," the EZLN has systematically shown *in practice* (and not out of some preconceived ideological purism) that "reform" is today a mere chimera for the dispossessed of Mexico, due to the fact all three constituted powers in Mexico (presidential, legislative, and judicial) function as mere administrators of the catastrophe that the neoliberal global *dispositif* (alternatively referred to as Democracy Inc. or *parlamento-capitalism*) has wrought on the country. Yet, at a time when the much discussed "biopolitical" qualities of contemporary capitalism make it seem inescapable, the Zapatistas have done more than simply critique the institutional left or lament the end of that left's world (a world that, as we will describe here, is for us nothing other than the listless afterlife of Carl Schmitt's *jus publicum Europaeum*). Nor has the EZLN fallen under the illusion that "revolution," in its twentieth-century sense (i.e., taking the state through armed struggle), can revive that world. Rather, by building on the experiences and organizational forms that have been created and recreated in the constant struggle against the mechanisms of colonization upon which the contemporary global neoliberal dispositif is built—a struggle for decolonization in which the EZLN has shown that it is in fact possible to break with the "least worst" option within this world and build something else in the here and now. Drawing on this long-term vision of struggle, the Zapatistas exclaim: "You might very well ask us where we were in 2006 and 2012 [the last two presidential campaigns], but we could just as easily ask you, where have you been for the last five hundred years?"

Through the formulation of different principles (*mandar-obedeciendo*) and the construction of alternative organization and institutions to support those principles (i.e., the Zapatista army, the Good Government Councils, the autonomous municipalities, a range of productive cooperatives, etc.), and with an unparalleled everyday persistence toward maintaining those principles and institutions, the Zapatistas have shown that it is possible to collectively produce new subjects capable of slowly extricating themselves from the stench of death that pervades the institutions of capitalist modernity (i.e., the state and market) in Mexico. And they have demonstrated that through this process (and only through this long and lonely process, and not through the simple presupposition of a preexisting ontological exteriority), it is possible to tendentially move from the minimal resistance possible when one finds oneself "within and against" and toward the more fully propositional location of "outside and for" (something else). This process of exteriorization should not be imagined as either posing the confrontation of two bounded extensions (a particular form of territory tied to jus publicum Europaeum) or as the global expansion of the isomorphic calculable space of the forms of sovereignty implicit in contemporary Empire. Rather it is the contradiction between the territory of bounded or calculable extension that still undergirds market exchange (be it in its legal or illicit forms) and the establishment of a level of political intensity necessary for the formation of a point of localization from which springs an entirely different conception of territory (another territoriality), beyond the spent Schmittian imaginary of the contemporary West.[8] This is a particularly important project given the political situation unfolding in Mexico (and increasingly the rest of the world), where the intricate and volatile interweaving of political, corporate, and drug mafias that has arisen in the very locations previously occupied by Mexico's dictatorial social state is more likely to resemble the bleak and cynical outlook of a *Game of Thrones* than the harsh yet heroic outlook of the revolutionary manuals of the twentieth century.

With 150,000 deaths, 3 million displaced, and 27,000 forced disappearances in the last seven years of the drug war, with United States interference in Mexico through the Merida Initiative unabated, with highly probable and large-scale electoral fraud/manipulation in the last two national elections, with some 54 million Mexicans living in poverty (almost twice the number of poor as in 1970), and with the continuing mass export of its own population, the enormity of the catastrophe Mexico is currently living is hard to comprehend, let alone address.[9] With this situation in mind, we would like to once again return to the function of the now recurrent thesis of Mexico's progressive left, "the Zapatistas no longer exist." Could it be that this thesis represents a final desperate attempt by Mexico's "progressive" left to avoid the one question whose most probable answer would leave them disempowered or even on the wrong side in this war without front lines that slowly engulfs us all: Does Mexico still exist?

We believe that the position and actions that the Zapatistas have taken continue to place them at the heart of discussions and imaginaries of social change in Latin America. That is, at the very moment when movements throughout the region have increasingly found themselves drawn into what they have been able to construe retroactively as new forms of "neoliberal governance" under the banner of "progressive governments," the Zapatistas have refused to walk down this path and have instead directly challenged the contemporary union of representative democracy and neoliberal global capitalism. Both drawing on and innovating certain social organizational patterns within what are today the Zapatista communities of Chiapas, they have presented their struggle in markedly different terms from the national liberation movements of the 1960s and 1970s or other similarly positioned indigenous struggles in the Americas today. We argue that the singularity of the Zapatista struggle arises in the practice of mandar-obedeciendo (rule by obeying), and we attempt a conceptual delineation that will help us understand the context and extent of the rupture implied by this practice. Mandar-obedeciendo has allowed the Zapatistas to formulate their struggle not as one for the establishment of sovereignty or even some form of sub-sovereignty (concepts that they show us are intimately tied to the history of conquest as well as to the regime of social control proffered by contemporary global capitalism), but rather as the practical and tendential unmaking of sovereignty, be it in classical or contemporary forms. This possibility for the active unmaking of sovereignty presents itself in Zapatista territory through a new spatialization of struggle that makes possible the creation and everyday maintenance of an intricate system for the development of what the Zapatistas have termed "autonomy." This is an autonomy that the Zapatistas claim is central not only for the struggles of indigenous peoples but also as an antidote to the dispersed form of global "paracoloniality" that accompanies the appearance of what the Zapatistas have called "the Empire of money."[10]

Sovereignty and the Jus Publicum Europaeum

If, as Michel Foucault believed, "sovereignty is the central problem of right in Western societies," then the delineation of this concept would seem paramount.[11] Yet, due to the hegemonic force that political liberalism has retained and even gained (perhaps especially among contemporary social movements) through the increasing discourse of "rights" and its undergirding legalism, sovereignty has continually been reduced to the requirements for the establishment of "national independence."[12] That is, sovereignty is characterized according to certain attributions, both internal (some form of state structure and constitutional regime providing effective territorial control) and external (legitimation provided by recognition from fellow nations). Given this framework, the very position (and perhaps cause) of subalternity is thus imagined as prohibition from the site of the effective exercise of sovereignty. In the context of decolonization in particular, it was presumed that Europe was this effective site, where the population of Europe enjoyed a degree of equality under a system of norms (i.e., "the rule of law"), whereas the colonies were the site for the application of an extranormative force of domination (i.e., the exception). Given this vision, there has been a tremendous pull (not least among subaltern movements) to equate the freedom struggles of subaltern "peoples" with the establishment of some form of sovereignty or subsovereignty within the framework of an independent nation-state. The genealogy presented here will demonstrate what we consider to be a series of errors at the center of this liberal imagination, while it will simultaneously delimit sovereignty as one particular strategy of political organization that, in the case of the Zapatista movement, is challenged in toto (by the delineation and application of the counter-strategy detailed hereafter) as the mechanism at the intersection of the continued subordination of non-Western peoples and the onset of new forms of domination associated with neoliberal global capitalism.

In sharp contrast to the liberal imagination, Carl Schmitt attempted to show that sovereignty itself was in fact an extrajuridical concept at the very heart of the jus publicum Europaeum: "The norm requires a homogeneous medium. This effective normal situation is not a mere 'superficial presupposition' that a jurist can ignore; that situation belongs precisely to its immanent validity. There exists no norm that is applicable to chaos. For a legal order to make sense, a normal situation must exist, and he is sovereign who definitively decides whether this normal situation actually exists."[13] If sovereignty was this "highest power" of decision, then such a power could not by definition be derived from norms, as that would make it subsidiary to those norms. Thus, the norm had to be explained in relation to sovereignty and not the reverse, as the guardians of the international legal order in the twentieth century had come to believe. From Schmitt's perspective, then, the "rule of law" (i.e., the application of the norm) can be viewed only by understanding sovereignty as that which subtracts itself (from the norm) to guarantee the situation in which the norm would have the necessary regularity to be recognizable as such. Sovereignty stands outside the norm so as to decide what will be "taken outside" (i.e., marked as exterior to) the norm.[14] In this way, the sovereign decision is the basis for the creation of a spatial ordering, a topographical relation in which insides (the norm) and outsides (chaos) are distinguishable in law by placing the outside "as that with which [the sovereign] maintains itself in a potential relation in the state of exception."[15] To use rather different language, we might say that Schmitt recognizes that the norm always (and everywhere) necessitates, and simultaneously stems from, an extrajuridical moment of the "primitive accumulation" of social force, the "transcendental exercise of authority" made possible due to "the victory of one side over the other, a victory that makes the one sovereign and the other subject."[16] Let us note, then, that for Schmitt it would make little sense to propose that there is a site of sovereignty (Europe) and a site of exception (the colonies), as sovereignty itself is the site of the exception par excellence.

This does not mean, however, that the formation of sovereignty should be thought of as apart from, or incidental to, the history of the subjugation of non-Western peoples. To the contrary, as Schmitt himself points out, the conditions of possibility for the establishment of the sovereign decision, far from an abstraction of the intellect, were "a legendary and unforeseen discovery of a new world . . . an unrepeatable historical event."[17] Schmitt thus takes us to the very source of sovereignty and its relation to the non-West, as for him there is little doubt that it was exactly this historical event, the attempted conquest of the Americas by subjects with "a superior knowledge and consciousness," that solidified the necessary "*Ur*-acts of law-creation," the appropriation of land and the establishment of the colonies.[18] Due to these ur-acts, a double-ordering of sorts could take place, the establishment of an *Ordnung*, an order implying domestic political domination, and an *Ortung*, a spatial localization allowing for the distinction of insides and outsides by drawing lines across the face of the earth. In order to clarify the stakes of this double-ordering in the history of jurisprudence, we turn briefly to Juan Ginés de Sepúlveda and Thomas Hobbes.

In 1552, Sepúlveda, official chronicler for the Spanish kings Charles V and Philip II, ended his justification of the conquest and his explication of the principal order of natural law by referencing what he believed to be the concept that best encompassed this natural order and its application to the indigenous peoples of the Americas—Aristotle's notion of "natural slavery," that some were born to rule and some were born to be ruled.[19] Yet within book 1 of *The Politics*, the theory of natural slavery is for Aristotle the political subsidiary of a related but distinct philosophical problem: "in every composite thing, where a plurality of parts, whether continuous or discrete, is combined to make a single common whole, there is always found a ruling and a subject factor."[20] Given the permanence of this primal duality, according to Sepúlveda, a relation of command-obedience (*mandato-obedecer*) must exist within all relations.[21] Consequently, in Sepúlveda's eyes, because the indigenous peoples do not have rulers of their own, they must submit to the rule of their conquerors. Sepúlveda's revival of the Aristotelian necessity of "a ruling and a subject factor" in all relations (a necessity that should not be confused with natural slavery), and the conquest it helped justify, should be considered the central building block on which the modern notion of sovereignty was constructed within and outside Europe.[22]

Thomas Hobbes carried Sepúlveda's project forward by breaking with the classical natural law tradition on which Sepúlveda had drawn, which took for granted that humans were born fit for society. In contrast, Hobbes posited that before "man" enters into "society," he lives in a "state of nature" consisting of a "war of man against every man."[23] According to Hobbes "the multitude," the disaggregated and thus impotent and vulnerable subject of this state of nature, has not yet coalesced into one person.[24] This multitude is incapable of any single action. It cannot make promises, keep agreements, or acquire rights except as individuals; thus there are as many promises, agreements, rights, actions, and, most important, conflicts as there are people.[25] By introducing the notion of a state of nature, a "war of every man against every man," as prior to the civil state (i.e., the rule of the sovereign), Hobbes can then claim that not only does man have to subject himself to the existence of a ruling and subject factor but that all rules by definition can exist only when man has submitted himself to the rule of the "common measure" provided by the One (will) (a submission Sepúlveda by his own admission was unable to accomplish). Thus, although Aristotle's "natural slavery" has been left behind, the command-obedience relation of the "ruling and subject" factor remains central, so that, as Schmitt insists, social disorder can give way to the "overwhelming force" of a distinct and transcendent political order (Ordnung).

For Hobbes, the state of nature and the presence of this multitude are not, as is frequently claimed, hypothetical conditions. Rather, as he clearly states,

> it may per adventure be thought there was never such a time nor condition of war as this. . . . But there are many places where they live so now. For the savage people in many places of America . . . have no government at all and live at this day in that brutish manner as I said before. Howsoever, it may be perceived what manner of life there would be where there were no common power to fear, by the manner of life which men that have formally lived under a peaceful government use to degenerate into, in a civil war.[26]

The identification of "America" with the existence of a people prior to the civil state is continued in John Locke: "In the beginning, all the world was

America."[27] As Schmitt explains, this identification is not incidental: Ordnung is in fact subsidiary to the physical land grab that was made during the Spanish conquest, as it was this "taking of the land" from the indigenous peoples of the Americas that allowed for the very distinction and therefore decision over what would be "inside" and "outside" the norm (Ortung).

Having laid out this trajectory of the nature and origins of sovereignty, we can now more clearly present a series of misconceptions (if not paralogisms) at the heart of the legalistic understanding of the concept of sovereignty that are key to its sustenance. First, the fact that there appears to be a space of norms (Europe) and a space for the application of the exception (the colonies) should not hide the fact that an extrajuridical force of domination (a unidirectional relation of command-obedience) lies at the heart of both. As Hobbes's work begins to demonstrate and as Foucault helps us clarify, by positing the state of nature as a condition actually present among the "savage peoples" of the Americas and thus as potentially ever present everywhere else, Hobbes can then claim that in both cases, in the colony and the metropolis, it is out of an internal and well-reasoned fear—of fellow man, be it conqueror or neighbor—that the "multitude" accedes to the rule of the sovereign. In this way, the conquest of the "savage peoples" of the Americas is once again legitimated while simultaneously used to bring a form of colonialism (sovereignty) *back* to the West under the banner of the necessity for protection from the potential threat of that which remains "beyond the line."[28] As Foucault claims, the right of colonization formulated during the conquest of the New World created a "boomerang effect" in which "a whole series of colonial models was brought back to the West, and the result was that the West could practice something resembling colonization, or an internal colonialism, on itself." Here the constitution of sovereignty, Foucault notes, no longer appears as the victory of one side over another in a reversible battle but rather as the product of a primordial will to live and thus to overcome the state of nature.[29] What appears within jurisprudence after Hobbes, then, is not the overcoming of the exceptional nature of the sovereign decision (the rule of law) but the conceptual disappearance of conquest, the ability within the West to present sovereignty as a question of "right" rather than domination. Second, subaltern people were never excluded per se from the site of sovereignty. The "New World" (and its "savages") was not thought to lie outside sovereignty (and thus to be of no importance to it) but was that upon which the sovereign decision would have to be applied in order to guarantee the regularity of the internal

European order. In other words, the non-West is here already "included" in the sovereign decision as the negation of European space and norms (as that which must be excluded).

In this schema, non-European people were not simply "excluded" from humanity as embodied in the exercise of sovereignty. Humanity was itself gathered in the sovereign decision under a single ontological universality (a single human race to which the sovereign decision might apply), while the historical/particular existence and habits of non-European people were simultaneously thought incompatible with the exercise of sovereignty.[30] After this initial gathering, that human race is then subdivided through the application of a single measure—the capacity or incapacity to exercise sovereignty—into a superrace and subrace.[31] The superrace (Europeans) is endowed with the capacity for a purely sovereign (internal and temporal) determination, while the subrace is viewed as determined by exteriority and spatiality (by the necessity for external domination).[32] At the same time the domination of the subrace becomes all the more urgent, in that due to its belonging within the single ontological universality of the human race, it constitutes an immanent threat to the internal order of the superrace itself (the actual, not hypothetical, threat pointed out by Hobbes of living like the "savages of the Americas").

We therefore have two very powerful reasons why a movement such as that of the Zapatistas might today reject the search for sovereignty as a viable strategy. First, to the extent that these movements imagine their aim as the establishment of freedom and not simply as a reversal of positions within domination, sovereignty stands as a direct obstacle. Second, the movements of both ontological gathering and historical segregation implicit in the conception of modern sovereignty create a powerful double-bind for these subaltern subjects. When considered as merely excluded from the site of sovereignty due to their violent domination by the West, non-Western subjects have little choice but to demand an ultimate inclusion, one in which their underlying humanity (i.e., sovereignty) might flourish. But when we examine the nature of the "inclusive exclusion" on which Western sovereignty functions, in which the play of ontological universality and historical particularity creates hierarchical differentiations assigned to geographic locations (Europe/non-Europe) within a single humanity, this demand for inclusion serves as a surreptitious call for the self-annihilation of these subaltern subjects and their particular historical differences. In other words, when these subjects are viewed as "excluded" from sovereignty, the only trajectory afforded them on the road to freedom is to "assume" sovereignty, to leave behind their historical existence, against which the concept of sovereignty has already been defined.

Decolonization and the Rise of Empire

The interstate European legal order based on absolute sovereignty that is defended by Schmitt and usually associated with the order emerging after the 1648 Peace of Westphalia has as its correlate a particular understanding of space. Not only does this spatial ordering contrast European and non-European locations, but the space internal to the European state is itself reduced (through violence) to a purely abstract or instrumental space. The advances in geometry at that time allowed the space of the state to be figured in metric, calculable, and therefore purely isotopic terms;[33] the territory of jus publicum Europaeum is figured as homogenous, abstracted space, available for and visualized from the bird's-eye view of the sovereign.[34] Like the multitude, state territory must be reduced to a common measure. If Schmitt, throughout the 1950s and 1960s, felt compelled to defend a "Eurocentric spatial order of the earth," it was exactly because such a system was coming to a certain end.[35] Although Schmitt identified the fall of the European international order as a result of the rise of international law, it is unquestionable that the success of the anticolonial movements throughout the late twentieth century and their achievement of formal sovereignty shifted the global relations of force and, according to Schmitt, "put everything European on the defensive."[36] Through the assumption of formal sovereignty by the recently decolonized nations, the space of the outside, which had been the basis for the European legal order, came to a definitive end, though with ambiguous consequences.[37] One of these was the tendential delinking of sovereignty from national territory and the formation of a suprastate system that has been called Empire.[38] This is not to say that in this process, frequently referred to as *deterritorialization*, territory has ceased to matter. Rather, Empire, as the instantiation of the capitalist world market, has extended the abstract and calculable space of the formally national territory to the entirety of the earth.[39] It is from this particular perspective that it can be claimed that Empire knows no outside. Simultaneously, sovereignty is no longer gathered in the guise of a Hobbesian transcendental accord, a single state-legitimating contract.[40] Through the extension of this world market, sovereignty is dispersed onto the processes of exchange themselves.

It is this situation that has been so clearly understood in the Zapatista assertion that the previous nation-state–centered system has been surpassed. In the words of Zapatista spokesperson Subcomandante Marcos, "we rose up against a national power only to realize that national power no longer exists. What we have is a global power that produces local and uneven dominations."[41] Struggles for decolonization today, the Zapatistas thus signal, must now be focused on overcoming the new structure of sovereignty imposed through this "Empire of money."

Autonomy: Another Power Is Possible

The Zapatista insurrection that erupted on New Year's Day 1994 involved only twelve days of armed conflict, as millions of people took to the streets all over Mexico to support the rebel demands but also to protest the violence and call for a ceasefire. The peace talks that ensued stopped and started over several years amid trouble at the negotiating table but, more important, generated significant public interest in Zapatista initiatives to create alternative political spaces. A series of government betrayals of the San Andrés Accords (negotiated and signed by the federal government and the EZLN) culminated in the passage of a regressive constitutional reform on indigenous rights supported by all three principal political parties and rejected by the EZLN and the representatives of the fifty-six indigenous peoples represented in the National Indigenous Congress. As a consequence, the Zapatistas retreated from public light and into what was, to both their enemies and their allies, an unsettling silence. All dialogue and negotiations with the government ended, and the Zapatistas would not again take up discussions or relations with any political party. The demands made in the San Andrés Accords were no longer a matter for legislative consideration or a question of rights to be granted. As Subcomandante Marcos explained, there is a time to ask power to change, there is a time to demand change from power, and there is a time to *exercise* power.[42] In the eyes of the Zapatistas, after open betrayals by the entire spectrum of the Mexican political class, this third time was long overdue. The Zapatista communities thus delved into the long process of unilaterally implementing autonomy without any official recognition or legal endorsement.

The EZLN statement at the moment of this final government betrayal echoed a sentiment expressed years earlier when it stated that its strategic goal was not to take power but to exercise it.[43] This statement points to what we think is a fundamental irresolvable antagonism between two practices of power: first, the practice of one that can be taken (sovereign power), and second, the practice of another, present in the Zapatista communities, that challenges both sovereign power and its contemporary deployment in Empire. The EZLN's insistence that it does not want to "take power" is often misunderstood as either the denial of the necessity or desirability of any system or organization of rule (something like a crude anarchism) or of the intent to leave or divide the Mexican state to create another, parallel system of (sovereign) rule. The former is usually related to a conceptualization in which all power is a negative force of pure domination, imposed from "above," and thus one's position in relation to power is always and only to resist and oppose. The subject's relation to power is thereby limited to victim (acted on) or protester (acting against). The latter is most commonly represented by a use of "autonomy" as separatism or secession, whereby people are defined by claims to exceptionality, a group deserving of a different system of sovereign rule or a subsystem of sovereign rule within the existing sovereign state. The EZLN, however, with the idea of the exercise of power, suggests that there is a form of social organization that completely bypasses the sovereign and its necessary relation of command obedience. This is a form of power that is not contracted to (via the "social contract") or derived from (via demand or petition) the sovereign.[44] According to the EZLN, this type of power is not only possible but was already present within the indigenous communities in Chiapas and strongly marked the initial stages of the EZLN's formation in the Lacandón Jungle.[45] This is not to say that this was the only form of power existing within these communities and that indigenous society can therefore be posed in exteriority to the state. To the contrary, the exercise of this other power put many indigenous communities in direct conflict with the traditional indigenous power structure, and the Mexican state tried to domesticate this other power by opening spaces for indigenous participation.

The Zapatista method for implementing "autonomy" took the form of what they called rule by obeying (mandar-obedeciendo). In direct contrast to mandato-obedecer, which lies at the base of the sovereign tradition, rule by obeying draws on the community practices of self-organization through assembly that tendentially disperse power (through a series of mutual obligations, shared responsibilities, and the accountability and revocability of delegates), effectively preventing the accumulation of power that might ensue from delegation.[46] In classical juridical terms, such a system places *this* "multitude" in the permanent position of command and delegated authorities in a subordinate position of immediate accountability. In effect, this power exceeds the options between the rule of the one (i.e., sovereignty) and no rule (i.e., anarchy) by posing the possibility of the permanence of the rule of all.[47] Despite the fact that these practices were present in some of the indigenous communities of Chiapas, their existence for the EZLN was not sufficient to spontaneously overtake sovereignty or its current manifestation in governance. Rather, through a system of "transduction,"[48] the EZLN takes practices that already exist at a limited degree of potentiality and work to intensify the consistency, connectivity, and truth content of those practices. That is, they create a network of practices that in effect select for this other type of power.

The principle of rule by obeying is formally implemented as a system of self-government centered on Good Government Councils headquartered in each of the five zones that constitute Zapatista territory. Each zone of Zapatista territory is composed of a number of autonomous municipalities, around forty in all, which are in turn composed of a variable number of communities, home to around 300,000 people, primarily of Tzotzil, Tzeltal, Chol, and Tojolobal indigenous groups.[49] Even before the Zapatista insurrection in 1994, there had been an explicit attempt to subordinate the military structure and the EZLN to civilian bodies within the Zapatista communities. This effort took a large leap forward with the establishment in 2003 of the Councils of Good Government, which formalized civilian authority over matters of daily life in Zapatista territory. Nevertheless, rule by obeying should always be viewed in constant tension with the hierarchical structure of command still in force within the Zapatista army.

The Councils of Good Government provide a form of rotating autonomous government charged with carrying out the mandate of the community assemblies, from which council delegates are chosen and to whom they are accountable.[50] The councils operate as a local justice system and a source of financial management and accountability for the distribution of funds and the coordination of collective projects, and they are in charge of protecting and handling disputes over the recuperated lands. The term lengths, form of rotation, number of members, and other details of the councils are decided locally by each zone, ranging from turns of one week to three months serving as part of the governing body. This variability helps us understand that mandar-obedeciendo is not a form; that is, it is not absolute horizontality. Rather, it is an ethic open to multiple forms adequate to move a particular political context toward the overall strategy of developing autonomy. Common across all zones, community members delegated to the councils take their turn governing and then return to the daily work of the community; each community in turn covers the daily work and sustenance of its currently governing members.[51] The distinction between this mandate and that which is given or assumed in what we can generally call "representative democracy" is not only the rotating function of governance, which prevents the professionalization of political participation and the formation of a political class, but also the relation of government to the community assemblies, which hold the core of decision-making power. The assembly system locates power firmly at the base and precludes the attachment of authority to a position of delegated responsibility—what would enable a command obedience structure to reemerge. The practice of recognizing and generating power from "below" structures all the other relations to be mediated and tasks to be completed: "In sum, to ensure that in Zapatista rebellious territory, whoever rules, rules by obeying."[52]

Given the EZLN's practices and statements, we can conclude that it views political struggle neither as purely spontaneous nor as the vertical transcendence of the social, but rather as the organization and potentialization of certain radical tendencies already existing within the social, in this case forged through hundreds of years of resistance to conquest. For the EZLN, then, autonomy is the daily struggle to act within mandar-obedeciendo over and against sovereign power and its derivative in governance. From this perspective it becomes clear that what was at stake for the EZLN in the San Andrés Accords, and what the Mexican government could not accept, was not some form of subsovereignty or secession, nor was it even the recognition of indigenous "identity" (a claim to "who we are"). Rather, the debate over autonomy for the EZLN centered around the demand for the nonimpediment of parallel but radically disparate practices of power that from its perspective would continually allow indigenous peoples to decide and control "who we want to become" (an effective self-determination).[53] This conception of power holds within it a radical antagonism to politics as it exists today, the ramifications of which are clear in the following EZLN statement: "We think that if we can conceptualize a change in the premise of power, the problem of power, starting from the fact that we don't want to take it, that could produce another kind of politics and another kind of political actor, other human beings that do politics differently than the politicians we have today across the political spectrum."[54]

The EZLN uprising was most immediately visible in the successful military takeover of seven municipal headquarters in Chiapas in what turned out to be a spectacular surprise and show of force on the day the North American Free Trade Agreement (NAFTA) entered into effect. What received less initial attention was the simultaneous occupation of somewhere between 500,000 and 700,000 hectares (1.2–1.7 million acres, or 2,000–3,000 square miles) of land "recuperated" from the *latifundistas*, or large landowners, who for centuries had run something similar to plantation-style haciendas with indigenous labor.[55] These takeovers affected some 12 percent of the total land area of Chiapas and marked a significant shift in the relations of production in the state.

In 1992, in preparation for the implementation of NAFTA, then president Carlos Salinas de Gortari modified article 27 of the Constitution of Mexico, which stipulated that *ejido* lands, a kind of collective or social property, could not be bought from or sold by their communal owners or titled by an individual owner. The inclusion of article 27 in the postrevolution Constitution of Mexico had classified 101.8 million hectares of Mexican land as "social property," representing 51.94 percent of the total landmass of the country, banning their privatization and thus preventing their expropriation as collateral or through debt payment. The modification of article 27 in 1992 eliminated this protection. Accompanying the constitutional change, a government program, the Certification Program for Ejidal Rights and Titling of Parcels (PROCEDE) was put in place in 1993 to "register" common lands, purportedly and with much publicity as a form of "development" for peasant farmers. In its fourteen years of operation, PROCEDE registered 28,790 agrarian units,[56] equivalent to 92.24 percent of the total social property in the country, in the hope that such a process would lead toward privatization. This policy shift not only pointed toward regressive land reform with devastating consequences for indigenous land tenure but also signaled a respatialization of social control.

The territorial aspects of the Zapatista conflict allow us to understand that despite the fact that sovereign functions have been deterritorialized (from the territorial nation-state), this does not mean that territory in and of itself has ceased to be central to social struggle. On the contrary, the production of space lies at the very heart of contemporary social antagonisms. It has become apparent, however, that space is inextricable from the social relations created on it (something that was at least somewhat disguised by the nation-state).[57] By adopting geographer Carlos Walter Porto Gonçalvez's triadic notion of territory (physical location), territorialization (a manner of taking hold of that space), and territorialities (the identities implied in the processes of taking hold),[58] we can better distinguish antagonistic strategic propositions within a situation of paracoloniality, where dominator and dominated find themselves in the same space.[59] In this sense, a number of projects of territorialization can exist in the same physical location. Therefore, the lack of a preexisting geographic or even subjective exteriority to neoliberal governance should not lead us to assume the unidirectionality of physically overlapping political phenomena. Rather, it should direct our attention toward the delineation of the logics that might underlie an antagonism of strategies present on the same territory and possibly within the same subject. Though the institutions and practices of neoliberal governance create enormous destruction in their attempt to fold all territory into the calculable space necessary for the functioning of the world market, this new situation simultaneously gives rise to countervailing projects that no longer need to wait to take hold of the territorial state to give expression to their political ends. This allows us to see that in the case of the EZLN land occupations, what was enabled was not simply traditional "land redistribution" in favor of a peasant class or even the "revolutionary" act of "taking the means of production" into one's hands, although the latter certainly played an important role. Rather, the new Zapatista territory became not only an escape from direct labor exploitation and an independent means of subsistence but the literal ground for the creation of autonomy, for the creation, sustenance, and growth of a self-organized collective subject. The development of the Zapatista autonomous municipalities essentially created a rupture in the system of representation configured by the state and the possibility of social relations unmediated by state stratification. Autonomous territorialization created a spatialization of struggle that essentially, or at least tendentially, disallowed the sovereign relation and provided the possibility for another kind of government—"good government" in Zapatista terms.

The establishment of rule by obeying, the existence of the Councils of Good Government, and the new spatialization of struggle by the EZLN have had significant successes. In their role as local justice systems, the Councils of Good Government have proved to be so successful and well received that people from non-Zapatista communities and even parties oppositional to the EZLN often opt to take their cases or complaints to the autonomous councils rather than to the official municipal or state courts.[60] Whereas general illiteracy rates within indigenous areas of Chiapas were estimated at around 42 percent throughout the 1990s, with only 11 percent of the population completing primary school and with the state school system negligent or completely absent in the area,[61] there are now autonomous primary and secondary schools in all Zapatista autonomous municipalities and autonomous high schools in several zones, each already with several generations of graduates.[62] Seven years after the uprising, while 11 percent of children in progovernment communities had received no primary school education at all and with only 20 percent going beyond primary school, in Zapatista communities *all* children had received some level of primary education, and 37 percent had entered secondary or higher levels of education.[63] The region in general has long held the highest infant mortality rates in the country, around 20 percent, and a child malnutrition rate in the poorest part of the state (primarily indigenous areas) upward of 70 percent (official indices qualify 80 percent as conditions of famine).[64] The ratio of doctors to population in the state in the early 1990s was one per 1,000 persons, the lowest in the country; in areas where the indigenous population was higher than 70 percent, the ratio reached one per 25,000 persons.[65] In 2007, the autonomous health systems were calculated as having two hundred community health clinics; twenty-five regional clinics, including ophthalmological, gynecological, dental centers and clinical analysis laboratories; and several municipal-level hospitals. While there are no official data measuring differences between autonomous areas and non-Zapatista areas in terms of health, independent studies have documented that in some autonomous regions where maternal mortality was once the highest in the country, under the autonomous systems there have been periods of up to eight years without any maternal deaths;[66] 63 percent of women in Zapatista communities receive prenatal care, compared to only 35 percent in non-Zapatista communities; and 74 percent of households in Zapatista communities have latrines, compared to 54 percent in non-Zapatista communities.[67] Both the education and health systems have been so popular that many non-Zapatista indigenous people go to the autonomous clinics, and non-Zapatista children attend the autonomous schools rather than state institutions.[68] Again, while official statistical data is unavailable with regard to social indicators in the autonomous communities, general indices of severe poverty in the region have shrunk, and the EZLN reports that hunger has been eradicated in Zapatista territory.[69]

Zapatista autonomy as a practice of decolonization seems to us of vital importance given the contemporary parameters of global political struggle. That is, at a time when many have attempted to eliminate colonial and paracolonial systems either through the reassertion of state sovereignty or through the new forms of participation afforded by neoliberal governance, Zapatismo has innovated conceptions of indigeneity and autonomy beyond these options. Although this has brought the Zapatistas into direct confrontation with the Mexican institutional left (and therefore cost them substantial sectors of support), their project does in fact provide a concrete alternative to the insistence (in Mexico or elsewhere) that the best that can be hoped for is the election of the "least worst" option within "parlamento-capitalism."

At a moment when Mexico's social indicators are at a crisis level, with skyrocketing unemployment, falling migrant remittances, massive social unrest, generalized distrust in the political system, and a narco war that has killed almost 25,000 people in the last three years, the political class has been obviously and wholly incapable of providing the most minimal guidance toward alleviating these conditions. Despite the fact that academics and journalists have for the most part turned their gaze elsewhere, the singularity and continued viability of the Zapatista project make an engagement with their struggle essential to understanding the forms of antagonism that have made themselves present in Latin America in the last decades and that are increasingly likely to arise elsewhere. Given this situation, it is highly unlikely that we've heard the last of the Zapatistas.

NOTES

1. Raúl Zibechi, "Carta de Raúl Zibechi: Un Nuevo Nacimiento" [Letter from Raúl Zibechi: A rebirth]. Nov. 13, 2012. Accessed Oct. 1, 2014. www.ezln.org.mx/2012/11/13/eco-mundial-en-apoyo-de-ls-zapatistas-carta-de-raul-zibechi-un-nuevo-nacimiento/.

2. For a discussion of the December 21, 2012, march, see Luis Hernández Navarro, "The Zapatistas Can Still Change the Rules of Mexican Politics," *The Guardian*, December 31, 2012.

3. EZLN, "Escucharon?" [Did you hear that?]. December 2012. Accessed October 1, 2014. www. Enlacezapatista.ezln.org.mx/2012/12/21/comunicado-del-comite-clandestino-revolucionario-indigena-comandancia-general-del-ejercito-zapatista-de-liberacion-nacional-del-21-de-diciembre-del-2012/.

4. See generally, EZLN, Ellos y Nosotros: Las Miradas [Them and us: The gaze], and Ellos y Nosotros: Los Mas Pequeños [Them and us: The smallest of them all]. Accessed October 1, 2014. www.enlacezapatista.ezln.org.mx.

5. For an interesting analysis of the "neoextractive" turn in Latin America, see Eduardo Gudynas, "The New Extractivism of the 21st Century: Ten Urgent Thesis about Extractivism in Relation to Current South American Progressivism," in *Americas Program Report* (Washington, DC: Center for International Policy, 2010).

6. See Raúl Zibechi, "The Art of Governing the Movements," in *Territories of Resistance: A Cartography of Latin American Social Movements*, trans. Ramor Ryan (Oakland, CA: AK Press, 2012), 266–98; and Pablo Dávalos, *La Democracia Disciplinaria: El Proyecto Posneoliberal Para América Latina* [Disciplinary democracy: The postneoliberal project for Latin America] (Quito, Ecuador: CODEU, 2011).

7. Although differing on their approaches to analyzing the structural crisis of capital, the following authors all seem to agree on the severity and long-lasting, if not insurmountable, effects of the crisis: Beverly Silver and Giovanni Arrighi, "End of the Long Twentieth Century;" Immanuel Wallerstein, "Dynamics of (Unresolved) Global Crisis;" David Harvey, "Enigma of Capital and the Crisis This Time;" and Gopal Balakrishnan, "Convolution of Capitalism;" all in Craig Calhoun and Georgi Derlugian, eds., *Business as Usual: The Roots of the Global Financial Meltdown* (New York: New York University Press, 2011). See also Pablo Gonzalez Casanova, "Otra política, muy otra: Los Zapatistas del siglo XXI" [A very other politics: The Zapatistas of the 21st century], *La Jornada* (Mexico City), January 26, 2013; Anselm Jappe, *Crédit á Mort: La decomposition du capitalism et ses critiques* [Credit unto death: The decomposition of capital and its critiques] (Paris: Éditions Lignes, 2011); and Richard Duncan, *The New Depression: The Breakdown of the Paper Money Economy* (Hoboken, NJ: Wiley, 2012).

8. It is interesting to note that the theorization of these new forms of "territoriality" has been most explicitly theorized from within Latin America, undoubtedly the region where the antineoliberal struggles reached their highest levels of intensity. For a prescient analysis of the centrality of "territoriality" in contemporary political struggles, see the work of Brazilian geographer Carlos Walter Porto Gonçalves, *Territorialidades y La Lucha Por El Territorio en América Latina* [Territorialities and the Struggle for Territory in Latin America] (Caracas: Instituto Venezolano de Ciencia y Tecnologia, 2012).

9. For statistics on the consequences of the drug war, see Hector Briceño, "Ejecutados 150 mil en 7 Años, alcaldes" [Mayors: 150 thousand executed in 7 years], *La Jornada* (Mexico City), April 9, 2012; for rates of poverty in contemporary Mexico, see Centro de Analisis Multidisciplinario, *Reporte Número 108, Política Contra la Pobreza: 42 años de fracaso* [Report 108: Anti-poverty policy: 42 years of failure], Mexico City: UNAM, April 2013.

10. Subcomandante Marcos, EZLN, "The Fourth World War," Chiapas, November 20, 1999, *La Jornada* (Mexico City), October 23, 2001.

11. Michel Foucault, *"Society Must Be Defended": Lectures at the Collège de France, 1975–1976*, trans. David Macey (New York: Picador, 2003), 26.

12. This is not to imply that all struggles for "rights" are inextricable from legalism and sovereignty. For an instance of a struggle that doesn't fall into this category, see Shannon Speed and Alvaro Reyes, "'In Our Own Defense': Rights and Resistance in Chiapas, Mexico," *Political and Legal Anthropology Review* 25, no. 1 (May 2002): 69–89.

13. Carl Schmitt, *Political Theology: Four Chapters on the Concept of Sovereignty*, trans. George D. Schwab (Cambridge, MA: MIT Press, 1985), 13.

14. Giorgio Agamben, *Homo Sacer: Sovereign Power and Bare Life*, trans. Daniel Heller-Roazen (Stanford, CA: Stanford University Press, 1998), 18.

15. Agamben, *Homo Sacer*, 21.

16. Michael Hardt and Antonio Negri, *Empire* (Cambridge, MA: Harvard University Press, 2000), 87, 98.

17. Carl Schmitt, *The Nomos of the Earth in the International Law of the Jus Publicum Europaeum* (New York: Telos Press, 2003), 39.

18. Jan-Werner Muller, *A Dangerous Mind: Carl Schmitt in Post-war European Thought* (New Haven, CT: Yale University Press, 2003), 88.

19. Muller, *Dangerous Mind*, 21; and Lewis Hanke, *Aristotle and the American Indians: A Study in Race Prejudice in the Modern World* (Bloomington: Indiana University Press), 1970.

20. Aristotle, *The Politics*, bk. 1, trans. H. Rackham (New York: Putnam, 1934), 19.

21. Juan Ginés de Sepúlveda, *De Regno*, (Pozoblanco, Spain: Ayutamiento de Pozoblanco, 2001), 48.

22. Richard Tuck, *The Rights of War and Peace: Political Thought and the International Order from Grotius to Kant* (Oxford: Oxford University Press, 1999), 43.

23. Thomas Hobbes, *Leviathan*, ed. Edwin Curley (Indianapolis, IN: Hackett, 1994), 78.

24. Thomas Hobbes, *On the Citizen*, ed. Richard Tuck and Michael Silverthorne (Cambridge: Cambridge University Press, 1998), 76.

25. Hobbes, *On the Citizen*.

26. Hobbes, *Leviathan*, 77; see also Hobbes, *On the Citizen*, 30.

27. John Locke, *Two Treatises of Government: Second Treatise* (Cambridge: Cambridge University Press, 2004), sec. 49.

28. Schmitt, *Nomos*, 93.

29. Foucault, *"Society Must Be Defended,"* 103.

30. This analysis is inspired by Denise Ferreira da Silva. Although her work centers on the closely related issue of the formation of the "transparent subject," we believe her thesis holds valuable insights for understanding political sovereignty. See Denise Ferreira da Silva, *Toward a Global Idea of Race* (Minneapolis: University of Minnesota Press), 2007.

31. Foucault, *"Society Must Be Defended,"* 61.

32. Da Silva, *Toward a Global Idea of Race*, 4.

33. Henri Lefebvre, *The Production of Space*, trans. Donald Nicholson-Smith (Malden, MA: Blackwell, 1991), 278–82; and Stuart Elden, "Missing the Point: Globalization, Deterritorialization and the Space of the World," *Transactions of the Institute of British Geographers* 30, no. 1 (2005): 15.

34. John Pickles, *A History of Spaces: Cartographic Reason, Mapping, and the Geo-Coded World* (New York: Routledge, 2004), 107–10.

35. Schmitt, *Nomos*, 140.

36. Schmitt as quoted in Alberto Toscano, "Carl Schmitt in Beijing: Partisanship, Geopolitics, and the Demolition of the Eurocentric World," *Postcolonial Studies* 11, no. 4 (2008): 417–33, 428.

37. The argument we construct here should not be thought to delegitimate tactical struggles for the recognition of formal legal sovereignty. As Frantz Fanon points out, *in struggle* the colonized come to understand that the attainment of "sovereignty" is from the beginning inextricable from a larger strategic struggle for dignity, for the recognition that "people are no longer a herd and do not need to be driven." See Frantz Fanon, *The Wretched of the Earth*, trans. Richard Philcox (New York: Grove Press, 2004), 139, 127.

38. See Alexandre Kojève, *Outline of a Phenomenology of Right*, trans. Bryan-Paul Fox and Robert Howse (Lanham, MD: Rowman and Littlefield, 2007); Jean-Marie Guéhenno, *The End of the Nation-State*, trans. Victoria Elliott (Minneapolis: University of Minnesota Press, 1995); and Hardt and Negri, *Empire*.

39. Elden, "Missing the Point," 16.

40. Kenneth Surin, *Freedom Not Yet: Liberation and the New World Order* (Durham, NC: Duke University Press, 2009).

41. *Zapatista*, dir. Benjamin Eichert, Richard Rowley, and State Sandberg, Big Noise Films, 2001.

42. Gloria Muñoz Ramírez, "Interview with Subcomandante Marcos: A Time to Ask, a Time to Demand, and a Time to Act," Americas Program, January 16, 2004. Accessed October 1, 2014. www.cipamericas.org/archives/1120.

43. EZLN, "To the Soldiers and Commanders of the Popular Revolutionary Army," communiqué, Flag.Blackened.Net, August 29, 1996. Accessed October 1, 2014. http://flag.blackened.net/revolt/mexico/ezln/ezln_epr_se96.html. The complete quote is: "What we seek, what we need and want is for all those people without a party or an organization to make agreements about what they don't want and what they do want and organize themselves in order to achieve it (preferably through civil and peaceful means), not to take power, but to exercise it."

44. Speed and Reyes, "'In Our Own Defense,'" 53–54.

45. Yvon Le Bot and Subcomandante Marcos, *El Sueno Zapatista: Entrevistas con el subcomandante Marcos, el mayor Moises y el comandante Tacho, del Ejercito Zapatista de Liberacion Nacional* (Barcelona, Spain: Plaza y Janes, 1997).

46. Despite similarities between our interpretation of the Zapatistas and the work of Pierre Clastres, we feel a fundamental ambiguity remains in his work as to whether "a society against the state" is the product of political initiative or of some natural tendency within society as such. Here we hope to show that the Zapatistas do identify tendencies that move in the direction of eliminating the autonomy of the political sphere but simultaneously make such tendencies into a strong political project. See Pierre Clastres, *Society against the State: Essays in Political Anthropology* (New York: Zone Books, 1989).

47. As Gustavo Esteva notes, in contrast with Antonio Negri's formulation, the Zapatista notion of *mandar obedeciendo* moves in the direction of definitively uncoupling the pair constituent and constituted power so that constituent power can become its own permanent state of affairs and not present itself simply as the continual unsettling of constituted power. See Gustavo Esteva, "A Celebration of Zapatismo," *Humboldt Journal of Social Relations* 29 (2005): 127–67.

48. We are adopting this term from Henri Lefebvre, who adapted it from Gilbert Simondon.

49. El Kilombo Intergaláctico, *Beyond Resistance, Everything: An Interview with Subcomandante Insurgente Marcos* (Durham, NC: Paperboat Press, 2008).

50. Raúl Ornelas, "La autonomía como eje de la resistencia Zapatista," in Ana Esther Ceceña, ed., *Hegemonias y Emancipaciones en el Siglo XXI* (Buenos Aires: CLASCO, 2004).

51. Subcomandante Marcos, "La Treceava Estela," pt. 5, July 2003. Accessed October 1, 2014. http://palabra.ezln.org.mx.

52. Subcomandante Marcos, "La Treceava Estela," pt. 6, July 2003. Accessed October 1, 2014. http://palabra.ezln.org.mx.

53. Speed and Reyes, "In Our Own Defense," 76.

54. EZLN, *Cronicas Intergalacticas: Primer Encuentro Intercontinental por la Humanidad y contra el Neoliberalismo*, Montañas del Sureste Mexicano: Planeta Tierra, 1997.

55. This number is unofficial and much disputed; estimates range from 200,000 to 700,000. The higher number is most recently cited in Hermann Bellinghausen, "La otra campaña, opción para agrupar a las organizaciones campesinas en lucha," *La Jornada* (Mexico City), March 1, 2007.

56. Secretaria de Reforma Agraria, Estados Unidos de Mexico, "Acuerdo por el que se declara el cierre operativo y conclusión de Programa de Certificación de Derechos Ejidales y Titulación de Solares (PROCEDE)," *Diario Oficial*, November 17, 2006.

57. Lefebvre, *Production of Space*.

58. Carlos W. Porto Gonçalves, "Da geografia às geo-grafias—um mundo em busca de novas territorialidades," in Ana Esther Ceceña and Emir Sader, eds., *La guerra infinita—hegemonía y terror mundial* (Buenos Aires, Argentina: Clacso, 2002), 217–56.

59. We owe this notion of paracoloniality to Kenneth Surin, as developed in "The Sovereign Individual, 'Subalternity,' and Becoming-Other," *Angelaki* 6, no. 1 (2001): 47–63.

60. See Gemma van der Haar, "El movimiento zapatista de Chiapas: Dimensiones de su lucha," 2005, LabourAgain Publications, International Institute of Social History, www.iisg.nl/labouragain/ruralmobilisation.php.

61. National Institute of Geography and Statistics (INEGI), "Censo General de Población y Vivienda 2000." www.inegi.org.mx/est/contenidos/Proyectos/ccpv /cpv2000/default.aspx.

62. EZLN, "Informe de 1 año de la junta de buen gobierno corazón céntrico de los zapatistas delante del mundo," episode of *Radio Insurgente: La voz de los sin voz*, broadcast September 24, 2004. Accessed October 1, 2014. www.radioinsurgente.org.

63. H. Sánchez Pérez, M. Arana Cedeño, and A. Yamin, "Pueblos Excluidos, Co-munidades Erosionadas: La Situación del Derecho a la Salud en Chiapas, Mexico," Boston: Physicians for Human Rights and El Colegio de la Frontera Sur, Centro de Capacitación en Ecologia y Salud para Campesino, 2006.

64. Pablo Gonzalez Casanova Henríquez et al., "La Situación de la Nutrición de las y los niños preescolares en la selva, frontera y altos de Chiapas durante la crisis bélica y social de 1994," *Revista CIMECH* 6 (1–2) 1996: 14.

65. Gustavo Castro and Miguel Pickard, "Los Derechos Economicos y Sociales en Chiapas: Salud y Educación," pt. 2, *CIEPAC Bulletin*, no. 163, July 25, 1999. Accessed October 1, 2014. www.ciepac.org/boletines/chiapasaldia.php?id=163.

66. J. H. Cuevas, *Salud y Autonomía: El caso Chiapas*, report for the Health Systems Knowledge Network: World Health Organization, March 2007.

67. Pablo Gonzalez Casanova Henríquez, "El Zapatismo avanza ante el desastre," *La Jornada* (Mexico City), January 24, 2009.

68. As reported by the Council of Good Government of Oventic in the "Second Encounter between Zapatista Peoples and Peoples of the World," Oventic, Chiapas, Mexico, July 21, 2007.

69. Laura Castellanos, *Corte de Caja: Una Entrevista al Subcomandante Marcos*, Nezahualcoyotl (Tlalnepantla de Baz, Mexico: Grupo Editorial Endira México, 2008).

3

Enclosing the Enclosers Autonomous Experiences from the Grassroots— beyond Development, Globalization & Postmodernity GUSTAVO ESTEVA

Profound transformations don't start at the top or with epic and monumental events, but through movements, small in their shapes, that seem irrelevant for the politicians and the analysts at the top. Historical transformations don't start in the plazas or with enraged crowds but in the organized conscience of groups and collectives that know each other and are mutually acknowledged, down and to the left, and construct another politics.

—SUBCOMANDANTE MARCOS (2007)

We live in times of change, of revolutionary change. And, within the tumultuous confusion of revolution itself, we find ourselves in a dangerous moment that requires us to deepen our commitment and speed up.

In this chapter, I explore the path described by Arturo Escobar when he perceived a postcapitalist, postliberal, and poststatist path embodied in some social movements in Latin America. These movements are beginning to theorize their own path. I want to explore his questions beyond modernity, when Europe is "displaced from the center of the historical and epistemic imagination," and I ask, with him: "Can the emergent cultural-political subjects in Latin America reach an activated and stable condition of alterity capable of re-constituting socio-natural structures from within, along the lines of de-coloniality, relationality and pluriversality?"[1]

Recovering a Sense of Proportion

Leopold Kohr, a teacher of Ernst Friedrich Schumacher, said long ago that economic fluctuations are not due to classic cycles but to the actual scale of the economic activity.[2] Rather than simple economic cycles, these are the same dimensions and scale of the political bodies involved. Economic integration and growth and the expansionary effect of government controls do not reduce or shorten these cycles; on the contrary, they magnify them.

Kohr offered clear evidence that John Maynard Keynes was right when he warned that his proposals would be adopted too late, and by then would be counterproductive. This is what is happening now: policy initiatives that bear his name worsen the problems instead of fixing them and are applied mechanically as if nothing had occurred.

If the problem currently faced is a matter of size, rather than an economic cycle, instead of increasing government controls to balance this new type of economic fluctuation, what needs to be done is to reduce the size of the particular political body that generates such devastating scale. The idea is to make the scale of the political body proportionate to the limited talent of those in government. The scale, and proportion, is also central in another aspect. Returning policy and ethics back to the center of social life can only be done in the midst of real entities, such as the community. Attempting to do this at the scale of abstract entities, such as the nation-state, is impossible and counterproductive. The case of peace and violence may illustrate the nature of the problem. Pax Romana signified a contract of domination: "I will not destroy you, as long as you accept my rules." This tradition seems still valid in the West and defines the dominant notion of peace, as can be seen today in Iraq or Gaza. If we recognize the plurality of the real world and the postmodern condition—beyond the universalist paradigm and celebrating difference—we have to recognize the culturally rooted character of social functions that can be associated with what is called peace: there are peaces, not peace. At a national or international scale, "peace" is only a disguise for permanent war. What we need to construct is an agreement for the harmonious coexistence of the different, each of which—distinct culture—expresses its own notion of "peace" and its desire "to be left in peace." Such an agreement corresponds to the world we are creating with the Zapatistas: a world where many worlds can be embraced.

The Ongoing Insurrection

An insurrection could be taking place. It is entirely evident but at the same time invisible: it would be under way right in front of our eyes, but we would not see it because of its novelty and the blinders and optical filters imposed by the ending era.

The recovery of verbs seems like the common denominator of the current initiatives taking place at the grassroots. The people replace nouns, like *education* and *health*, with the corresponding verbs: *learning* and *healing*. The former defines "needs" whose satisfaction depends on public or private entities that are increasingly incapable of satisfying them. The latter express the attempt to recover personal and collective agency and to enable autonomous paths of social transformation. To explore what is going on in the spheres of everyday life in which this takes place may make the character of this ongoing insurrection more visible.

EATING

We have reached a point, notes Eduardo Galeano, where those who do not fear hunger—a fear affecting an increasing number of people: a billion are going to bed every night with an empty stomach—have a fear of eating, given the growing consciousness and general awareness of the harmful ingredients offered by the market.[3]

People are reacting. Some struggles still attempt to change laws and government policies in order to regulate the operation of the handful of corporations that already control 80 percent of the world's food trade and try to also control food production. More and more, however, people follow another direction.

First of all, on the basis of ancient traditions and in order to create alternatives to the market, people are forming new connections between the countryside and the cities. Urban consumers are associating themselves with local producers and are assuming responsibilities for the production itself, its characteristics, and risks. At times, this evolves into a commons with enormous potential. The contemporary design of these new units was apparently born in Germany, coming from Japan, but has spread like an epidemic in the United States (community-supported agriculture) and in Canada (community-shared agriculture). Tens of thousands of such groups already exist and are complemented by independent organic producers that directly sell in nearby cities and other initiatives of organizations like Family Farm Defenders. This relationship, conceived as a way to lose our fear of eating, has acquired such a dynamic that even Walmart is attempting to appropriate it.

Food production in the cities is becoming increasingly important. The most spectacular example is that of Cuba. During the so-called special period, the Cubans discovered that after thirty years of revolution they were importing 70 percent of their food supply in addition to all of the chemicals required to support their highly industrialized agriculture. And they had no dollars with which to purchase these imported foods; on average, every Cuban had lost twenty pounds. There was hunger. Today, Cubans are the world champions of organic agriculture, Cuba is the only country reaching the requirements for sustainability, and its cities produce more than half of what the urban inhabitants consume. In the United States, such actions are spreading at an impressive speed. In Detroit, a universal example of the failure of industrial development, nine hundred community gardens thrive, most of them dedicated to local food production.

In the countryside, the struggle for land is spreading and intensifying. At times it takes the form of a silent occupation, more or less clandestine, like the one that recently took place in Peru: indigenous peoples recovered 1 million hectares, which are currently producing 40 percent of the country's food supply utilizing traditional practices. In other cases a spectacular struggle with uncertain results is taking place, for example in Brazil the landless peoples' movement: they have organized one of the most interesting social movements in the continent.

In recent years, this ancient struggle for land experienced a political mutation: it shifted to territorial defense and thus became an experiment in popular sovereignty and autonomy. These efforts express resistance to the aggressive actions taken up by corporations and backed by the governments to gain control of the land for mass food production as well as other purposes—from mining to ecotourism. The Mexican government, for example, conceded a substantial portion of its national territory, probably as much as 40 percent, to national and transnational corporations that received fifty-year mining concessions. Upon granting them, the government assumed the responsibility of displacing the people living in these territories to make them available for these corporations. In accordance with recent international agreements, corporations have a right to sue the state if deadlines are not met, opening up a new line of business: profits for doing nothing.

Those participating in this new struggle affirm that they are trying to weave collectively their efforts, knowledge and resistance in the defense of natural resources and territory, to oppose the big development projects, and to deepen the processes of local and regional organization. A growing number of communities are now resisting and increasingly warn that they will not be defeated by the new neoliberal offensive. At the same time, they affirm the value of their community assemblies, the principle of public office as service, the communal ownership of land, and a reconstitution of peoples' territories. The Quito Declaration, formulated in October 2009 by the International Commission of Integral Agrarian Reform, in the midst of the Global Campaign for Agrarian Reform led by Via Campesina, illustrates well the attitudes that blame the Green Revolution and commercial policies for the food crisis and climate change and denounce the contamination and privatization of water by large corporations, while affirming the farmers' struggles for agrarian reform and the defense of their territories.

New attitudes and initiatives express an increasingly relevant conceptual shift. In addition to the land itself, a specific relationship with it is claimed, in contrast with the relationship imposed by public and private developers for the past fifty years. This type of relationship expresses the collective will as an exercise of people's sovereignty, which challenges government authority and power and generates de facto institutional arrangements: a growing number of people, especially campesinos, are in control of their territory and govern themselves in their own way.

All of this can be framed with the notion of food sovereignty according to Via Campesina, the largest organization of farmers in history, which now includes hundreds of millions of people from more than 140 countries. It is expressed in rather simple terms: to define for ourselves what we eat . . . and produce it on our own terms. The World Organization of Fishermen—the largest of its kind in history, now including more than half of the world's fisheries, has taken the same path.

Given the current conditions of the world, with a large portion of the population having surrendered themselves to diets and eating practices imposed by capital and its production system, few proposals are as radical and complex as that of food sovereignty. It substantially transforms the traditional quest for self-sufficiency and gives it a more radical and political content.

LEARNING

The education system is in crisis; it marginalizes a majority of people and does not prepare them for work or life. The school system mostly produces dropouts, as more than half of the children who enroll in school this year will not attain the educational level considered mandatory in their respective countries. This will mean a permanent discrimination against them because they will lack this new kind of passport, essential for navigating throughout modern society.

Those who learn to consume this new merchandise called education accumulate twenty or thirty years of "ass-hours" for a solid diploma but are increasingly unable to find work. The majority of those graduating from Mexican universities will never be able to work in their chosen fields of study. The crisis of the education system is already well known around the world, and since the 1990s it has had as much visibility as today's financial crisis.

Despite the obvious and well-documented failure of schooling and the experience of the damage it provokes, a general struggle for "educational access" persists. The majority have been educated with the idea that this is the only way they can "be somebody" and escape the discrimination exercised against the "nobodies." Because production and distribution of education was included in the policy packages of the current era of development (i.e., since 1949), a UNESCO team of experts met in 1953 to diagnose the situation of education in Latin America. They concluded that the central educational problem was the indifference and resistance of parents to sending their children to school. Eleven years later the same experts modified their diagnosis, concluding that no country in Latin America could satisfy the demands for education. The campaign to convince parents to send their kids to school has been, and continues to be, successful. But there is no possibility of satisfying these demands, even though the World Bank and governments around the world carry the main message and programs of "education for all."

People have been reacting, though, going in many different directions.

Students, parents, and teachers are still attempting to reform and broaden the dominant educational system, and change its theories and practices, both public and private, from within. They dispute and challenge the unions entrenched in the system, as well as the state and corporations—all of which intend to aggressively transform it to serve their own interests. Other groups struggle inside and outside the state and market in order to drive forth different forms of "alternative education."

A vigorous, growing movement advances in another direction. The practices of autonomous and liberated learning have become more popular than ever. The movement is generating its own institutional arrangements at the margins, against and beyond the system. Supported by their own theoretical apparatus, such practices go well beyond existing frameworks, reclaim ancient learning traditions, and introduce contemporary technologies in the ways to learn and study as free and joyful activities.

This is indeed a unique movement. It is possibly the biggest on earth, in terms of the number of people involved, perhaps billions. But it is basically invisible, and a large part of those participating in it do not feel like they are part of a social or political movement, in the conventional sense of the term, even though they love to find others like themselves and engage in horizontal relationships and share experiences with them. In general, they are very conscious of the significance of their actions: they fully experience the radicalism of breaking with all forms of education in order to learn and study in freedom.

The movement itself is generating new centers for the production of knowledge outside public and private research centers and conventional institutions. These centers are developing new technologies based on significant theoretical innovations that reformulate the world and introduce new methodologies to interact with it. As Foucault suggested, this is an expression of the insurrection of subordinated knowledge, which strengthens and deepens it. They are reclaiming the historical content buried or masked within functional coherences and formal systematizations. They are revaluing knowledge disqualified because it has been considered useless, insufficiently elaborated, naïve, or hierarchically inferior to scientific knowledge. For them, popular wisdom is not common knowledge, because it doesn't imply unanimity. Such knowledge is specific, local/regional, differentiated. They are also juxtaposing and combining learned knowledge with local memory, erudition with empirical knowledge, to form a historical knowledge of struggle. This requires demolishing the tyranny of globalizing discourses with its hierarchy and privileges derived from the scientific classification of knowledge, which has intrinsic effects of power.

HEALING

The health-care system is increasingly inefficient, discriminatory, and counterproductive. The iatrogenic effect is increasingly documented: doctors and hospitals are producing more diseases than they cure. What caused great scandal when Ivan Illich published *Medical Nemesis* forty years ago has now become a common personal experience. The production, consumption, and distribution of health care is the second largest economic sector in the world and involves a growing number of people. The medical profession and health-care industry have taken control of every institutional apparatus: they formulate the norms, apply them, and punish those who violate them. Each failure of this professional dictatorship offers the opportunity for the dictatorship to strengthen and expand. And the failures multiply every day.

People's effort to face this situation intensifies through many different paths. As in the case of education, innumerable efforts are under way to reform the system, many of them frustratingly ineffective. For example: after a considerable effort, utilizing much of his political capital, President Barack Obama achieved the most important reform of the U.S. healthcare system in fifty years . . . Yet the system is still the most costly and ineffective in the industrialized world.

Similarly, there is a proliferation of alternative therapies that try to avoid the dominant system's incompetency and most damaging effects. In most cases the results are counterproductive, deepening the pathogenic character of the search for health. More often, however, they become paths clarifying the idea of the inherent problems in the dominant health-care system and looking for authentic alternatives.

In any case, there are an increasing number of initiatives that openly defy the system and break with the dominant notions of sickness and health, including body and mind, all the while nurturing autonomous healing practices. Traditional therapies that have been marginalized and disqualified by the health profession are recovered and enable healthier behavior patterns and forms of humane treatment rooted in the home and community. These efforts are already shaping new institutional arrangements.

SETTLING

Disasters usually associated with public and private development projects are still proliferating throughout the world and increasing the number of homeless people. At the same time, mobilizations to stop them, to reformulate the urban environment and create different living conditions in the cities, are also multiplying and even reshaping the very notion of what a city is.

Efforts to consolidate and strengthen building practices by the people themselves (*autoconstrucción*) that have long defined urban expansion in the so-called Third World are enriched with contemporary technologies. Settling or squatting styles, typical of the so-called marginal communities, are extended to other social spheres.

The *okupa* movement is spreading, particularly in Europe, and with it efforts toward community regeneration and the creation of new commons. Struggles proliferate that bring to the cities the political mutation in the countryside and create coalitions of territorial defense against public and private developments such as an airport or a new highway. They tend to become seeds for establishing autonomous forms of government.

True, the conviction that the monstrous human agglomerations still called cities cannot survive as they are and must shrink considerably continues to spread, but in the meanwhile there are serious efforts to make them livable and sustainable, starting with fragmenting them into multifunctional *barrios* (neighborhoods) where inhabitants can live for the greater part of their lives.

EXCHANGING

Though the Walmartization of the world continues and a few corporations still widen their predatory capacity, causing all sorts of damages, a new era of direct exchange is spreading, outside the capitalist market. Markets where producers and consumers abandon their abstract condition to engage in direct interaction with other people prosper, next to local currencies that serve as means of payment and communal cement and facilitate bartering. Different methods of exchange earn various names, and many abandon the direct use of money as commodity and seek to replace the abstract market with nonexploitative relationships between parties who know and trust one another. In any case, these are initiatives that openly defy the fiction of the self-regulated market and attempt to escape from corporate domination.

This narrative of what's happening in the world raises obvious questions. What are the possibilities and what is the character of this insurrection? What is its nature? Will it really be anticapitalist or will it be put in service of the dominant regime and prolong its agony? Why call behaviors that are initially seen as survival instincts, often-desperate actions with no obvious articulation, an insurrection? These are questions with no direct answers because they are about open processes whose path is yet unknown. Though the impulses that constitute these initiatives are clear, their result is still uncertain.

Beyond Development: Living Well

If there was an expression that could express the vibes of the social movements spreading throughout Latin America, it would be that of *buen vivir*, living well, usually complemented with *crianza mutua*, mutual nurturing. The horizon beyond living well looks to reconstitute political, social, juridical, and economic power—but overall to reconstitute life itself, which has been severely damaged by Western projects. This emphasis generates all sorts of tensions and contradictions with governments across the whole ideological spectrum that tend to increasingly disqualify and criminalize these increasingly vigorous movements.

The definition of the good life, a traditional sphere of action and imagination of the civil society, was attributed to the government in the modern nation-state, which usually shared it with private corporations and the media, surrendering it to capital.

During the last fifty years, after Harry S. Truman coined the idea of underdevelopment and thus redefined the development enterprise as a new emblem for American hegemony, development operated as a universal definition of the good life, associated with the average living conditions in the developed countries and particularly in the United States. It soon became evident that the adoption of such a way of life, postulated as a general ideal, was not feasible in the areas called underdeveloped by Truman. The emphasis of development was thus pragmatically shifted to ensure the satisfaction of basic needs for everyone, but the universal definition of the good life was not abandoned for the construction of social ideals and even to define the basic needs. This orientation still defines development policies in Latin America, in spite of ideological differences that give more emphasis to the market or to the government in their implementation.

Such attitudes clearly belong to a typical Western tradition: the construction of One World—with different flags and pretexts. The westernization of the world would be the hidden agenda of development, under the assumption that the Western, developed countries represent the culmination of human evolution, guided by the arrow of progress. The arrow is currently broken, and the idea of progress itself seems ready for a museum. The cultural homogenization associated with the development enterprise finds increasing resistance everywhere. As the Zapatistas suggested in 1994, the time has come to celebrate the otherness of the other and to create a world in which many worlds can be hospitably embraced. Instead of continuing to dissolve peoples and cultures, to integrate every man and woman on Earth into a universal and uniform design, the exploration of ways to enable the harmonious coexistence of the different has become a priority. This attitude points toward a political horizon beyond the nation-state, reformulates the democratic struggle, and recovers autonomous definitions of the good life emerging from autonomous centers for the production of knowledge. It challenges the dominant mood among governments, political parties, and experts—still associated with social engineering, the trickle-down effect, and other beliefs of the old development religion.

Almost twenty years ago, Paul Streeten rigorously documented for the International Labor Organization the perverse connection between economic growth and injustice.[4] He demonstrated that greater growth corresponded to greater poverty, and that there is a relation of cause and effect between one and the other. He demonstrated as well that the famous "trickle-down effect"—the idea that concentrated riches spill out onto the majority generating well-being in their wake—is a perverse and unfounded illusion. Cultivating the obsession of economic growth implies writing a blank check to the market leaders or the state, so that they do their thing in the name of the well-being of the majority, a well-being that doesn't come, and following that path, will never come.

We need to recover a sense of proportion that is simply another form of common sense: that sense that exists in community. To struggle against a culture of waste, disposability, destruction, and injustice, and the culture that has produced the global warming to which disasters caused by irresponsibility are now attributed, we can reclaim the sensible and responsible rejection of what is unnecessary in the name of socially viable goals, and discard forever the idolatry of economic growth.

The time has arrived to seriously propose the advantages of a negative growth rate, clearly specifying what we would continue to stimulate. For example, we might usefully support highly efficient, productive, and sensible economic activities, such as those that make up the majority of those in the much persecuted "informal sector." This will imply a focus on strengthening the productive capacity of the majority, instead of supporting the inefficient giants. The economists' nightmare, a drop in the GNP, could be a blessing for the majority.

The main positions in relation to development can be associated with three Sachs. Goldman Sachs would symbolize the dominant position in government, corporations, and international institutions: a sixty-year step back to when development was simply economic growth and private profits. Jeffrey Sachs, going back forty years (to the Basic Needs Approach of the World Bank), would illustrate a kind of philanthropic capitalism. Fully aware of existing poverty and degradation, this position acknowledges that the market cannot alleviate them and calls on the state and philanthropy to deal with them. Wolfgang Sachs and the *Development Dictionary*, which he edited with friends of Ivan Illich, constructed the theoretical space for the innumerable initiatives looking for the good life, each in its own way, beyond the dogma of development and economic growth.[5]

Radical Pluralism

The new attitude in many social movements implies the abandonment of conventional universalism without falling into cultural relativism. It expresses in practice, based on local traditions and ancient experiences of resistance and liberation, what Raimón Panikkar conceptualized as radical pluralism.[6] This position acknowledges the existence of human invariants but not cultural universals. In accepting cultural diversity as a precondition for harmony among peoples, and recognizing that no person may represent the totality of human experience, cultural relativity (not relativism) is assumed, which means that every view of the world is relative to its context and no one can hold a complete and absolute view of reality.

It does not seem feasible to incorporate radical pluralism into the design of the nation-state, formally based on a pact of homogeneous individuals (not heterogeneous people and communities [knots in nets of relations]), claiming full sovereignty over all of them, and based upon violence and the universal application of juridical norms. Constitutional reforms in countries like Bolivia, Ecuador, and Mexico are advances in the right direction: to recognize the very existence of Indigenous peoples and their autonomy, but to also make evident their limits.

Something similar happens with the questions of collective rights, those of "minorities" or Indigenous peoples. The nation-state may accept classifications of individuals, to grant them special rights: workers, women, children. In the same way, it may grant special rights to the individual members of "minorities," tribes, peoples. What it cannot incorporate is the very idea of collective rights, the rights of the collectivity that is something more than and different from the individuals constituting it. Many Indigenous peoples, as well as other "minorities," have successfully created de facto institutional arrangements expressing the reality of their collective will and existence, usually at odds with the governments of the countries within which they exist. It is increasingly clear that they conceive their reality within a new political and epistemological paradigm.

In 1996 Subcomandante Marcos clearly outlined the conditions of the current political conjuncture by pointing out that when the Zapatistas raised the point of not taking power they thought that another way of doing politics could thus take shape and another kind of politicians might emerge. For the Zapatistas, the question is not about who is in power or how that power has been attained, either by an individual, group, or political party (whether through elections or any other means), but the very nature of power itself. For example, upon distancing themselves from guerrilla warfare, the Zapatistas warned that the place of the people was always pending and uncertain. They stressed that one cannot create a new world or society with merely a dispute between competing hegemonies. In the Fourth Declaration of la Selva de Lacandona they suggested the creation of local committees dedicated to imagining and putting into practice everything that can be done without political parties or the government.[7]

The idea is not about changing the world without taking power, a lucid phrase that warns against Leninist manias. Rather than attempting to take the artificial power deposited in the state through elections, it is necessary that people exert their real power through the practice of transformation. Instead of losing that power and converting into its opposite—a mechanism of domination—the idea is to use it at the proper scale and to avoid its expropriation by candidates, parties, leaders . . . or the so-called factual powers (the media, the corporations . . .).

In order to reclaim our real power, we need to rethink who we are. Throughout indigenous communities and local neighborhoods, the nets of real relationships constituting the person form a thick social fabric defined by *comunalidad*, a communal way of being, a collective we that forms the first layer of one's own existence. This social construction starts in the cradle: the traditional rebozo or shawl that allows the baby to be symbiotically attached to the mother's body for an extended period of time. From a young age, children learn to be with the world, not separated from it.

A growing number of those who are not connected to anything that can be called community are creating alternatives through the construction of a new commons. Some manage to physically form these communities, organizing a new communal way of life. Others generate these commons through more flexible means, much like those working in the midst of a huge city, and could engage with many of them. Most of these people are not informed by a single ideology or theoretical formation. Friendship, with its characteristic component of gratuity and reciprocity, is the cement that brings people together and creates the point of departure for the new commons.

In the theoretical tradition articulated by Hegel, the economic society of individuals socialized as private property owners imposed their mercantile rationality over a communal rationality that stems from the "natural" society. This is how Hegel's political premise was formulated in 1820: those competitive individuals cannot govern themselves, someone must govern them. This premise has dominated political theory and practice for the last two hundred years. The discussion is around how one must determine who will govern and how they should do it, whether democratically or through an authoritarian regime, through elections, a coup, or a revolution. Overall, the assumption is taken for granted and is now a general prejudice: the people cannot govern themselves.

However, millions of people, perhaps billions, have set forth a different conviction and act in accordance with it. They have always governed themselves with their own political procedures. Whether in the colonial era or among modern states, they have continued in opposition to the dominant system in the midst of all kinds of restrictions, tensions, and contradictions. They've managed to resist the attempts to dissolve their practices and are now moving from resistance to liberation, determined to create a political system adjusted to their own principles, not those of the modern states that are based on violence, the economy, and individualism.

If the people have the appropriate political bodies, they can govern themselves. They do not need to surrender their power to a person or an elite, for them to govern everyone. It is in this context that social relationships are constructed differently. The "power" then is not a relation of domination but an expression of solidarity and comunalidad. It is the relation among dignified men and women seeking the common good—that is what defines their political activity, not the search for "power" up there somewhere.

The political horizon being adopted by current social movements goes beyond the design prevalent since the Treaty of Westphalia of 1648, when the modern nation-state was born. However, it is possible to recover certain terms from that era in order to articulate and describe present conditions, terms such as "nation" and "state," since we have not yet come up with new terms. How to characterize, for example, the communities that were involved in producing the Achachi Manifesto in Bolivia? Thousands of commoners from Omasuyo Province strived to make collective decisions based on the principle to lead by obeying (*mandar obedeciendo*). As Raúl Zibechi notes, this is a mobile and unstable articulation, one that is combined with the stability of a structure and the fluidity of change.[8] Horizontally intertwined, these are powers not yet separated from their community and are also not state powers. The best example can probably be found with the Zapatistas, especially the Juntas de Buen Gobierno (Good Government Councils), which demonstrate the actual possibilities of having effective democratic mechanisms, despite all the forces operating against them. This is clearly an example of the shape of the new society, in which a daily experiment of transformation is practiced.

Reclaiming the Commons

Since the 1980s, many peasants, urban marginal residents, and deprofessionalized intellectuals have been trying to disconnect themselves from the dominant institutions and to prevent their unavoidable interaction with them from affecting their ideas, hopes, and projects.

There is not a word to fully express the diversity of social struggles in Latin America attempting to create, at the grassroots, new ways of life and government. The *commons* have been called *communes, wastes, open fields, usi civici, mir, ejido, Allmende, communaux, altepetl, gemeentegronden.* All these venerable Spanish, English, Italian, Russian, Germanic, Norwegian, Catalan, French, Náhuatl, or Dutch words, along with many others, with their local variants, allude to spaces that are neither private nor public. "Commons" is thus a generic term for very different forms of social existence. In the same way, the immense richness of the social organizations currently existing or being created in Latin America cannot be reduced to the formal categories *community* or *commons.* The Spanish ejido is not identical to the British "commons," to the pre-Hispanic communal regimes, or to the Mexican ejido invented in the Constitution of 1917, implemented in the 1930s, and reformulated in 1992. The emerging new commons are clearly different from their predecessors. All these forms, both actualizations of ancient traditions and contemporary creations, are beyond the private threshold but cannot be defined as public spaces, collective refuges, or hunting preserves. They are not forms of property or land tenure. Specific ways of doing things, talking about them, and living them—art, *techne*—express, in these forms of commons, cultural traditions and recent innovations. Their precise limits (their contours, their perimeters) as well as their internal strings (their straightjackets) are still insufficiently explored territory.

Instead of the individual, the commons is currently replacing the individual as a cell for the society. An increasingly vigorous movement seeks to recover the enclosed commons and regenerate those who resisted its enclosure, who are not a small amount of people: for example, 70 percent of the world's fisheries still operate by way of commons, and 85 percent of the territory in Oaxaca, a state in southern Mexico, is in communal hands. There are also attempts to apply the rules of the commons—restricted and regulated access to common patrimony—to what are now considered global commons: water, air, forests, seeds . . . all of them threatened by the savage exploitation of private corporations and their regimes of free access. The term "commonism" was coined to refer to an increasingly extended alliance between those who seek to claim their rights to the commons and those who intend to protect what remains of the biosphere and remove themselves from individualistic consumerism. All of them try to form what André Gorz calls the "archipelago of conviviality," which also begins to adopt political shape. The National Indigenous Congress of Mexico, which is an articulation of innumerable and different communities dispersed throughout the country, has adopted a very clear motto: "We are a web when we are separated and an assembly when we are together." In the tradition of the Iroquois nation, which brought together many diverse cultures throughout the northern United States that were in conflict, indigenous peoples in Mexico cultivate the autonomy exercised in their communities. They give specific mandates to representatives who can come to agreement with others, much like them, through assemblies. Real parliaments capable of giving form to social norms, respecting them as common initiatives, and put them into practice.

The Reconstitution

Since 2011 there have been very visible manifestations of profound indignation in many different parts of the world. In these movements the creativity and vigor of people have been demonstrated.

- In places like Tunisia or Egypt the outbreaks and liquidation of authoritarian governments have been a prerequisite and precursor to deep social transformations only beginning to take shape,

- while very serious and dangerous attempts to restore the old regime are on their way.

- In other places such as Greece or Spain, recovering plazas and other sites of great symbolic value as appropriate spaces for political assemblies and continuous debate had a cathartic effect for expressing massive indignation. These spaces also became the beginning of a far-reaching movement that has only begun to find its direction. In Greece an autonomous movement is taking root, applying previous experiences to create new paths.

- In Mexico, the Movimiento Nacional por la Paz con Justicia y Dignidad (National Movement for Peace with Justice and Dignity), convened and lead by the poet Javier Sicilia after the loss of his son in a horrendous crime in April 2011, is still mobilizing many people to stop the violence that has plagued the country since the government became the entrepreneur of violence with the pretext of the drug cartels. On December 21, 2012 the Zapatistas peacefully occupied the same towns they had occupied at the beginning of their uprising, on January 1, 1994. They are taking a series of initiatives, renovating their presence in the political scenario, and articulating again many other initiatives and movements.

- In Bolivia, 2011 began with massive expressions of discontent against unacceptable stances taken by the government of Evo Morales. The tensions and contradictions between his regime and the social movements have been increasing since then. The same is happening in other countries in the region that have "leftist" heads of state, like Argentina, Brazil, Ecuador, Uruguay, and Venezuela, some of them committed to what they call "twenty-first-century socialism." The massive mobilizations in Brazil of June 2013 took the political classes by surprise, but the social movements, like the Mouvemento dos san Terra, knew very well what was at stake: the attempt to give neoliberalism a human face clearly failed.

- On September 17, 2011, the symbolic occupation of Wall Street was the beginning of a movement without clear precedent. It produced a new awareness, giving voice to general concerns about the condition of American "democracy." Many people identified with what Naomi Klein told the people gathered in Zucotti Park on October 7, 2011: "What took you so long? We've been wondering when you were going to show up. . . . And most of all: 'Welcome.' "[9] The Slovenian philosopher Slavoj Žižek emphasized that the movement gave visibility to the lack of freedom and invented a language to talk about it. He also offered other memorable phrases: "The marriage between democracy and capitalism is over." "We are not dreamers. We are those who are awakening from a dream that became a nightmare." "We are not destroying anything, but witnessing how the system is destroying itself." In an article in *Foreign Affairs*, Michael Hardt and Antonio Negri, for their part, examined how the movement gives voice to a widespread feeling of economic injustice: "It has become evident that the outrage against corporate greed and economic inequality is real and deep."[10] But according to them, the movement is above all a protest against the lack or failure of representation. "It's not just that this or that politician or this or that party are ineffective or corrupt. . . . But that the representative system itself is inadequate. This movement of protest can, and perhaps should, become a genuine constitutional democratic process." A few months later, those still in the plaza made a recap: "On September 17 people from all over the country and the world came together to protest the massive injustice of our era, perpetuated by political and economic elites. That day we stood against the deprivation of human rights and the social and economic injustices. We speak, resist and occupy Wall Street successfully. We are happy to be here in Liberty Plaza and we consider ourselves an autonomous political entity committed to nonviolent civil disobedience and the construction of solidarity based on mutual respect, acceptance and love. From this reconquered land we tell all Americans and the world: *Basta!*" While some people are still seeing the movement as a kind of global revolution beginning at the heart of the beast, others did not want to celebrate too soon, and still others, for example the media, consider the Occupy movement to be basically dead. What is clear is that thousands of initiatives inspired by it are currently flourishing and spreading throughout the United States.

For John Berger, to name the intolerable is itself hope.[11] When something is considered intolerable, action should follow. Those outraged at Wall Street, much like those in Madrid and Athens and São Paulo, dared to name the intolerable and thus forged a hope that is the essence of all popular movements.

It is impossible to anticipate the evolution of the movements currently erupting all over the world. Governments that initially responded with indifference or repression are now obligated to pay attention. The mainstream media could not maintain its initial indifference, because among other reasons there was a flood of information coming from alternative media sources. The attempts to reduce the movements to a limited set of manageable demands, many of which were presented by some of the protesters, clearly failed.

Some specific measures and policy changes may deactivate the movement in many parts of the world. But there is another option. There is a widespread conviction that, given the failures of the representative system and capitalism, the current crisis requires a regime change that can only be mediated through a people's organization that allows for the recomposition of a social fabric, which has been ripped apart and nearly destroyed. A reconstitution from below begins with neighborhood assemblies, which take diverse forms of organization adequate for each location. There are places where the social fabric is still strong; what is needed is to activate and regenerate it. At the other extreme, there are places in which the social fabric has been ripped apart so completely it has left no sign of ever being there. One cannot organize an assembly here, not even of one block or between neighbors in an apartment complex. But two or three neighbors can organize themselves, and in their small assembly, which will slowly but surely connect with others, they will be spreading seeds for the new reconstitution. It's about, once again, creatively bringing together the constituent power of the people. These assemblies, from the smallest to the largest, are constituent assemblies.

From this point what's next begins to emerge. From a regenerated social fabric, a political power of the people can be legitimized. In certain areas of the world, for example in Mexico, there are some immediate and urgent tasks at hand, like protecting everyone from the spreading violence in a vicious civil war without clear sides, to create a safer community. The challenge today is above all for social creativity and imagination. "For a long time, Teodor Shanin had a very relevant and clearly formulated intuition: 'The future should be, one way or another, communitarian. Socialism was clearly carrying a message of communitarianism. The problem is that it was translated into collectivism, statism and self-destruction.'"[12]

Communitarianism becomes fundamentalism only in a nation-state framework. The actual transformative subjects are those who radically disengage from national state paradigms, and instead promote social and political experiments capable of addressing current challenges and beginning to construct a new society. However, the proponents of this transformation are damaged subjects, influenced and constituted by power that cannot always clearly express their new vocation. "We are not pure," say the Zapatistas. Their decision to openly challenge the conditions of exploitation and the internalization of dominant political practices does not mean they are alien to them. "All of us are crippled—some physically, some mentally, some emotionally," observed Ivan Illich, Robert Fox, Robert Theobald, and some of their friends fifty years ago, in the time of the March on the Pentagon against the war in Vietnam. In their "Call to Celebration" they affirmed: "We must therefore strive cooperatively to create the new world. There is no time left for destruction, for hatred, for anger. We must build, in joy and hope and celebration."[13]

Their manifesto was an invitation to celebrate what we can do together: "For every one of us, and every group with which we live and work, must become the model of the era which we desire to create." It described an opening: "If any one phrase can sum up the nature of the new era, it is the end of privilege and license. . . . The expanding dignity of each man and each human relationship must necessarily challenge existing systems. . . . This call is a call to live the future. Let us join together joyfully to celebrate our awareness that we can make our life today the shape of tomorrow's future."

The time is ripe for these words. We learned the lesson: the 1960s ended in disaster, the great defeat that paved the way for the nightmare of neoliberalism. The new initiatives proliferating in the world can be seen as regenerative processes to search for others in the same conditions, similarly damaged, similarly hopeful, to construct together what has ceased to be a utopia, because it already has a place in the world, though it still lacks a name.

"I can no longer believe in magical transformations, like a victorious uprising which transforms a society," recently said Mercedes Moncada, from Nicaragua. "I believe that revolutions are gradual, deep and associated with the daily life. They must be rooted in all the spaces of the societies, in the families, in the personal relations, in the little ones, in the neighborhoods, all of which also define the shape of power."

Howard Zinn stresses that "revolutionary change is something immediate . . . something that we need to do today, right now, wherever we are, where we live, where we work or study. It implies to begin right now to get rid of all the authoritarian and cruel relations, between men and women, parents and children, between different kinds of workers. This is not an armed uprising. It happens in the little corners which cannot be reached by the powerful but clumsy hands of the state. It is not centralized or isolated: it cannot be destroyed by the powerful, the rich, the police. It happens in a million places at the same time, in the families, in the streets, in the neighborhoods, in the work places. Suppressed in one place, it reappears in another until it is everywhere. Such revolution is an art. That is: it requires the courage not only of resistance but of imagination."[14]

And so, the social revolution of the twenty-first century, the revolution of the new commons, commonism, beyond development, beyond the economic society, beyond capitalism and socialism, is not associated with the great epic of magnificent leaders and mass movements. It has three strong pillars, the very simple, common pillars, all too familiar, of friendship, hope, and surprise.

Friendship is the stuff generating new commons, particularly in the cities, for individualized people who don't have anything they can call community.

Surprise means to acknowledge our condition, as humans. We don't know the future. We are now back from the future, from any promised land, any technical design for social engineering. This is a call to our imagination, living in the present.

And hope, the essence of social movements, is not the conviction that something will happen but the conviction that something makes sense, whatever happens.

All over the world, we are smelling hope, exploring hope, instead of falling into despair or apocalyptic randiness.

It is an adventure into unknown territory.

NOTES

This chapter reworks previous essays: "Enclosing the Enclosers," in Turbulence Collective, *What Would It Mean to Win?*, Oakland, CA: PM Press, June 2007; "La crisis como esperanza," *Bajo el volcán* 8(14) 2009: 17–54; "From the Bottom-Up: New Institutional Arrangements in Latin America," *Development* 53(1) (March) 2010: 64–69; "Los quehaceres del día," in Gabriela Massuh, ed., *Renunciar al bien común: Extractivismo y (pos)desarrollo en América Latina*, Buenos Aires: Mardulce, 2012, 237–82; and "Der laufende Aufstand," in Projectgruppe "Zivilisationspolitik," ed., *Kann es eine "neue Erde" geben? Zur "Kritischen Patriarchatstheorie" under der Praxis einer postpatriachalen Zivilisation*, Frankfurt: Peter Lang, 2012, 233–72.

1. Arturo Escobar, "Latin America at a Crossroads," *Cultural Studies* 24, no. 1 (2010): 45, 47–48.

2. Leopold Kohr, "Size Cycles," *Fourth World Review* 54 (1992): 10–11.

3. Eduardo Galeano, *Global Fear*, n.d., on the Red Tulips Mailing List. https://groups.google.com/forum/#!topic/red-tulips/cdsVGZiID9g. Last accessed October 16, 2014.

4. Paul Streeten, *The Political Economy of Fighting Poverty*, Issues in Development Discussion Paper 1. (Geneva, Switzerland: ILO, 1995).

5. Wolfgang Sachs (ed.) *The Development Dictionary: A Guide of Knowledge as Power* (London: Zed Books, 1992).

6. Raimón Panikkar, "The Myth of Pluralism," in Panikkar, *Invisible Harmony* (Minneapolis, MN: Fortress Press, 1995), 52–91.

7. Zapatistas, *Fourth Declaration of la Selva de Lacandona*, Flag.Blackened.Net, January 1996. Last accessed October 16, 2014. http://flag.blackened.net/revolt/mexico/ezlnco.html.

8. Raúl Zibechi, *Dispersar el poder* (Guadalajara, Mexico: La Casa del Mago, 2006).

9. Naomi Klein, "The Most Important Thing in the World," in Sarah van Gelder et al., eds., *This Changes Everything* (San Francisco: Berret-Koehler, 2011), 46, 49.

10. Michael Hardt and Antonio Negri, "The Fight for 'Real Democracy' at the Heart of Occupy Wall Street," *Foreign Affairs*, October 11, 2011. Last accessed October 16, 2014. www.foreignaffairs.com/articles/136399/michael-hardt-and-antonio-negri/the-fight-for-real-democracy-at-the-heart-of-occupy-wall-street.

11. John Berger, *And Our Faces, My Heart, Brief as Photos* (New York: Pantheon Books, 1984), 18.

12. Teodor Shanin, "Pensar todo de nuevo: Anticapitalismos sin socialismo," *Bajo el volcán* 11, no. 18 (March–August 2012): 109.

13. Ivan Illich, Robert Fox, and Robert Theobald, "A Call to Celebration," in Illich, *Celebration of Awareness* (London: Marion Boyars, 1971), 13–18.

14. Howard Zinn, "The Art of Revolution," in Herbert Read, ed., *Anarchy and Order: Essays on Politics* (Boston, MA: Beacon Press, 1954), ix-xxii. Spanish translation by David Brooks (2010), "Rescatar las incontables pequeñas acciones de gente desconocida, la labor de Howard Zinn," *La Jornada*, México, December 30, 2010. Last accessed October 16, 2014. www.jornada.unam.mx/2010/01/30/mundo/017n1mun.

4

Life and Nature "Otherwise" Challenges from the Abya-Yalean Andes

CATHERINE E. WALSH

The communion between nature and people . . . abolished in the name of God and later in the name of Civilization. —E. GALEANO (2008)

Openings

In 2008, when Ecuador's Constitutional Assembly was about to begin the debate on the rights of nature, the Uruguayan intellectual Eduardo Galeano sent a short text to the Assembly's president. The text, of which the epigraph is part, was not written for publication. It was meant as a reflection on the epoch-breaking significance of Ecuador's constitutional debate and discussion, the first in the world to give centrality to life and nature. In it Galeano emphasized the import of nature in the European "conquest/invasion" of Latin America and the subsequent and ongoing colonial project. And he "located" the divorce of nature and people's communion within—and as fundamental to—the venture of Western civilization.[1]

The growing recognition, particularly in the "Souths" of the world today, that Western civilization is in crisis, and the propositions coming from Abya-Yala (the name, originally from the Cuna language, that indigenous peoples collectively give to the Americas today) for radically distinct life-models and visions interlaced with and in nature, give Galeano's words pragmatic substance. Galeano's words also, in a sense, establish the importance of location and place; that is to say, of the place and location from which we think the world, and act, struggle, and live in and with it.

Here I am not referring necessarily to a geophysical place—although this does matter—or to the "localism" of community-based perspectives and practice. Rather, my reference is more broadly to the historical, cultural, epistemological, and existence-based spaces, places, and locations that configure, shape, and give substance to meaning, thought, struggle, and praxis. Such "localization" disrupts the objective universality of categories, including those of civilization, nature, autonomy, and state. It also contests and challenges the dominant, monocultural, and unicentric frame of Western modernity and/as rationality and its nomos.

In his important book *The Nomos of the Earth* (1950), Carl Schmitt makes evident the problematic and the possibilities of place, space, location, and localization, and their relation with the advances and wanes of Eurocentric and Western frames.[2] As G. L. Ulmen points out in his translator's introduction, Schmitt was "thinking globally, but he was also thinking about Europe's place in any new world order, and about the significance of the European legacy."[3] That is, Europe in relation to history, to the imperial partition of the world, and to the shifts—real and projected—since this time in the geopolitical, territorial, spatial arrangement. Europe was the "localization" of Schmitt's global thinking and rethinking, the lens through which he mapped and remapped the world, and with it international law, modernity, and the westernization of civilization. Yet unlike many of his time, Schmitt used this localization not in a fixed or Eurocentric sense, nor as a universalizing tool. Instead his project was to dislocate and disturb, to reveal the geopolitical complicities that constructed and enabled global linear thinking, and to push forth deeper comprehensions of global divisions, unity, and power, of earth, existence, and of its "peacemakers."[4]

"There always has been some kind of *nomos* of the earth," Schmitt says. "In all the ages of mankind, the earth has been appropriated, divided, and cultivated."[5] Nomos in this sense is understood as a fundamental process of apportioning space: "the structure-determining convergence of order and orientation in the cohabitation of peoples. . . . Every new age and every new epoch in the coexistence of peoples, empires, and countries, of rulers and power formations of every sort, is founded on new spatial divisions, new enclosures, and new spatial orders of the earth."[6] In the first nomos, the oceans were opened up, the earth circumnavigated, and America "discovered." The second nomos began with this "discovery," the use of land and sea, and the subsequent universalizing of a Eurocentric organizing structure that continued until World War II. With the third nomos, Europe, according to Schmitt, was decentered and collapsed into the broader category and power ordering of the West. Yet as Schmitt seems to suggest at the end of his text, with this *new* nomos comes the possibility that Western rationality, its normative world ordering, and its entire "system of accepted measures, concepts, and customs" might also begin to lose ground.[7] To "understand the normative order of the earth," Schmitt contends, "human thinking again must be directed to the elemental orders of its terrestrial being here and now."[8]

Schmitt provides here a way to locate and engage an "other" thinking and understanding, not predicated on the idea—at least in the Schmitt sense—of a "normative order" or of earth as only human-terrestrial. While recognizing Schmitt's critical contribution, this chapter also seeks to transgress the lineal structure of history, the confines of dominant geopolitics, and the frames of Western-world conceptions and suppositions—including those of earth, humanity, being, and nature—omnipresent in his analysis and argument.

In this sense, Walter D. Mignolo's use and critique of Schmitt are particularly helpful.[9] For Mignolo, the present world order does not negate but rather complicates Schmitt's view. On the one hand today's global order is simultaneously polycentric and capitalist; the principles of capitalism are shared by the various centers, anchoring the power of decisions. "Some are attempting to impose, and others reject, the imposition," Mignolo argues, "which means that—in the sphere of the state and the corporations—the struggle that is being fought is located in the domain and control of authority and the control of knowledge."[10] Capitalism, in this sense, is not just economic. It extends to the spheres of knowledge and subjectivity, but also, I might add, to the spheres of nature, being, and life, the organizing spheres of political, epistemic, and existence-based struggle and transformation in today's Andes.

By locating struggle in the domain and control of authority and knowledge, and alluding to the ways both are being reconceived in politics, practice, and law, Mignolo also takes us beyond Schmitt's purview and frame, evidencing shifts in the very ideas of political society and state while making evident, at the same time, modernity-coloniality-decoloniality's intertwine. In this sense, Mignolo affords a significantly different "localization," a localization that pushes a consideration of the "otherwise": that is, of the constructions and constellations taking form and force in the margins or exteriority (in the Dussel sense), *despite* modernity, capitalism, and the still-present but shifting West. They are constructions and constellations that transverse the local, affording an "other" logic of proposition, life, civilization, and reason *to think with* in different historical, cultural, epistemological, and existence-based spaces, places, and locations.

This chapter takes as its overarching concern the construction, positioning, and possibility of this "otherwise"—or differential logic, thought, creation, and existence— in Abya-Yala today and most particularly in the Andean plurinations of Bolivia and Ecuador. As such, its interest is not with "alternative" models per se, since the idea of "alternatives" takes us back to the centrality of colonial frameworks and dominant models of power. It is also not simply with *studying about* "the emancipation practices of those peoples engaged in struggles for the re-appropriation of nature," a study that as Porto-Gonçalves and Enrique Leff maintain, has increasingly become the purview of political ecology. For these authors, political ecology is "the disciplinary and political field of encountering of different rationalities in the social appropriation of nature and for the construction of a sustainable future."[11] Such field and study are without a doubt crucial in advancing understandings of the correlation of life, knowledge, and nature, and in moving "ecology" beyond the confines of "environment." Yet, as is true with the academic disciplines at large, a problem can arise when lived struggles become case examples to justify and give credence to theory, something that Porto-Gonçalves and Leff allude to and that is also taken up by Arturo Escobar.[12] With the academic making of objects of study, the subjectivity, agency, insurgency, and historical and praxical force of the lived struggles can easily become shrouded, obscured, and displaced. Also easily shrouded, obscured, and displaced can be the way such struggles are making history and constructing theoretical moments and movements—to recall Stuart Hall[13]—as well as the way they are opening and enabling decolonial prospects and horizons.

The interest of this chapter is *to think from and with* these lived struggles and their political, epistemic, and existence-based insurgence. It is concerned with the emergent shifts, movements, and decolonial fissures or cracks, and with ongoing tensions, conflicts, and contradictions, including in relation to the refounding of the state, the rethinking of autonomy, and the building of radically distinct projects of civilization; of being with and in nature and/as life "otherwise."

As I will argue, the impetus and base of this Abya-Yalean insurgence and "otherwise" are not in the Left, academia, or progressive government but are instead located in the struggles, propositions, knowledge, practice, and thought of indigenous and African-descended peoples and movements. It is these peoples and movements—their propositions, knowledges, practices, and thought—that conceptually orient, signify, and lead the social, political, epistemic, and existence-based shifts, disruptions, transgressions, and transformations, giving, as Raúl Prada has argued in relation to Bolivia, new orientation and sustenance to a peoples' international in formation, in defense of Mother Earth, and in struggle against capitalism and the dominant order.[14]

It is this insurgence and "otherwise" of social movement struggle that has opened new paths in the Andes, including those reflected in the Bolivian and Ecuadorian constitutions, paths that now offer no simple way of return. Moreover, as the ideas of *buen vivir* and nature's rights—Andean constructs with parallels among other ancestral peoples of the world's Souths—begin to travel the globe,[15] alter conceptions of autonomy, environment, and earth, and penetrate the positivist and monolithic/monocultural realm of jurisprudence, their paths seem to multiply and intercross. All this raises interesting questions about the future, about possible issues of co-optation and marketization, and about counter-strategies and counter-configurations—present and to come—of capitalism, coloniality, and modernity (not only of the West).

In what follows, I highlight key aspects of the insurgence and the emergent shifts in paradigm and practice with regard to life, knowledge, and nature; consider their antecedents; and contemplate the counter-positions they offer and the questions they open up, including in terms of the Western rational nomos and autonomist politics, thinking, and practice, the overarching themes of this book. I examine advances in law and public policy and changes in the conception of rights. In addition, I explore some of the emergent challenges and dilemmas in the social, political, and economic spheres, considering the present context of Bolivia, and most particularly Ecuador.

Also taken up, in the final part of the chapter, are how these constellations of life and nature "otherwise" are beginning to emerge elsewhere, including in the United States and global North. Here a brief overview of the related advancements in legislation, public policy, and what is increasingly called "Earth law" raise related but different questions about autonomist politics and the nomos. Finally, I briefly consider what all this suggests in terms of new positionalities—those of the Andes and the global South; decolonial fissures—most especially in the global modern colonial order; and ongoing struggle—the struggles of life and nature "otherwise" that still remain, are continually renewed, and, of course, are still yet to come.

Of the many insurgencies, shifts, and movements occurring in the region today, the most historic and widely spreading are those that give a radically distinct significance to nature, life, and the model and mode of civilization itself. Western civilization—the constitutive order and model-mode of power that has attempted to universalize and naturalize itself for the last five-hundred-plus years—is in global crisis, and Abya-Yala/Andean America is one of the central places that is bringing the crisis to the fore. As Edgardo Lander argues,

> fortunately and despite the intent over 500 years to universalize this model of systemic war against nature, of knowledge understood as control and, as such, as destruction, as monocultural knowledge and monocultural life-standard; and despite the extraordinary capacity of the market, technology, the media, and colonial subjugation, we find that the places from which to think, feel, and ethically reflect on this process, have not been exterminated. They exist, are vigorous, and present; they are places from which it is possible to establish spaces to think that [this civilizatory model] is not inevitable, that we have options.[16]

Similarly, Aníbal Quijano maintains that of all places on the globe, Latin America is producing today a profound critique of Eurocentrism, the coloniality of power, and Western modernity's capitalist-civilizatory frame. "We are not simply proposing something new against all this; new rationalities are reappearing—of those that were colonized—and new rationalities are also being produced."[17] It is in this "new" period that Latin America is also subverting the Eurocentric patrons of race, knowledge, subjectivity, and authority, Quijano contends, and producing new critical subjectivities, other forms of political authority, new political imaginaries, and other horizons of historical meaning/consciousness and of social coexistence.

The reference to "newness" and "otherness" here should not be understood as suggestive of a fourth nomos in the Schmittian sense, and/or as a lineal historic advance or progression. It is instead indicative of the political, epistemic, and existence-based insurgencies, shifts, and movements pushed from that which has been historically subjugated, oppressed, violated, and negated. Of course the impetus for this shift comes not from progressive governments but from social movements. Ecuador is a case in point.

Ecuador's indigenous movement has long posited and explained its struggle as both political and epistemic, as rooted in the construction of a radically different project of life and living "with." Such a project disrupts the very tenets on which uninational and monocultural society and state have been predicated, neoliberalism avowed, and the cultural and civilizatory model and order of the West universalized. Certainly this movement is not the only one on the globe that has led such struggle and challenge, but still it stands out. It stands out most especially for the insurgency it has afforded since the late 1980s in the political, epistemic, and existence-based realms, an insurgency that has begun to penetrate social structures, institutions, and principles, enabling shifts and movements—in politics, thinking, and being—never before considered or thought possible for society at large.

Indigenous politics have always been insurgent. That is to say, they have always been oppositional, rebellious, resistant, and propositive, postured against what the Kichwa intellectual Luis Macas has called the "colonial tare," and directed toward the creation and construction of radically distinct life conditions. The strategy, reach, and effect of this insurgency and politics, however, have not always been quite the same.

In contemporary times, it was in the late 1980s that Ecuador's indigenous movement emerged with force. The historic 1990 uprising that paralyzed the country for weeks and presented a series of demands to government interrupted the hegemonic idea and narrative of the mestizo nation. It also called into question the conceptions of law, territory, and state. The movement, led by the Confederation of Indigenous Peoples and Nationalities of Ecuador, was conceived as autonomous with regard to government and state, and against political and electoral participation. However, the autonomist politics were not "indianist" in nature—that is, exclusionary of other social sectors—but rather convoking; a politics that summoned others to join the indigenous-led struggle that, in essence, was a struggle for all. Its call for a plurinational state (a central demand of Bolivia's Katarista movement in the 1980s as well) and its naming of interculturality as a central ideological principle of sociopolitical transformation were little understood and largely negated by the populace at large, including by most sectors of the Left. The general assumption then was that both signaled a separatist-autonomic project and stance.

What is interesting here is the inability of most to comprehend the Ecuadorian indigenous movement's conception of autonomy itself, a conception thought from a logic distinct from that of the West and its Left. The political posture against state, most specifically against the uninational Western-centric model of the state, did not preclude intervention in state structures and institutions. Collective land titles, semiautonomous bilingual-intercultural education, and collective rights were demands and victories that worked to open up the state while at the same time contributing to a rethinking of national and international law. In this sense, autonomist politics were not only about self-governance; they were also about opening a wedge—through the proposals of plurnationalism and interculturality—in the very ideas of uninational state and monocultural society.

The mid-1990s saw shifts in the heretofore strategic practice of indigenous—and autonomist—politics. The new decision to work simultaneously on two fronts—outside the state and inside government—led to the formation of the political movement Pachakutik in 1995 and important changes at the local level (the then focus of the movement's intervention). The election in 1996 of seventy-five local officials, from mayors to city councilors, many indigenous, began a process of interpolation from the bottom up. This process was fortified with the 1998 Constitution's naming of fifteen indigenous and Afro-descendant collective rights and recognition of collective territoriality and autonomy.[18]

While the assumption of state power was never the movement's proposition, intervention and incursion in the realms of government, law, and state were important tactics in rupturing the hegemonic and exclusionary order. Some have referred to this decade of the 1990s in Latin America as the era of multicultural constitutionalism and multicultural statism, enabled on the one hand by social movement intervention and on the other by neoliberal designs. Bolivia serves as a key example. The 1990 historic March for Territory and Dignity from the lowland region of Beni to La Paz made evident an indigenous and peasant insurgency. It also led to the passing of three presidential decrees for territorial rights and a subsequent broader political struggle around territory, law, and indigenous rights. The naming of Aymara intellectual Victor Hugo Cardenas to the vice presidency (1993–1997), however, was not the result of or a response to indigenous demands but rather a pivotal strategy of neoliberalism's multicultural logic. By bringing an indigenous leader-intellectual into a government clearly defined as neoliberal in orientation (the government of Sanchez Lozada), the "state" and its transnational allies sought to both co-opt and pacify insurgent struggle, and include those historically excluded within the purviews of state and market. Such a scheme was constitutive of what a number of authors described at the time as the multicultural logic of transnational capitalism, but it was blocked by indigenous and *campesino* collective resistance and organization.

Today's Insurgent Project

Today in Bolivia and Ecuador, we are witnessing the construction and shaping of a distinct and more complex insurgent project. It is a project made possible by the resistance, insurgency, and organizational demands and proposals of the past, including the incursions and interventions that "opened" the established judicial, legislative, and social institutional structure. It is a project not grounded in indigeneity per se, or simply in what has been defined in a somewhat limited sense as the sphere of ethnic/cultural politics and rights. It is a project-in-process that is beginning to transgress, interrupt, and transform dominant structural logics, rationalities, and foundations, and the singular episteme, order, and worldview they enact.

In this sense, the present moment of transformation and struggle is not statist per se, although it may seem so with the recent "win" of the Plurinational State in the new constitutions of Bolivia (2009) and Ecuador (2008). With the recognition of the plurinational character of the state comes a process that simultaneously refounds and rethinks—transgresses, interrupts, transforms—state and nation, as we know them.[19] The Bolivian intellectual-activist Raúl Prada makes clear why: "The plurinational State is not a State-nation (or Nation-State). . . . The plurinational State is not now a State in the strict sense of the word; the plural 'event' dislodges the unitary character of the State. The State is now not the political synthesis of the society, nor is there currently a separation of State, political society, and civil society, particularly since the forms and practices of social organization now absorb the functions that correspond to the field of State."[20] As he goes on to say, "the Plurinational State is beyond the threshold of the Nation-State. Without a doubt it has opened another horizon, other tasks, other aims, other strategic objectives, with the primordial one now being that of decolonization."[21] Moreover, and in the present structural crisis of capitalism, "the plurinational condition, the proliferate condition of the plural, acquires another connotation, becoming an alternative to the singular world, and the singularity of thought."[22] Here the "alternative" intimates not just a transgression but also a radical shift—a radical "otherness" postured from difference—to use Abdelkebir Khatibi's expression from another place and context[23]—with relation to the heretofore-established norm, and its logic, rationality, and foundation. As I will argue later, a characteristic of this otherness of state has to do with autonomous pluralism.

The philosophical, cosmological, and life-based visions underlying such a shift became publically evident at the beginning of the twenty-first century with the indigenous-led mobilizations against free trade agreements and the posturing of the "culture of life" to counter the "culture of death" that is the neoliberal project. But it has also been present within indigenous as well as Afro-descendant communities themselves, in what the Afro-Ecuadorian leader-intellectual Juan García Salazar refers to as the work *casa adentro* or "in-house." That is the work that helps strengthen the ties of belonging and of collective memory, the vision of life, history, and being in the world, and the thinking with the "knowledges that we have been told are not knowledges, that are of no value."[24] Such work by necessity also has to be carried out-of-house, *casa afuera*, to intercede in and, in so doing, to help in building a different vision and practice of humanity, nature, life, and living for all.

The recent constitutions of Ecuador and Bolivia have, without a doubt, helped enable a public presence of an "other" life-vision. In the case of Ecuador, this includes, among other areas, the recognition of ancestral knowledges as necessary components of science, technology, and education, and the making of nature as the subject of rights.

Similarly, the principle, concept, and ancestral philosophy of *sumak kawsay* or buen vivir in Ecuador, and *sumac qamaña* or *vivir bien* in Bolivia, literally translated as "living well" and better understood as life in plentitude and collective well-being, are today the organizing frame of both countries' constitutions. The intention: the construction of a radically different social contract of "living with," based not on the "good life" premise of progress, individual well-fare, and "to have," but on the communion of humans and Nature (with a capital N) and the spatial-temporal-harmonic totality of existence. Excerpts from the preambles of each constitution are illustrative:

> We women and we men . . . recognizing our millennial roots . . . celebrating nature, *Pacha Mama* (Mother Earth) of which we are a part . . . calling forth the *wisdom* of all cultures . . . and as inheritors of the social struggles of liberation against all forms of domination and colonialism, and with a profound commitment to the present and future, have decided to construct a *new form of living-with, in*

diversity and harmony with nature and to reach life in plentitude or collective well-being [el buen vivir, el sumak kaway].[25]

The Bolivian people, of plural composition, from the depth of history, inspired in the struggles of the past, anticolonial indigenous uprisings . . . popular, indigenous, social and union struggles . . . build a new State . . . based in equality and respect among all, in the principles of sovereignty, dignity, complementarity, solidarity, harmony, and equity in the (re)distribution of the social product, where the search for *life in plentitude* [el vivir bien] . . . with respect to the economic, social, judicial, political, and cultural plurality . . . and in *collective coexistence* . . . leaves the colonial, republican, and neoliberal state behind.[26]

My interest here is not to analyze these constitutions (something I have done elsewhere).[27] Instead it is to highlight the attention given to non-Western life-visions as a counter-frame to—and a recognition of—the legacies of colonial domination and capitalist interests. Without a doubt, such attention is reflective of the political-epistemic-existence-based insurgence of indigenous and Afro-descendant social movements over the last several decades, a proactive stance of affirmation, creation, and construction that leads to new arrangements of thought, knowledge, and being and thinking, of life, living, and societal articulation—arrangements that interweave ancestral principles, cosmologies, life-philosophies, and historical struggles against the persistence of colonial-imperial matrices of power imposed from without and within the nation (including the political project of *mestizaje*). And arrangements that are indicative of the urgency to rethink and reconstruct society and state through the guiding principles and political projects of interculturality and plurinationalism for society in its totality.

Such arrangements afford an important challenge to the coloniality of power in general, and most especially to the "coloniality of Mother Nature or Mother Earth." By this I refer to the coloniality that finds root and ground in the intertwined projects of civilization, scientific exploration, Christianity and evangelization, development (understood as modernization and "progress"), and education. A coloniality that works at the intersection of the cultural, ontological, existential, epistemic, territorial, cosmological, and sociospiritual, imposing a notion of a singular world governed by the central dichotomous binary of humans over nature.[28] This binary interrupted the historical, ancestral, material, and cosmological interrelation of peoples, animals, plants, and land, and among the dead and living, and justified man's intervention in and control, domination, and appropriation of nature since the so-called Conquest. The civilizing and ordering of the savage and wild, and the incorporation of this natural world into the world of European science, property, and possession were constitutive elements of the dissemination of power.[29] The natural/scientific explorations first led by Charles Marie de Condamine, Carl Linnaeus, and Alexander von Humboldt, and locally carried out by "New World" *criollo* elite such as José Celestino Mutis and Francisco José de Caldas in Nueva Granada, objectified and naturalized nature. By exploring, explaining, classifying, and ordering the natural world, these men—whether intentionally or not—imposed a cultural order and control, constitutive of what Mary Louise Pratt has referred to as a "European planetary consciousness." That is "an orientation toward interior exploration and the construction of global-scale meaning through the descriptive apparatus of natural history, . . . a basic element constructing modern Eurocentrism."[30]

This "planetary consciousness" is of course a component part of what we understand today as the universalizing project of Western civilization, whose hegemony Andean Abya-Yalean insurgent processes endeavor to upset and overturn. It is also fundamental to the belief, vital then and now, that the control, exploitation, and use of nature as natural resources, commodities, and environment are a human necessity and right. "The desire to dominate Nature, to change it into exportable products, has always been present in this region," says Alberto Acosta, former president of Ecuador's Constitutional Assembly. "In the early stages of Independence, when faced with the earthquake in Caracas of 1812, Simon Bolivar said the famous words, which marked that time, *'If Nature objects, we shall fight against it and make it obey us.'*"[31]

The desire, right, and conceived need to dominate, control, and appropriate nature are constitutive of Western rationality, science, and the modern/colonial order—or nomos—of the globe as earth. Schmitt's three nomoi are both demonstrative and constitutive of the dichotomous divide; "earth" for him was the "planet on which we live, as a whole, as globe," an essentially modern view and construct. "Before the age of great discoveries, before the 16th century of our system of dating, men had no global concept of the planet on which they lived. Certainly they had a mythical image of heaven and earth, and of land and sea, but the earth still was not measured as a globe, and men still had not ventured into the great oceans. Their world was purely terrestrial. Every powerful people considered themselves to be the center of the earth and their dominion to be the domicile of freedom, beyond which war, barbarism, and chaos ruled."[32] For Schmitt earth is essentially anthropocentric, that is, given meaning and order by man. The struggle then it so seems is, at least in part, with and against nature, conceived as barbarism, chaos, conflict, and nonorder, a struggle thought from the context of the spatial and terrestrial as human realms, where order, orientation, and law coincide. It could be argued that because Schmitt's concern was with the emergence of a global linear thinking that began in 1492 with the start of the "modern age," it was necessarily (hu)mancentric. We do not know if he thought—or what he thought about—outside this frame. We do not know if he in any way perceived the operation or even the possibility of other logics for understanding, orienting, and being in and with nature as the totality and relationality inherent to life itself, or if the terrestrial as human-earth was for him only one component of a much more plural cosmos.

In a practical sense, the coloniality of Mother Earth or Mother Nature has worked to reify a singular paradigm of nature and life as civilization that simultaneously constructs, justifies, and serves the global order and its central fundaments: Western modernity, coloniality, patriarchy, heteronormativity, and capitalism all interwoven. It is in this sense and context that the shift begun in the Andes today with relation to life and nature and evidenced in the constitutions, law, and public policy is noteworthy, significant, and substantial.

Shifts in Law, Public Policy, and Rights

The constitutional and legal shifts begun with the multicultural reforms of the 1990s and more radically postured in the plurinational conceptualizations of Ecuador and Bolivia today bring to the fore at least three fundamental concerns with relation to law and legal reform, concerns not necessarily limited to Latin America. The first is legal monism, that which reduces law to either international law or state law, totalizing the ideas-conceptions of rights and justice and, by so doing, negating other spaces, places, and forms of legal reason and production. The second is the irreconcilable hierarchical opposition established between the positivist model of law and the models or systems of customary law, particularly that of indigenous customary law recognized since the 1990s in a number of Latin American constitutions. And the third is the prevalent assumption that legal pluralism—the coexistence of diverse normative orders—is inherently progressive, the maximum expression of ethnic and legal diversity and a goal in itself.[33] Much could be said about the multicultural problematic at play here, something I have analyzed elsewhere.[34] Suffice it to say that the addition of special "ethnic" or "minority" laws to the positivist legal frame, or the simple recognition of "traditional" or customary law and along with it the mapping of a limited sphere of operation, does little to transgress, interrupt, rethink, shift, or transform the modern/colonial design of law and/ as nomos. It also does little to construct and enable a legal "otherwise"— that is, an "other" thinking and practice of legalism and law and, along with it, a radically distinct social project.

Law and the right to have rights are certainly component parts of the modern-colonial-world-system. The obsession with rights, and most particularly with human rights (a Western modern construct), has opened an important platform for addressing issues of gender, sexual orientation, and religious and ethnic diversity and inclusion. It has also pushed and enabled a broad-based acceptance within international law of the rights of ancestral collectivities that, in turn, is pushing a reconceptualization from non-Western logics, both of rights themselves and their subjects. However, it is not the sphere of international law itself that is rousing and driving the shifts, nor is it the nomos that is leading its own inward-focused change. The shifts, movements, and transformations in law occurring in Ecuador and Bolivia are rather grounded in the recent history of political, epistemic, and existence-based insurgencies previously described, and in the processes these insurgencies have activated in the frame not of multicultural (neo) liberal inclusion but of decolonization. Decolonization here is indicative of the necessary relation of pluralism with a radically distinct interculturalization. As Prada argues, "decolonization implies the constitution of new subjects, new fields of intersubjective relation, the creation of new subjectivities, new social imaginaries; this is the development of a constitutive and institutive interculturality, enriched by and accumulative of the differences and diversity inherent to it."[35]

It is precisely for this reason that the plurinational and the intercultural are necessarily intertwined. The plurinational state proposes a model of political, social, economic, judicial, and cultural organization that includes autonomic pluralism and plural autonomies in the instances of territoriality, community, and authority. In the case of Bolivia, this entails department-based, regional, and indigenous autonomies, each with their own spheres of competencies and jurisdiction, with the addition of law in the case of indigenous autonomy. In Ecuador, autonomy is conceived similarly in territorial-decentralization terms, including regions, provinces, rural parishes, municipalities, and "special" ethnic-cultural regimens and jurisdictions. Autonomy, in this sense and as it is constitutionally conceived, is not only a component part of the plurinational state; it is a component part of decentralization as well. Autonomy is thus, and on the one hand, granted by the state and conceived within its purview. Yet, and on the other hand, it is also a construct and practice constitutive of state refounding.

Carlos Crespo criticizes this reductionist, state-centric conception of autonomy, arguing that it pacts indigenous communities with the government-state and under the government-state's authority and administration, which in essence still remains Western in rationality. Luis Tapia follows this reasoning when he says: "Suffice it to recall that departmental autonomy was a principal strategy and project of the patrimonialist oligarchy, used to stop the wave of political ascent of indigenous and peasant organizations and anti-privatization social movements that together were putting in crisis neoliberal governments."[36] Yet, as Tapia also notes, the political negotiation reflected in Bolivia's new constitution (something we might extend to Ecuador's as well) signals a very different moment, one that conceives state reform from the perspective of autonomies and their diverse forms of organization, instead of just adding autonomies to the established structure.

The plurinational state—or better said: the process of state plurinationalization—gives centrality to the heterogeneity of the state and of its social structures, a conception that in turn opens up the idea and practice of autonomy itself, of heterogeneous and plural autonomies. The plurinational, in this sense, calls for a different state, one that as the Confederation of Indigenous Peoples and Nationalities of Ecuador argued in 2007, "eradicates the regionalism and exclusion that we have been subjected to by the imposed model of the pyramidal state, [and is] a new model of political organization for the decolonization of our nations and peoples."[37]

The most inspiring shifts in law are with regard to nature. The recognition and naming of nature as the subject of rights in Ecuador's 2008 Constitution, including her right to reparation and restoration, interrupts the human-defined subject of law and with it the Cartesian logic that separates humans and nature. Brought into consideration here is Pacha Mama, or Mother Earth, as a living being, with intelligence, sentiments, and spirituality, a being of which humans are a part. Nature in this sense is neither an object nor a use-based exploitable good controlled and dominated by humans; it is an integral part of life itself that cannot be divorced from humanity or society. Natural resources and the environment are also differentially positioned; "Persons, communities, and [ancestral] nationalities and peoples have the right to benefit from the environment and natural resources in the frame of buen vivir," but exploitation cannot put in permanent danger natural systems or permanently alter nature's genetic makeup (art. 74).

While battles continue against extractivist politics and for making the application of nature's rights a reality—something I discuss in the following section—there is already legal precedent. The first successful case, decided in March 2011 in favor of the Vilcabamba River and against the Provincial Government of Loja, argued that a local road widening project was depositing large quantities of rock and excavation material in the Vilcabamba River, increasing the river's flow and provoking a risk of disasters from the growth of the river with the winter rains; large floods were affecting the riverside populations who utilize the river's resources. The Provincial Court decided on the side of nature, establishing, among other points, that "it is the responsibility of the constitutional judges to incline towards the immediate protection and the legal tutelage of the rights of nature, doing what is necessary to prevent contamination or call for remedy." In so doing, they named six means of reparation, declaring as a final point "that the defendant is violating the right that nature has to be fully respected in its existence and maintenance of its vital cycles, structure, functions, and evolutionary processes."[38]

Bolivia's 2012 Law of Mother Earth also gives nature subjectivity and agency. Mother Earth is understood here as a collective subject of public interest and a living dynamic system made up of the undivided community of all living beings, who are all interconnected, interdependent and, complementary, sharing a common destiny. The Law's objective, stated in its article 1, is "to establish the vision and foundations of integral development in harmony and equilibrium with the Mother Earth, for living well, guaranteeing the continuity of the capacity of regeneration of Mother Earth's components and systems of life, recuperating and strengthening local and ancestral knowledges, in the framework of the complementarity of rights, obligations, and responsibilities."[39] This Law, a much weakened version of that initially proposed by the social movement and organization network Pacto de Unidad, continues the differential logic initiated by Ecuador, and historically reflected in Andean cosmologies and practices. It also gives centrality to "development," now reconceived in the policy arena as vivir bien.

In fact, a rethinking of development with nature—and as vivir bien or buen vivir—is an important component of both Bolivian and Ecuadorian government initiatives now termed Plurinational Plans of Living Well. Both public policy plans portend to bring to the fore an "other" logic and life project that challenges many of the tenets of Western civilization and capitalism. Yet, in their conceptualizations and elaborations, neither engenders a total divorce or separation from these tenets; purported instead is a kind of movement "in-between" that mixes the liberal rubrics of "integral development," humanism, and social inclusion with the differential logics engaged by nature, Mother Earth, and vivir bien/buen vivir. While some contend that this is part of a necessary "transition" politics, others, including myself, fear that such in-between posturing will weaken, co-opt, and manipulate the very distinction in difference—the "otherwise"—that "living well" affords to the Western civilizatory logic.

Conflicts, Challenges, Contradictions

Constitutions are one thing and governments are another. The differential logics of nature and of life opened by the constitutions and constitutional processes in Bolivia and Ecuador of course are not constitutionally dependent. Their multiple, diverse, and dynamic existence is in ancestral cosmologies, epistemologies of thought, and community practices.[40] However, what constitutional recognition did do is interrupt the Western logic of constitutions and law themselves, while simultaneously positing an "other" logic, thought from and with ancestral peoples and valid for all beings. The hope was that such logic would filter into and be assumed by government not just in discursive terms but also in policy and practice, necessitating and engendering on the one hand a continuous dialogue with ancestral peoples and leaders and on the other a move away from extractivism and the exploitation of nature and its resources. Such has not been the case.

Today extractivism, or what is more often referred to in the region as neoextractivism, is a central and component part of the government politics and policy of both Rafael Correa in Ecuador and Evo Morales in Bolivia. It is also the central focus of indigenous-led protest and mobilization, and of a new government politic of criminalization.

In Ecuador, neoextractivism was officially ushered in with the passage of the Mining Law of December 2008, three months after the popular approval of the new constitution. With a previous history of only small-scale and mostly artesian mining in Ecuador, the new law positioned open-sky megamining (gold and copper) as a new, necessary alternative to and an eventual replacement for the extraction of oil, given declining oil reserves estimated to be depleted in the next twenty years. Within this same logic and in the arguments on behalf of the Law, mining is presented as indispensable in the struggle against poverty (an argument central to other South American government's mining pursuits, most notably Peru and Argentina), a fundamental pursuit of Correa's project of "Citizen Revolution," reiterated again after his 2013 reelection for the next four years.

Noteworthy is the overlooking and negation of the devastating impact of open-sky mining on water, land, livelihood, and peoples, clearly witnessed for example in neighboring Peru. Of course also overlooked and negated are the tenets and rights of the constitution itself, including the rights of nature, territorial rights, and the collective rights of indigenous and Afro-descendant peoples, including the autonomy implied in these communities' rights over their lands and their rights to consultation. While megamining is a more recent threat, one ought not to forget the ongoing impact of other extractivist pursuits, including oil field expansion, palm oil cultivation, and the newest: *transgenicos* or genetically modified agriculture (banned in arts. 15 and 401 of the constitution). The XI Oil Round announced by the Ecuadorian government in November 2012 was demonstrative. Its goal: to auction off twenty-one new oil blocks in the southern Amazon covering 10 million acres of virgin rainforest, home to seven indigenous nationalities.[41] In response to this initiative and to the Ecuadorian government's oil field auctioning at the North American Prospect Expo held in February 2013 in Houston, the Achuar leader Jaime Vargas made clear the clash in logic and project: "For us, the indigenous people, the rainforest is life. There we are in touch with everything. But, for the powerful capitalists and materialists it is seen as a business market, a money market, for power and capital. But for us, it is the market of life because we find everything there; our pharmacy, our goods, our education, our science, our knowledge, our force, our creator, are all found in the life of the jungle."[42]

Since the passage of the 2008 Mining Law, protest and mobilization against extractivist plans and policies have resulted in criminal arrests under the rubric of "state sabotage and terrorism." As of 2012, more than two hundred persons, many of them indigenous leaders, had been charged. Today these numbers are much greater.[43] "The fighters for Nature and Life are persecuted as terrorists so that the transnationals can loot natural resources," says the former energy minister and president of the Constitutional Assembly Alberto Acosta. "Repressive practices inherited from old politics, oriented to disqualify and punish social movements. . . . The hand of twenty-first-century neoextractivism."[44]

With the March 2012 signing of an agreement between the Ecuadorian government and the Chinese company Ecuacorriente for Project Mirador and Cordillera del Condor, one of five scheduled megamining projects for the Ecuadorian Amazon, megamining officially took hold.[45] President Rafael Correa deemed this signing historic not just for Ecuador but for Latin America as a whole since 52 percent of the profits will remain in the country. "We've already lost too much time for development," says Correa; "those who make us lose time are demagogues. 'No to mining, no to oil,' enough of these stupidities! We will not permit the infantile Left, with feathers and ponchos, to destabilize this process of change."[46] "In Correa's words: "La megamineria va porque va" (megamining goes because it goes).[47]

As Acosta argues, "if we abide by historical experience and the reality being lived in other latitudes, megamining directs us to consider in much more depth the schizophrenia of extractivism within the colonial matrix of power. Despite changes with relation to past extractivism, particularly in terms of national interest, what remains and what cannot be covered up is the persistence, the ongoing heritage, of the colonial *raigambre* or entanglement. Worse yet, this twenty-first-century extractivism is recolonizing."[48] The massive indigenous-led march against mining and for water and dignity in Ecuador in March 2012, the Bolivian mobilizations that began in the fall of 2011 and continued through 2012–2013 against the building of a Brazilian-funded highway through TIPNIS-El Territorio Indígena y Parque Nacional Isiboro-Secure (an indigenous territory, nature reserve, and national park with significant oil and hydrocarbon reserves), and the actions that began in Peru in February 2012 against the gold and copper open sky megamining Project Conga, signal the emerging and ongoing struggle in the region for nature and for life.[49] This struggle is synthesized in the March 2012 Declaration of the Coordinadora of Andean Indigenous Organizations, supporting the marches and mobilizations: "To defend water is to defend life. Enough of extractivism, false environmental solutions, and the criminalization of indigenous leaders. For the construction and implementation of Buen Vivir, the protection of Mother Earth, and authentic plurinational states." At their third Congress, held in July 2012, the Coordinadora reiterated its opposition to the politics of extractivism being pushed by neoliberal, alternative, and progressive states against nature and/ as Mother Earth, a politics that seeks to divide indigenous organizations, criminalize leaders, and criminalize the exercise of rights. The Coordinadora's call at this Congress, and as children of Mother Earth, was for the construction of a new civilizatory paradigm grounded in buen vivir.[50]

However, and despite the still present (and inherent) conflicts, challenges, and contradictions, the "otherwise" of nature and life and its distinct civilizatory concept and project continues on, with or without government and state. Moreover, from the Andes it has begun to traverse the globe.

Closings

The ideas and reflections presented here open a series of considerations regarding not only the constellations of knowledge, nature, and life coming from the Andes and its "indigenized" peoples to other parts of the world but also the complexity of the issues at hand when we endeavor to bring these constellations to realization and practice. Of course at the base of this complexity is capitalism, the still vibrant heart of the coloniality of power that is manifested and fortified today in the ever-increasing exploitation of nature as a civilization-perceived necessity. In this, China and Brazil are as much implicated as Europe and the United States.

Thus, and while on the one hand we appear to on the edge of crucial shifts with regard to the matter of life and nature, shifts that reconceive humanity and push significant transformations in the conceptual, legal, and public policy spheres, the appropriation, control, and exploitation of natural resources and of ancestral lands for extractivism have and on the other hand never been greater. What we are up against is nothing less than a crisis of civilizations and of nature and life itself; that is clear. However, what distinguishes this crisis and historical moment are the very presence and insurgencies of its "otherwise." That is, the very presence and insurgencies of the knowledges, peoples, cosmologies, and life visions and practices that coloniality has worked to negate, decimate, co-opt, and deny, those that today are opening the door to dialogues, critical reflections, and praxis that not only subvert the prevailing nomos-order but also, and maybe more important, advance and enable decolonial prospects and horizons.

Life and nature "otherwise", in this sense, are not about—or at least are not only about—new postures of thought, theory, autonomy, or even resistance. They are also not about the introduction—or co-optation—of new catchphrases, modisms, or terms of fashion and convenience for so-called twenty-first-century socialism, or left politics. Rather, they are more crucially about addressing—in an insurgent and proactive sense—what, for the majority of the world, are the daily concerns of existence, dignity, survival, and life itself.

Still, the fact that it is the life-based philosophies, practices, and thought of ancestral indigenized and racialized peoples from the Abya-Yalean Andes that are giving base and foundation to debates today—here and around the planet—is, in and of itself, indicative of change: that is, of shifts, movements, and decolonial fissures or cracks in the global modern colonial order, and of concretions toward radically distinct frames of being in and with nature and/as life. That is the "otherwise" that is at play not only in this chapter but also in nature herself.

In ending, the poetry and reprimand of both Ernesto Cardenal and Eduardo Galeano seem particularly fitting:

La liberación no sólo la ansiaban los humanos. Toda la ecología gemía. La revolución es también de lagos, ríos, árboles, animales.

Not only humans desired liberation. The whole of ecology cried for it. The revolution is also of lakes, rivers, trees, and animals. (Ernesto Cardenal)[51]

Nature still has much to say and it is high time we, its children, stopped playing deaf. (Eduardo Galeano)[52]

NOTES

1. This text was later widely circulated on the Internet. For the English version see Eduardo Galeano, "We Must Stop Playing Deaf to Nature" (2008), in *The Rights of Nature* (San Francisco: Council of Canadians, Fundación Pachamama, and Global Exchange, 2011), 68–70.

2. With the translation into English of this text in 2003, Schmitt has been increasingly recognized as one of the most important twentieth century theorists of international geopolitics and relations. See for example Stuart Elden, "Reading Schmitt Geopolitically," *Radical Philosophy* 161 (May–June 2010), 18–26.

3. In Carl Schmitt, *The Nomos of the Earth in International Law of the Jus Publicum Europaeum*, trans. G. L. Ulmen (New York: Telos Press, 2003), 24.

4. Schmitt, *Nomos*, 39.

5. Schmitt, *Nomos*, 351.

6. Schmitt, *Nomos*, 78–79.

7. Schmitt, *Nomos*, 355.

8. Schmitt, *Nomos*, 39.

9. Walter D. Mignolo, *The Darker Side of Western Modernity: Global Futures, Decolonial Options* (Durham: Duke University Press, 2011).

10. Mignolo, *Darker Side*, 32–33.

11. Carlos Walter Porto- Gonçalves and Enrique Leff, "Political Ecology in Latin America: The Social Reappropriation of Nature, the Reinvention of Territories and the Construction of an Environmental Rationality," in UNESCO-EOLSS Joint Committee, ed., *Culture, Civilization and Human Society, Encyclopedia of Life Support Systems (EOLSS)*, Developed under the Auspices of UNESCO (Oxford: EOLSS, 2013), www.eolss.net.

12. See especially Arturo Escobar, "Whose Knowledge, Whose Nature? Biodiversity, Conservation and the Political Ecology of Social Movements," *Journal of Political Ecology* 5 (1998), 53–82.

13. Stuart Hall, "Cultural Studies and Its Theoretical Legacies," in Lawrence Grossberg, Cary Nelson, and Paula Treichler, eds., *Cultural Studies* (New York: Routledge, 1992), 277–294.

14. Raúl Prada, "Horizontes del vivir bien," *Revista Praxis en América Latina* 8 (May–June 2012), 4–12. Accessed Oct. 11, 2014. www.praxisenamericalatina.org/4–12/horizontes.html.

15. Examples, among others, include Thomas Fatheur, "Buen Vivir: Latin America's New Concepts for the Good Life and the Rights of Nature," Heinrich Böll Foundation, July 2011. Accessed Oct. 11, 2014. http://www.boell.de/en/content/buen-vivir-latin-americas-new-concepts-good-life-and-rights-nature; and Giuseppe De Marzo. *Buen vivir. Per una nuova democrazia della Terra*, (Rome, Italy: Edeisse, November 2009).

16. Edgardo Lander, "Crisis civilizatorio: El tiempo se agota," in *Sumak Kawsay/ Buen Vivir y cambios civilizatorios*, coord. Irene León (Quito, Ecuador: Fedaeps, 2010), 34. Translation mine.

17. Aníbal Quijano, "América Latina: Hacia un nuevo sentido histórico," in *Sumak Kawsay/Buen Vivir y cambios civilizatorios*, coord. Irene León (Quito, Ecuador: Fedaeps, 2010), 65.

18. See Marc Becker, *Pachakutik: Indigenous Movements and Electoral Politics in Ecuador* (Lanham, MD: Rowman and Littlefield, 2011); Jose Antonio Lucero, *Voices of Struggle: The Politics of Indigenous Representation in the Andes* (Pittsburgh: University of Pittsburgh Press, 2008); and Catherine E. Walsh, "The (Re)articulation of Political Subjectivities and Colonial Difference in Ecuador: Reflections on Capitalism and the Geopolitics of Knowledge," *Nepantla: Views from South* 3, no. 1 (2002): 61–97.

19. Of course what nations like Ecuador and Bolivia are facing today is not just the transition or movement toward a plurinational state but also the battle between the making of a strong liberal state (the government projects) and state refound-

ing and plurinationalization, projects whose impetus and ground was outside government.

20. Raúl Prada, "Umbrales y horizontes de la descolonización," in Alvaro García Linera, Raúl Prada, Luis Tapia, Oscar Vega Camacho, eds., *El Estado: Campo de lucha* (La Paz: Muela de Diablo and CLACSO, 2010), 88. My translation.

21. Prada, "Umbrales," 90.

22. Prada, "Umbrales," 85.

23. Abdelkebir Khatibi, "Maghreb plural," in Walter Mignolo, ed., *Capitalismo y geopolítica del conocimiento: El eurocentrismo y la filosofía de la liberación en el debate intelectual contemporáneo* (Buenos Aire, Argentina: Ediciones del signo, 2001), 71–92.

24. Catherine E. Walsh and Juan García, "El pensar del emergente movimiento afroecuatoriano: Reflexiones (des)de un proceso," in *Estudios y otras prácticas intelectuales latinoamericanos en cultura y poder*, coord. Daniel Mato (Buenos Aires, Argentina: Clacso, 2002), 324.

25. Constitución de la República del Ecuador, 2008; emphasis mine.

26. Constitución de la Republica de Bolivia, 2009; emphasis mine.

27. See Catherine E. Walsh, *Interculturalidad, Estado, Sociedad: Luchas (de)coloniales de nuestra época* (Quito, Ecuador: Universidad Andina Simón Bolívar/Abya-Yala Ediciones, 2009).

28. While space does not permit this exploration here, it is interesting to consider how the patrons of heteronormativity are differentially played out in the humanity-nature divide. The androgynous character of many indigenous and African spirits and gods, and the symmetry based in complementary asymmetries characteristic of the open and fluid gender relations and dualities in the Andes and Mesoamerica, were considered by the Europeans and the national elite as unnatural nature-manifestations; their elimination was viewed as a necessary action of civilization, that is of becoming (hu)man and consequently of dominating nature and its manifestations in inferior (read: savage, irrational, pagan) beings (including plants and animals, women, "indios," and "blacks"). See Michael Horswell, *Decolonizing the Sodomite* (Austin: University of Texas Press, 2005); Sylvia Marcos, *Taken from the Lips: Gender and Eros in Mesoamerica* (Boston: Brill, 2006); and Catherine E. Walsh, "Life, Nature, and Gender Otherwise: Reflections and Provocations from the Andes," in Wendy Harcourt and Ingrid Nelson, eds., *Beyond the Green Economy: Connecting Lives, Natures and Genders Otherwise* (London: Zed Books, forthcoming). Curiously enough, for Pratt, the naturalist-collector figure has a "certain androgyny about it; its production of knowledge has some decidedly non-phallic aspects." As such, we can ask how he figures into the "natural" order, says Pratt, *Imperial Eyes: Travel Writing and Transculturation* (New York: Routledge, 1992, 33. Such question opens a much broader consideration, of course, about the interplays of gender, sexuality, and nature.

29. See Mauricio Nieto, "Historia natural y la apropiación del nuevo mundo en la ilustración española," *Etudes andines* 32, no. 3 (2003): 417–429, and Pratt, *Imperial Eyes.*

30. Pratt, *Imperial Eyes*, 15.

31. Alberto Acosta, "Toward the Universal Declaration of Rights of Nature, Thoughts for Action," 2010, English version: http://www.therightsofnature.org/wp-content/uploads/pdfs/Toward-the-Universal-Declaration-of-Rights-of-Nature-Alberto-Acosta.pdf. Accessed Oct. 11, 2014.

32. Schmitt, *Nomos*, 351.

33. See Boaventura de Sousa Santos, *La globalización del derecho: Los nuevos caminos de la regulación y la emancipación* (Bogotá, Columbia: Universidad Nacional de Colombia, 1998); and Maria Soledad Bellida, "Interculturalidad y pluralismo jurídico" in *Derecho: Revista de la Facultad de Derecho* (2008), www.unsa.edu.pe /escuelas/de/rev . . . /093–100_08_MBellidoA01.pdf (link no longer valid).

34. Catherine E. Walsh, *Interculturalidad crítica y (de)colonialidad: Ensayos desde Abya Yala* (Quito, Ecuador: Abya-Yala Ediciones, 2013), particularly the chapter "Interculturalidad critica y pluralismo jurídico," and Walsh, *Interculturalidad*, 2009.

35. Prada, "Umbrales," 90.

36. Luis Tapia, "El estado en condiciones de abigarramiento, in Álvaro Garcia Linera, Raúl Prada, Luis Tapia, and Oscar Vega Camacho, *El Estado. Campo de lucha* (La Paz, Bolivia: Muela del Diablo editores/CLACSO, 2010), 118.

37. Confederation of Indigenous Peoples and Nationalities of Ecuador, cited in Walsh, *Interculturalidad*, 103.

38. Quoted in Natalia Green, "The First Successful Case of the Rights of Nature Implementation in Ecuador," Global Alliance for the Rights of Nature, 2013. Accessed Oct. 11, 2014. http://therightsofnature.org/first-ron-case-ecuador/.

39. Article 1, law no. 300, October 15, 2012, my translation. Accessed Oct. 11, 2014. www.lexivox.org/norms/BO-L-N300.xhtml.

40. It is interesting to note that in a recent call for papers on sumac kawsay or buen vivir, the journal *Iconos* in Ecuador raised the question of whether buen vivir is not just a recent invention since, as the journal's call contends, there are no ethnographic studies to prove its existence.

41. Further illustration can be found in the fact that more than 27,000 hectares of ancestral Afro-descendant and indigenous land in the northern part of the province of Esmeraldas have been concessioned or sold in recent years to African palm cultivators. During the Correa government the National Bank of Public Works has financed credit to palming companies for 16,655 hectares, more than double that previously. According to Ivan Roa, with the present government, credit for palm cultivation has increased more than at any other time in history, both in the amount of money and the amount of ancestral land "given" or leased to national and transnational companies. Roa, "El desborde de la violencia: Raza, capital y grupos armados en la expansion transnacional de la palma aceitera en Nariño y Esmeraldas," master's thesis (Quito, Ecuador: Flacso, 2011).

42. See "Indigenous Leaders Confront Ecuadorian Government in Houston," *Earth First Journal*, Feb. 6, 2013. Accessed October 11, 2014. http://earthfirstjournal .org/newswire/2013/02/06/amazonlandgrab/.

43. The political persecution, repression, and arrest of those challenging extractivism continues to grow, impelled, in part, by the August 2013 government decision

to exploit oil in the Yasuni National Park, the most biologically diverse reserve in the world. This decision, which ended Ecuador's official international campaign begun in 2007 for nature and for keeping the oil in this reserve in the ground, sparked actions that the government has endeavored to silence and quell. Other cases, including the May 2014 militarization of the subtropical region of Intag in order to enable copper mining, have resulted in further repression, persecutions, and arrests under the charges of state sabotage and terrorism.

44. Alberto Acosta, "El uso de la justicia como mecanismo de terror," *El Universo*, February 8, 2011. Accessed Oct. 11, 2014. www.eluniverso.com/. My translation.

45. With over 2,030 plant species, 142 mammal species, 613 bird species, 56 frog species, and 9 reptile species, the Mirador and Cordillera del Condor is one of the richest areas of biodiversity in South America. The project—slated to use 140 liters of water per second, consume electricity equivalent to a city of 140,000 habitants, excavate 54,000 tons of rock per day, generating at least 336 million tons of waste, with an acid drain (in 227 sources) expected to contaminate the ground and water for thousands of years—not only threatens this biodiversity but also destroys the future possibilities of all forms of life in this region of ancestral indigenous territory. Of relevance here is also the broader question about the role of China and Chinese capital in Ecuador in specific and South America in general, capital largely directed to extractivist endeavors. China is currently Ecuador's largest creditor, a position set to further grow with the projected financing of $13 billion by China's Industrial and Commercial Bank and a Chinese oil firm for a major oil refinery on Ecuador's Pacific Coast. See "Ecuador Business: Chinese Firms to Fund Pacifico Refinery," *Ecuador Economist*, June 6, 2012.

46. "Rafael Correa defiende contrato para explotación minera," *El Universo*, March 10, 2012.

47. Alberto Acosta, "El retorno del Estado: Primeros pasos postneoliberales, mas no postcapitalistas," *Observatorio Económico de América Latina*, May 8, 2012. Accessed Oct. 11, 2014. www.obela.org/contenido/retorno-del-estado-primeros-pasos
-postneoliberales-mas-no-postcapitalistas. My translation.

48. Acosta, "El retorno del Estado," 16.

49. "Juan Perelman has synthesized what is really behind the indigenous struggle in defense of TIPNIS: to protect indigenous people's autonomy, probably today these people's most precious possession, precisely because it is autonomy that guarantees—maybe the only guarantee of—not disappearing as a people, society, and culture in front of the steamroller that is the globalization of capital, in which the Bolivian government is just one nut or bolt more. This autonomist struggle, in its base, is anti-statist, against the legitimization of this territory and its populations by the state." Carlos Crespo, "Tipnis y autonomía," blog entry, December 10, 2012. Accessed October 11, 2014. http://anarquiacochabamba.blogspot.com/2012/12
/tipnis-y-autonomia.html. The Conga Project, negotiated between the Peruvian government and the Denver–based Newmont Gold Corporation, threatens to dry up four lagoons, contaminate water sources, and destroy the life and livelihood of over 100,000 people. As of July 2011, Peru already had forty-three principal mining

projects, with 65 percent of the mining inversions concentrated in four majority-indigenous-peasant regions (Cajamarca, Apurimac, Moquegua, Arequipa). By 2012, close to a thousand leaders were facing police persecution and penal processes for defending water and life.

50. See "Declaración, III Congreso de la CAOI," *Enlace Indígena*, July 24, 2012. Accessed Oct.11, 2012. http://movimientos.org/es/enlacei/show_text.php3%3Fkey%3D21290.

51. Ernesto Cardenal, quoted in Adrian Taylor Kane, ed., *The Natural World in Latin American Literatures* (Jefferson, NC: McFarland, 2010), v.

52. Galeano, "We Must Stop Playing Deaf to Nature," 68.

5

Mind the Gap Indigenous Sovereignty & the Antinomies of Empire

JODI A. BYRD

Since 2011, and in the time since the Occupy movement's demonstrations around the United States and world, it is now somewhat passé if not naïve to evoke the protest mobilizations as some sort of optimistic shift toward global transformation of debt, biofinancialization, and conspicuous consumption. After Michael Taussig observed angry signs, James C. Scott gave two cheers for anarchy, and Michael Hardt and Antonio Negri declared the end to manifestos, the outcomes and impacts of the Occupy movement continue to circulate within leftist critique to ambivalent ends.[1] What has emerged, however, has been a sustained and attentive engagement with the entanglement such notions as value, accumulation, crisis, and financialization have with and to the processes of enclosure that conscripted the New World into productive value, a process that served to reworld lands and reciprocal relationships into property and conscripted labor. "In the beginning," John Locke announced in his *Second Treatise*, "all the world was America, and more so than that is now; for no such thing as money was anywhere known. Find out something that hath the use and value of money amongst his neighbors, you shall see the same man will begin presently to enlarge his possessions."[2] Locke's predictive common sense of human nature, articulated here in the voice of god, is the sine qua non of colonial capitalism, and use, value, and possessive enlargement have been the operative modes of colonization and genocide, indentureship and slavery, enlightenment and democracy since Europeans first imagined natural man and civil society. Over three hundred years later, and as we find ourselves now managed and managing (barely) within the systems of governmentality that Foucault defined as biopolitics, the gap between use, value, and possession continues to collapse as neoliberal institutions consolidate control over our lives at the same time that they entrench our investments in notions of some outside, alternative escape from all this to a more judicious, less indebted, more equal space of the commons, the space beyond.

To enter such an outside, one must steal away, become fugitive, stop the theft by thieving; as Fred Moten and Stefano Harney write, "to enter this space is to inhabit the ruptural and enraptured disclosure of the commons that fugitive enlightenment enacts, the criminal, matricidal, queer, in the cistern, on the stroll of the stolen life stolen by enlightenment and stolen back, where the commons give refuge, where the refuge gives commons."[3] Their notion of the commons, or in fact the undercommons, attached to fugitive planning and black intellectual thought, seeks to recover the surround of the fort, to reframe the notion of surround as the act of surrounding toward a politics from below the below. But what does it mean to delineate such notions of the wilderness, the wild, and the surround within the larger trajectories of U.S. frontier expansion? How might a notion such as indigeneity function within the calls for the redistribution of sense and sensibility at the site of stealing away? How does one begin to access and activate the "indigenous" within systems of subjectifications and objectifications that formed themselves in relation to what Elizabeth Povinelli apprehends as those prior presences necessary to render liberalism and the human intelligible at the horizon of governance?[4] And finally, how does the embracing and jettisoning of the idea of the "native" and "tribal" function within reiterations of states of nature that often underwrite calls for redistribution, access, justice, and the commons?

Often such calls for the commons arise within the context of certain governmental norms and givens that are predicated upon Enlightenment investments in the human and the individual—fugitive and stolen back though they might be. As Carl Schmitt argues, the geopolitical logics of Enlightenment humanism arose within the originary moment of the New World discovery. The state of nature, he asserts in *The Nomos of the Earth*, "is a *no man's land*, but this does not mean it exists *nowhere*. It can be located, and Hobbes locates it, among other places, in the New World."[5] Within the context of the Americas, freedom, equality, and liberty were hewn in a crucible of violence, subjugation, enslavement, extermination, and expropriation that made such promissory ideals intelligible, desirable, and enforceable. Savage, animal, and female were differentiated in order to cohere civilized, human, and male into the normative structures through which power, politics, and livability could be structured. Indigenous peoples and lands became recognizable as they were conscripted into Western law and territoriality and then disavowed from the space of actor into that space which is acted upon within the systems of colonial governmentality that continue to underwrite the settler empires that have emerged through the direct benefit of lands stolen from peoples who could not maintain territoriality or humanity in the face of the grinding appropriations of modernity. In order to begin to answer some of the questions I have posed, and here I would like to add a question Nandita Sharma and Cynthia Wright have asked of indigenous critique—"What are the consequences of naturalizing an ethnicized, racialized, and nationalized relationship between people and with land?"— the first thing we should do is consider how people and land function and are naturalized within the concepts of the political that reside within sovereignty and territoriality and the commons.[6]

That the concept of the political, which includes the biopolitical, the exception of bare life, and even the possible alternatives that might emerge to transform sociality and relationality into "new world orders," is tied to the order of the New World and the conquest of indigenous peoples matters within considerations of the commons, particularly as they deconfigure and reconfigure the concepts of property, territoriality, and sovereignty. Certain philosophical antecedents—including the origins of "natural man," "human rights," and "freedom and equality," derived from and through the colonization of indigenous peoples in the Americas—have been disavowed within the realms of the political and biopolitical. Those realms, according to Michel Foucault and Giorgio Agamben, transformed from the territorial state into the state of population during the nineteenth century as sovereignty came to enact itself through the exception and the threshold between life and death.[7] Indigenous peoples, as neither fully alive nor completely eradicated, remain spectral within the settler colonies of the global North, even as the transition from territorial expansion that made settler colonialism a spectacle of triumph over the savage and the wilderness sublimated into the biopower of the welfare state that redefined sovereignty as "the right to make live and to let die."[8]

That transition, fueled as it was through capitalism, populism, and possessive whiteness that demanded the outside as expansive liberty, structured itself through the zones of indistinction that were constitutive of the genocidal dispossession of the seventeenth, eighteenth, and nineteenth centuries. Agamben argues that "the 'ordering of space' that is, according to

Schmitt, constitutive of the sovereign *nomos* is not only a 'taking of land' (*Landesnahme*)—the determination of a juridical and a territorial ordering (of an *Ordnung* and an *Ortung*)—but above all a 'taking of the outside,' and exception (*Ausnahme*)."[9] Within the settler colonies of the global North, the transition from territorial expansion to contemporary biopolitics exposed everyone to the precarities of bare life. The sovereign nomos was, from the start, predicated upon indigenous precarity that existed alongside land- and sea-appropriations.

New World Nomos

The discovery of the New World marked a fundamental and radical shift within the historical trajectory of European epistemology, engendering in its wake the notion of the human and mobilizing the concepts of property, money, and life as possessions that would come to stand as the boundaries between civilization, savagery, and the nonhuman. The resultant worlding of the globe into four continents that met in the contest to civilize and make that new land productive, as Lisa Lowe has suggested, structured and formalized humanism into geographical and temporal scales in which "*freedom* was constituted through a narrative dialectic that rested simultaneously on a spatialization of the *unfree* as exteriority and a temporal subsuming of *enslavement* as internal difference or contradiction."[10] The significance of this event cannot be overstated; but in the meantime, post-Enlightenment liberal humanism has striven to obscure, divert, and forget that the New World's state of nature was produced by processes of racialization, conquest, colonization, and genocide.

Perhaps it is with some irony, then, that political theorist Carl Schmitt's *Nomos of the Earth* is one of the few philosophical tomes of its era that takes as its premise the foundational role of the New World for the inauguration of a world order. That old order of the earth is foundering, Schmitt concludes at the end of his introduction, though it "arose from a legendary and unforeseen discovery of a New World, from an unrepeatable historical event. Only in fantastic parallels can one imagine a modern recurrence, such as men on their way to the moon discovering a new and hitherto unknown planet that could be exploited freely and utilized effectively to relieve their struggles on earth."[11] In the absence of such a possibility, according to Schmitt, it is now incumbent upon those who remain grounded on earth to reconfigure a new nomos responsive to the terrestrial planetarity of a unified globe, to restore balance to the current foundering nomos through appeals to tradition and *e pluribus unum*, or finally, to create an equilibrium of balanced *Großräume*, large rooms or blocs, a rational new nomos to restore the jus publicum Europaeum.[12]

Schmitt's evocation of the New World as an implied parallel planet that "could be exploited freely and utilized effectively to relieve their struggles" speaks to the colonial foundational pathology that continues to inflect also the contours of liberalism, postautonomia, and anarchist resistances. These political philosophies rely upon and project an imagined Americas as a future perfect new world order that will traverse a successive path toward the fulfillment of political promise and the restoration of the state of nature. Even within the fierce urgency of post-Fordist economic production and capitalist consumption, the hoped-for narratives of liberation depend upon the Americas as an already emptied, infinitely exploitable new territory and new site of a transfigured commons, a multicultural asylum that will utilize effectively the remaining resources of the here and now as the violent disenfranchisements of what Achelle Mbembe has defined as the necropolitical costs of keeping alive will be leveled and shared more equally by everyone.[13]

Certainly there is a nostalgic turn to the native and to the primitive within a range of political and cultural theories that attempt to grapple with the historical consequences of capitalism and the biofinancialization of dispossession that have defined the twenty-first century. To imagine a world of redistribution from whatever political ideology is to grasp for the reins of an empire that depend upon a simultaneous absenting of any prior presence and the suturing of that New World to that prior as already given. Jean M. O'Brien has described that process as one that requires "a stark break with the past" in which colonizers rely upon elaborate replacement narratives to define "their own present against what they constructed as the backdrop of a past symbolized by Indian peoples and their cultures."[14] Indians, O'Brien concludes, "can never be modern"; yet European modernity hinges upon Indians as the necessary antinomy through which the New World—along with civilization, freedom, sovereignty, and humanity—comes to have meaning, structure, and presence.[15] Concomitantly, and with its implied claim to being original and antecedent, indigeneity is simultaneously deferred and negated, essential and required for sovereignty and territoriality to cohere at the site of settler legitimacy, power, and precedence. In other words, indigeneity and the "native" who claims it are naturalized to land precisely because sovereignty and territoriality require the condition and being of the native to be intelligible within the processes of recognition.

The *Beast* Is the Sovereign

Joanne Barker, in her discussion of the global ramifications of the early nineteenth-century Marshall trilogy's impact on the indigenous world, argues that rather than functioning as a stable and coherent governmental or political concept, sovereignty should be understood as a term and force that is historically contingent. "Sovereignty—and its related histories, perspectives, and identities—is embedded within the specific social relations in which it is invoked and given meaning."[16] Chief Justice John Marshall, when he innovated both the doctrine of discovery and his categorical interpretation of the U.S. Constitution to produce the sui generis "domestic dependent nation," unleashed a parceling system of what might be called, after Schmitt, a Großräume that facilitates removals, terminations, allotments, and reservations that would follow as the consequences of Marshall's articulation of colonial law. Sovereignty, as a legal and governmental force, was in this historical moment tied to geography as much as to people, and circulated as something that could be postponed for certain races, while they remained not just in the state of nature but in the state of pupilage. Sovereignty in the New World required Indians as the sign of the external savage in order to cohere an internal ordering of the nomos. "Perfect settler sovereignty," Lisa Ford writes, "rested on the conflation of sovereignty, territory, and jurisdiction."[17] With the Cherokee removal, Georgia "effected perfect settler sovereignty by dissolving indigenous polities and forcing indigenous peoples from its borders."[18]

Over the course of two hundred years, U.S. legal and political thought has pursued a more perfect articulation of such settler distinctions. Articulating the structural networks of a transformed sovereignty within the materialization of an imminent twenty-first century postmodern "Empire," Hardt and Negri suggest that "the dialectic of sovereignty between the civil order and the natural order has come to an end. . . . The modern dialectic of inside and outside has been replaced by a play of degrees and intensities, of hybridity and artificiality."[19] If it is true that we are witnessing what Hardt and Negri have identified as the beginnings of "the transformation of a global frontier into an open space of imperial sovereignty," then questions of territoriality and governance inevitably haunt how we might apprehend the unbinding of sovereignty from land.[20] With the rise of such a deterritorialized sovereignty that enacts itself within the frontiers of an unbounded global empire, questions of indigeneity become more significant, and more unsettling.

That the frontier continues to serve as mnemonic for space and governmentality within discussions of the global—and now the commons—is telling. Often configured as a zone of indeterminacy, the frontier begins with the premise of a *terra nullius*, a "no-man's-land" at the threshold between civilization and the outlaw, the internal and the external. According to Agamben, this zone is an anthropological machine in which the state defines itself at the line of differentiation between animal and human. That zone of indeterminacy, Agamben suggests, "functions by excluding as not (yet) human an already human being from itself, that is, by animalizing the human, by isolating the nonhuman within the human: *Homo alalus*, or the ape-man."[21] For Agamben, the nonhuman isolate includes the *néomort*, the Jew as "the non-man produced within the man," "the slave, the barbarian, and the foreigner," as well as the "*enfant sauvage* or *homo ferus*."[22] Modern political governance operates through a "the zone of indifference," in which "the articulation between human and animal, man and non-man, speaking being and living being, must take place. Like every space of exception, this zone is, in truth, perfectly empty, and the truly human being who should occur there is only the place of a ceaselessly updated decision in which the caesurae and their rearticulation are always dislocated and displaced anew. What would thus be obtained, however, is neither an animal life nor a human life, but only a life that is separated and excluded from itself—only a *bare life*."[23] Perfect settler sovereignty meets perfect empty space at the site where the homo ferus is rendered a *homo sacer*.

Jonathan Goldberg-Hiller and Noenoe K. Silva have read this moment of "central emptiness" within Agamben's thesis as a potential space in which indigenous peoples might be found, because Western law and Romantic imagination has linked them to nature or evoked them "as human/animal signs of the zone of indifference."[24] The enfant sauvage, as one possible signification of the savage in the state of pupilage, and the homo ferus, as that savage child resignified as werewolf, have both served as metonymy for Indians within Enlightenment philosophy. In *Savage Anxieties: The Invention of Western Civilization*, Lumbee scholar Robert A. Williams, Jr., posits that "for writers and theorists who were obsessed with using the 'state of nature' to prove their theories of human nature and society, the Indian was as close to that natural state as you could get in the world: an ideal stand-in for humanity's first, primitive, backward stage of social development."[25] As the founders of liberalism elaborated the anthropological machine that would differentiate human from animal and being with language from being speechless, the Indian as savage served as the American "missing link" through which settlers would perfect their colonial assemblages of sovereignty.

Nowhere is that link so clear as in the example Williams gives of General George Washington's nascent policy to deal with Indians and negotiate the settlement of their lands on the western frontier. In a September 7, 1783, letter to James Duane, Washington writes,

> the Settlemt. of the Western Country and making a Peace with the Indians are so analogous that there can be no definition of the one without involving considerations of the other. For I repeat it, again, and I am clear in my opinion, that policy and œconomy point very strongly to the expedience of being upon good terms with the Indians, and the propriety of purchasing their Lands in preference to attempting to drive them by force of arms out of their Country; which as we have already experienced is like driving the Wild Beasts of the Forest which will return as soon as the pursuit is at an end and fall perhaps on those that are left there; when the gradual extension of our Settlements will as certainly cause the Savage as the Wolf to retire; both being beasts of prey tho' they differ in shape.[26]

Tying policy to the economy of purchasing land rather than engaging in direct warfare, Washington's letter to Duane reflects what Williams describes as an "Americanized language of Indian savagery," dependent upon the notion that the Indian was a failed capitalist who was doomed to retreat westward as civilization advanced and developed the lands they would be all too willing to sell at bargain basement prices.[27] As nonhumans naturalized to the lands they inhabit but do not cultivate, the Indian as savage beast of prey moves like the wolf, *à pas de loup*.[28]

The significance of Washington's "Savage as the Wolf," within the anthropological machine of modern sovereignty that produces and requires the indigenous to be intelligible, derives in part from the fledgling United States' articulation of its own policy after the Treaty of Paris was signed to end the Revolutionary War on September 3, 1783. Washington's letter to Duane four days later, as others have observed, is notable for a number of reasons, including his compassionate conservative delineation of the need for a boundary between the Indians and settlers that would serve as the terms of peace with those nations still at war with the revolting colonies.[29] "We will from these considerations and from motives of Compn.," Washington writes, "draw a veil over what is past and establish a boundary line between them and us beyond which we will *endeavor* to restrain our People from Hunting or Settling, and within which they shall not come, but for the purposes of Trading, Treating, or other business unexceptionable in its nature."[30] Echoing the Royal Proclamation of 1763 that drew a line to delimit the British colonies, Washington imagined an extension of that boundary as a necessary and rational delineation of his own colonial sovereignty that would set the frontier between past and present, savagery and civilization. And in evoking the Western Country as synonym for both Indian Country and frontier, Washington begins to operationalize what will come to define U.S. empire as the exceeding of that threshold through the continual inclusion of the outside, the external remade as internal.

That the Indian is the foundational pathology within the logics of modern sovereignty is not a given within Western thought, though clearly the juxtaposition of "the Savage as the Wolf," and the establishment of the line of exception/unexception that marked the limits of U.S. settlement, signals the role the bestial Indian played as the dialectical bind that constituted U.S. sovereign civility at the beginning of its formation as a nation-state. The final seminar Jacques Derrida gave at the École des hautes études en science sociales in Paris set out to study the ontological, political, ethical, and zoological presuppositions of sovereignty. Stealthily proposing to consider the différance between humanity and animality through a consideration of how the sovereign and the beast are mutually constitutive, Derrida ruminates on a dialectic that produces them both as "being-outside-the-Law," on the frontier threshold where they refract each other beyond the scope of the human.[31] In the political bestiary of sovereignty, "the figures of the wolf," Derrida contends, "thus encounter, and pose for us, thorny frontier questions. Without asking permission, real wolves cross humankind's national and institutional frontiers, and his sovereign nation-states; wolves out in nature [dans la nature] as we say, real wolves are the same on this side or the other side of the Pyrenees or the Alps; but the figures of the wolf belong to cultures, nations, languages, myths, fables, fantasies, histories."[32] Washington's "the Savage as the Wolf" renders Indians intelligible as the enfant sauvage, the homo ferus, against which the United States asserts its own will to civility.

Rather than producing a perfect state sovereignty that achieves territoriality and jurisdiction through the total annihilation of the Indian, however, the taxonomy of settler sovereignty requires indigenous sovereignty as its necessary condition. In other words, within the recursive logics of a twisted reciprocity, settler sovereignty necessitates and hails the existence of indigenous sovereignty, at the exact moment that settler sovereignty abjects indigenous sovereignty beyond the internal of its own logical reach. "The fact remains," Derrida explains, that "sharing this common being-outside-the-law, [the] beast, criminal, and sovereign have a troubling resemblance: they call on each other and recall each other, from one to the other; there is between sovereign, criminal, and beast a sort of obscure and fascinating complicity, or even a worrying mutual attraction, a worrying familiarity, an *unheimlich*, uncanny reciprocal haunting."[33] As antipodal beings outside, beyond, and above, the beast and the sovereign function as antinomies, as the outlaw and as the ontological prior through which the law is established and enacted. Procedurally, indigenous sovereignty, rendered into an uncanny mimesis of settler sovereignty, is simultaneously recognized and refused as the nation-state incorporates the cast-off excesses of savagery into itself as the basis for its own authority through the logics of "man is wolf to man." Indigeneity, meanwhile, is deferred and desired as the affective limit and remediation to the biopolitical violence of the state, and the native disappears into the state of nature as allegorical remembrance with no antecedent.

Colonialism as Commons

In trying to solve the problem that indigenous sovereignty poses to recognition, nationalism, and radical decolonization, Nandita Sharma and Cynthia Wright have argued that the native and his/her claims to "*autochthony can be said to be a neoliberal mode of belonging*, one whose attempts to contain contestation are based on allegations that any demand for rights and/or resources by 'non-Natives', including a radical rethinking of how rights and resources are thought of and distributed, is tantamount to a disregard for, and even colonization of, the *autochthones*." Resisting what they see to be a troubling and radically nativist turn that enables the xenophobic, anti-immigrant sentiments that underwrite the distribution of wealth and access in the global North, Sharma and Wright assert that the possessive identities of "native" and "non-Native" are "*part of the ruling practices of the colonial state* in many places across the globe." They continue: "The failure of revolutionary movements to imagine and create full liberation *for all* (including negatively racialized 'migrants' and 'Natives') allowed for an alliance between what became constructed *in response* (by elites and by Aboriginal people) as 'aboriginality' and the related ideas of hereditary sovereignty that secured the power of European monarchies and aristocracies."[34] In other words, because indigenous sovereignty functions as the ontological prior to nation-state sovereignties—and is in fact required as the reciprocal haunting that makes state sovereignty intelligible as the zone of differentiation between savage and civilized, man and animal—Sharma and Wright assume the effect for cause and argue that the native, connoted as now complicit with, rather than constitutive of, modes of possession, becomes not just exclusionary but oppressive any time she asserts rights to territoriality and resources above and beyond those every other arrivant has rights to. By such logics, in order to resist the state, one must also resist any claims to indigeneity in a recursive system that continually produces Rey Chow's question: "Where have all the 'natives' gone? They have gone . . . between the defiled image and the indifferent gaze. The native is not the defiled image and not not the defiled image."[35]

In assuming a defiled indigeneity, Sharma and Wright conclude that assertions of autochthonous rights stand in contradiction to commoning rights that are the true path to decolonization: "By understanding *colonialism* as the theft of the commons, the agents of decolonization as the *commoners*, and decolonization as the gaining of a *global commons*, we will gain a clearer sense of *when* we were colonized, *who* colonized us, and *how* to decolonize ourselves and our relationships. By comprehending colonialism as occurring each time the commons is expropriated and the commoners are exploited, our understanding of colonialism and who has been colonized should expand."[36] Eradicating indigeneity altogether, in order to transform the lands of the New World into a larger good that would be the procurement of a global commons, Sharma and Wright appropriate by renaming the processes of colonization into "theft of the commons," thus reiterating a logics derived from the contest between the beast and sovereign. In their framing of indigeneity as intolerant excess hindering true decolonial resistances that realign migrants-as-natives and natives-as-migrants, Sharma and Wright interpolate and then abject indigeneity at the exact moment they operationalize expansion as a hoary mode of territoriality that does not escape colonization so much as entrenches it.

Alyosha Goldstein, in his essay "Where the Nation Takes Place: Proprietary Regimes, Antistatism, and U.S. Settler Colonialism," analyzes the discursive strategies through which antisovereigntist movements around the United States construct themselves as salt of the earth yeomen farmers terrorized by possible allegiances between the ruling elites and indigenous peoples. Groups in New England who are opposed to land rights and Indian casinos charge "the federal government with allocating 'special rights' for Indian peoples or accusing Indian nations of demanding such inequitable rights."[37] Indian nations come to represent in such arguments the illiberal excesses of a United States historicity that strives to dispossess property owners and taxpayers alike. And while the consequences of eighteenth- and nineteenth-century policies of indigenous removals, displacements, and genocide are often acknowledged in such arguments, they are framed legally through the system of latches and phenomenologically through the disavowal of colonialism as structuring event, both of which serve to place a time limit on claims to agency and reparation that indigenous peoples might assert in the present. Reading slightly against the U.S.-based Occupy movements of 2011 that sought to challenge the top wealthiest 1 percent of the population, it is American Indians, rendered statistically nominal within their own lands through centuries-long genocidal policies, who might suddenly be reframed as the 0.9 percent against whom the 99.1 percent continue to struggle in order to (re)distribute land, wealth, and access to resources within and through the persistent structures of colonialism.[38]

In her critique of Sharma and Wright's analysis, Andrea Smith claims that the problem of settler colonialism is not inevitably migration, but that such critiques of indigeneity "fail to consider how the capitalist conception of land forces all peoples (including indigenous peoples) who migrate (whether it be through enslavement, migration, or relocation) to become 'settlers.'" She continues, "if land is property, then migration, for whatever reason, relies on a displacement and disappearance of indigenous peoples that arise from that land." In response to such failed figurations, Smith turns to a refusal of nation-state recognitions that extend themselves through the logics of late capitalism by identifying the possibility that indigeneity, if taken relationally rather than temporally, might provide radical alternatives for decolonial action. "We must understand ourselves as peoples," she writes, "who must care for the land rather than control it."[39] Reconfiguring indigeneity as praxis, Smith concludes that the processes of liberation depend upon the dismantling of the commodification of land through a restoration of some prior, essentialist, and romanticized mode of being.[40]

The quagmire of indigenous sovereignty as exception continues to haunt iterations of temporal, spatial, and relational claims to land. Even the practice of "caring for" is co-opted by the colonial state, which frames relationality to land through a mode of either playing Indian (imagining Indians as eschewing property ownership to be emulated in the pursuit of the commons) or through a return to the figure of the Indian in the state of pupilage who has not yet learned to properly care for the land. Nowhere are such liberal fictions more evident than in the current struggles for resource and water rights in Oklahoma, where the Keystone pipeline threatens aquifers throughout the state and the Chickasaw and Choctaw Nations have filed a lawsuit in U.S. District Court to protect the groundwaters of southeastern Oklahoma from attempts to syphon water supplies to Oklahoma City and northern Texas. Leaders of the Chickasaw and Choctaw Nations argue that they have held treaty rights to the water resources since the 1830s, when they were forcibly removed to Indian Territory—what now constitutes the state of Oklahoma—from their original homelands in the South. Arguing that they are the best stewards to maintain the ecological sustainability of the land's resources, the Chickasaw and Choctaw have had to file suit to protect tribal water interests against the state's unilateral appropriations that plan to export the valuable resource from the Kiamichi, Muddy Boggy, and Clear Boggy Basins that stretch from Ada, Oklahoma, to the Arkansas state line.[41]

In response to their efforts to protect water from unilateral expropriation, the current Republican governor of the state, Mary Fallin, has started a counter-media campaign titled "Our Oklahoma. Our Water." Drawing upon the collectivity of an "Our" who rely on water as valuable commodity for their everyday lives and businesses, the ads identify the threat of "some interests" who "view water as a way to gain power and profit, putting their interests ahead of Oklahoma's."[42] Using the scare tactics of contemporary political ads, OK H2O constructs the Chickasaw and Choctaw as the defiled threat to the good of all and in the process evokes notions of "the common" tied to the materiality—air, land, and water—that is necessary for the survival, not to mention economic profit, of all taxpayers, native and nonnative alike. In the process, the Chickasaw and Choctaw become the illiberal agents of a corporatized and lawyered oligarchy that seek to derive power and profit from an unjust tribalization of water and the privatization of the resources that should benefit neighbors and strangers alike. That Oklahomans, many of them direct descendants of the Sooners who benefited from the commodification of land into property that culminated in the Land Rush of 1889, see themselves as having a relational tie to land that supersedes those of indigenous peoples is exactly part of what Lauren Berlant has identified as a cruel attachment that colonialism has demanded of its settlers and arrivants.[43]

The Antinomies of Empire

Slavoj Žižek, in his critique of the Kantian parallax, writes: "We should assert antinomy as irreducible, and conceive the point of radical critique not as a certain determinate position as opposed to another position, but as the irreducible gap between the positions itself, the purely structural interstice between them."[44] Likewise, the antinomies of empire that continue to inform and constrain indigenous politics as savage and illiberal excesses are indicative of the persistence the irreducible gap between state and indigenous sovereignty has within delineations of the commons, and reflects some of the dialectical double binds that remain operationalized within the larger body of critical theory. Gayatri Chakravorty Spivak notes that within Kant's *Critique*, there is a dangerous example of "what a legally adjusted and grounded determinant judgment would produce" in the form of the Australian Aboriginal/New Hollander or the man of Tierra del Fuego whom Kant evokes as example. Such a subject, Spivak argues, "is not only not the subject as such; he also does not quite make it as an example of the thing or its species as natural product. If you happen to think of him," Spivak continues, "your determinant judgment cannot prove to itself that he, or a species of him, need exist." The result of such an "antinomy that reason will supplement" is that "the New Hollander or the man from Tierra del Fuego *cannot* be the subject of speech or judgment in the world of the *Critique*. . . . It provides the only example of 'a natural dialectic . . . an unavoidable illusion which we must expose and resolve in our *Critique*, to the end that it may not deceive us' (*CJ* 233)."[45]

Žižek, however, suggests that rather than invest in liberal, conservative, or leftist responses to such dialectics, we should embrace what he gives us as his fourth option, a recognition that there is no possibility of an outside through which to mobilize dissent: "The distinction between the zero-level of the empty place and its filling-up with a positive project must be rejected as false: the zero-level is never 'there,' it can be experienced only retrospectively, as the presupposition of a new political intervention, of imposing a new order."[46] Because indigenous peoples in the Americas continue to fail to be the subject of speech or judgment within Western philosophy, those who continue to draw upon such traditions sustain the premise that there was never anything in the New World except a refraction produced by the European gaze. As nonthing, nonsubject, nonspecies, the space of this "native" or "savage" that stands in for indigeneity is deferred in the Derridean sense so that both sides of the beast and the sovereign dialectic might continue to be claimed by the settler.

Within calls for a new order of property as well as reassertions of the commons as truly liberatory for everyone equally, the filling up of the zero-level savage depends upon what Žižek has elsewhere identified as a self-deceiving desire for the non-duped as "the innocent ignorance of the big Other . . . [who] *must not know all*."[47] The reason Lacan's non-duped err, Žižek explains, is that those who believe there can be such a positionality claim to have already achieved a "kind of movement 'from outside inwards' " through which to remain undeceived by the social relations that have defined us all. Supposing that there is a possible distance from such structures from which to observe stealthily, and plot unconstrainedly, "we effectively," Žižek asserts, "*become* something by pretending that we *already* are that." "By 'pretending to be something,' by 'acting as if we were something,' we assume a certain place in the intersubjective symbolic network, and it is this external place that defines our true position—if we remain convinced, deep within us, that 'we are not really that,' if we preserve an intimate distance towards 'the social role we play,' we just doubly deceive ourselves."[48] Within the antimonies of empire that structure the legal, political, and territorial dimensions of colonial sovereignty in the United States, the state produces the savage native as a settler self-deceiving colonial construct of the non-duped outsider who moves like a wolf beyond and through the frontiers produced through the logics of capitalistic dispossession.

Thus, as Rey Chow observes, "our fascination with the native, the oppressed, the savage, and all such figures is therefore a desire to hold to an unchanging certainty somewhere outside our own 'fake' experience. It is a desire for being 'non-duped,' which is a not-too-innocent desire to seize control."[49] Indigeneity as the space of the non-duped outsider is caught between abject depravity and romanticism, serving in the first instance to make visible the biopolitical power of the sovereign at the boundary between life and death. In the second and coterminous instance, the native-as-beast prefigures the end of that biopolitical power by disrupting, banning, and revealing the sovereign to have always been a beast itself. The native is not, as Chow persuasively argues, the non-duped; however, because subjectivity, agency, existence, and speech elude her, the space of the native remains irreducible beyond the dialectic binds of sovereignty that naturalize, abject, and displace her while also producing her as a (im)possible ontological being.

How we think about the commons, then, will require attention to the structures of colonialism that habituate certain relationalities at the site of reason and nature. And how we mind the gap between the beast and the sovereign, the indigenous and the arrivant, the romantic and the abject will determine how effective anticolonial critique will be against the grinding forces of biopolitics that target all of us.

NOTES

I am especially grateful to Mimi Nguyen for pointing me to Rey Chow's discussion of the non-duped native. Her help in making this argument coherent was invaluable.

1. Michael Taussig, "I'm So Angry I Made a Sign," in W. J. T. Mitchell, Bernard E. Harcourt, and Michael Taussig, *Occupy: Three Inquiries in Disobedience* (Chicago: University of Chicago Press, 2013), 3–43; Michael Hardt and Antonio Negri, *Declaration* (New York: Argo Navis, 2012); James C. Scott, *Two Cheers for Anarchism* (Princeton: Princeton University Press, 2012).

2. John Locke, *Second Treatise of Civil Government* (1690), chap. 5, sec. 49 (Buffalo: Prometheus Books, 1986), 30.

3. Stefano Harney and Fred Moten, *The Undercommons: Fugitive Planning and Black Study* (Brooklyn, NY: Autonomedia, 2013), 28.

4. Elizabeth A. Povinelli, *Economies of Abandonment: Social Belonging in Late Liberalism* (Durham, NC: Duke University Press, 2011).

5. Carl Schmitt, *The Nomos of the Earth in the International Law of the Jus Publicum Europaeum*, trans. G. L. Ulmen (New York: Telos Press, 2003), 96.

6. Nandita Sharma and Cynthia Wright, "Decolonizing Resistance, Challenging Colonial States," *Social Justice* 35, no. 3 (2008–9): 121.

7. See Michael Foucault, *Society Must Be Defended: Lectures at the Collège de France, 1975–76*, ed. Mauro Bertani and Alessandro Fontana, trans. David Macey (New York: Picador, 1997), and Giorgio Agamben, *The State of Exception*, trans. Kevin Attell (Chicago: University of Chicago Press, 2005).

8. Foucault, *Society Must Be Defended*, 241.

9. Giorgio Agamben, *Homo Sacer: Sovereign Power and Bare Life*, trans. Daniel Heller-Roazen (Palo Alto: Stanford University Press, 1998), 19–20.

10. Lisa Lowe, "The Intimacy of Four Continents," in Ann Laura Stoler, ed., *Haunted by Empire: Geographies of Intimacy in North American History* (Durham, NC: Duke University Press, 2006), 206.

11. Schmitt, *Nomos*, 39.

12. Schmitt, *Nomos*, 355.

13. Achille Mbembe, "Necropolitics," trans. Libby Meintjes, *Public Culture* 15, no. 1 (2003): 11–40.

14. Jean M. O'Brien, *Firsting and Lasting: Writing Indians out of Existence in New England* (Minneapolis: University of Minnesota Press, 2010), xxi.

15. O'Brien, *Firsting and Lasting*, xxii.

16. Joanne Barker, "For Whom Sovereignty Matters," in Barker, *Sovereignty Matters: Locations of Contestation and Possibility in Indigenous Struggles for Self-Determination* (Lincoln: University of Nebraska Press, 2005), 21.

17. Lisa Ford, *Settler Sovereignty: Jurisdiction and Indigenous People in America and Australia, 1788–1836* (Cambridge, MA: Harvard University Press, 2011), 2.

18. Ford, *Settler Sovereignty*, 196.

19. Michael Hardt and Antonio Negri, *Empire* (Cambridge, MA: Harvard University Press, 2000), 187–88.

20. Hardt and Negri, *Empire*, 182.

21. Giorgio Agamben, *The Open: Man and Animal*, trans. Kevin Attell (Palo Alto: Stanford University Press, 2004), 37.

22. Agamben, *Open*, 37.

23. Agamben, *Open*, 38.

24. Jonathan Goldberg-Hiller and Noenoe K. Silva, "Sharks and Pigs: Animating Hawaiian Sovereignty against the Anthropological Machine," *South Atlantic Quarterly* 110, no. 2 (Spring 2011): 435.

25. Robert A. Williams, Jr., *Savage Anxieties: The Invention of Western Civilization* (New York: Palgrave Macmillan, 2012), 203.

26. George Washington to James Duane, September 7, 1783, in *Documents of United States Indian Policy* (1975), 3rd ed., ed. Francis Paul Prucha (Lincoln: University of Nebraska Press, 2000), 1–2.

27. Williams, *Savage Anxieties*, 213.

28. Jacques Derrida, *The Beast and the Sovereign*, vol. 1, trans. Geoffrey Bennington (Chicago: University of Chicago Press, 2009), 2.

29. See for instance David E. Wilkins and Tsianina Lomawaima, *Uneven Ground: American Indian Sovereignty and Federal Law* (Norman: University of Oklahoma Press, 2001); Donald Fixico, ed., *Treaties with American Indians: An Encyclopedia of Rights, Conflicts, and Sovereignty* (Santa Barbara: ABC-CLIO, 2008); Robert J. Miller, *Reservation "Capitalism": Economic Development in Indian Country* (Santa Barbara, CA: ABC-CLIO, 2012); and Robert A. Williams, Jr., *Like a Loaded Weapon: The Rehnquist Court, Indian Rights, and the Legal History of Racism in America* (Minneapolis: University of Minnesota Press, 2005).

30. Washington to Duane, 1.

31. Derrida, *Beast and the Sovereign*, 17.

32. Derrida, *Beast and the Sovereign*, 4–5.

33. Derrida, *Beast and the Sovereign*, 17.

34. Sharma and Wright, "Decolonizing Resistance," 126.

35. Rey Chow, *Writing Diaspora: Tactics of Intervention in Contemporary Cultural Studies* (Bloomington: Indiana University Press, 1993), 54.

36. Sharma and Wright, "Decolonizing Resistance," 133.

37. Alyosha Goldstein, "Where the Nation Takes Place: Proprietary Regimes, Antistatism, and U.S. Settler Colonialism," *South Atlantic Quarterly* 107, no. 4 (Fall 2008): 849.

38. U.S. Census Bureau, "The American Indian and Alaska Native Population: 2010," *2010 Census Briefs*, issued January 2012. Accessed October 13, 2014. www.census.gov/prod/cen2010/briefs/c2010br-10.pdf.

39. Andrea Smith, "Indigeneity, Settler Colonialism, White Supremacy," in Daniel Martinez HoSang, Oneka LaBennett, and Laura Pulido, eds., *Racial Formation in the Twenty-First Century* (Berkeley: University of California Press, 2012), 83.

40. Smith, "Indigeneity," 84–85.

41. "Chickasaw and Choctaw Nations File Motion for Partial Summary Judgment," press release, Chickasaw Media Relations Office, official website of the Chickasaw Nation, March 14, 2012. Accessed 10/13/2014. https://www.chickasaw.net/News/Press-Releases/2012-Press-Releases/Chickasaw-and-Choctaw-Nations-File-Motion-for-Part.aspx.

42. "Our Oklahoma. Our Water," YouTube video, 0:31, posted by "OK Water," March 16, 2012. Accessed 10/13/2014. www.youtube.com/watch?v=ezj8tZoEFJU.

43. Lauren Berlant, *Cruel Optimism* (Durham, NC: Duke University Press, 2011).

44. Slavoj Žižek, *The Parallax View* (Cambridge, MA: MIT Press, 2006), 20.

45. Gayatri Chakravorty Spivak, *A Critique of Postcolonial Reason: Toward a History of the Vanishing Present* (Cambridge, MA: Harvard University Press, 1999), 26.

46. Slavoj Žižek, *Less Than Nothing* (London: Verso Books, 2012), 967.

47. Slavoj Žižek, "How the Non-duped Err," *Qui Parle* 4, no. 1 (Fall 1990): 2.

48. Žižek, "How the Non-Duped Err," 4.

49. Rey Chow, *Writing Diaspora*, 53.

6

The Enclosure of the Nomos Appropriation & Conquest in the New World ZAC ZIMMER

In the beginning, there was fence. . . . —JOST TRIER

"In the beginning, there was fence." So Carl Schmitt advances in an early section of *The Nomos of the Earth*.[1] It is Fence that divides, it is Fence that brings order: in Schmitt's account, land appropriation is the primeval act of all possible law. In the formation of the Nomos, Fence and the land appropriation it represents are ontologically prior to any and all community. So what, then, precedes Fence?

In theoretical terms, we can define the commons as the unenclosed: the opposite of Fence. Commons is what Fence erases in the act of appropriation and enclosure. Schmitt gives historical form to the process of land appropriation in his retheorization of sixteenth-century Spanish justification for the Conquest and appropriation of the Americas. In order to think against Schmitt's nomos, then, it is necessary to think the commons from the perspective of the Americas and from within the historical legacy of the Conquest. In this chapter, I seek to mobilize a particular constellation of Andean thinkers from both the colonial and the contemporary period: Inca Garcilaso de la Vega, José Carlos Mariátegui, Alberto Flores Galindo, and Antonio Cornejo Polar, among others. What these thinkers have in common is that the enclosure upon which Schmitt's nomos is premised in reality calls for their erasure as American subjects. Yet Schmitt's supposed erasure, for all the violence it implies, cannot be completed, for the commons and the commoners cannot simply be erased.

Against the Schmittian tradition of thinking the American continent as the blank slate upon which fences are erected—a tradition that runs through John Locke and back to the original European settler colonists—this Andean constellation counters nonplace with land itself, an America grounded in the material reality of conquest. The Andean alternative vision of that land is not enclosed private property but rather a *commons*. It is the nomos not turned upside down, as the radicals of the English Revolution would have it, but rather the nomos turned inside out. Yet if this reality counters the American blank slate with a critical history of appropriation, it also participates in its own species of utopianism, namely, a golden age of Incan communism. One could say this process substitutes a land problem for an identity problem: the insistence on an unenclosed Incan commons actually rests upon a closed, homogenous identity. Is it possible to conceive of a commons that is both materially *and* subjectively open?

Conquest and Nomos

The question of Fence opens up an ontological problem at the heart of the process of conquest and enclosure in the New World. Simply put: does Fence precede community? Is the idea of an unenclosed commons a utopian fantasy, a mythologized ideology? To consider this broader question, I will turn to one of the more problematic yet important thinkers of the emergence of the New World: Carl Schmitt. Although Schmitt has not been traditionally recognized as a key thinker of the conquest of the Americas, he is one of the few twentieth-century theorists of international law to insist on the centrality of the emergence of the New World—both as location and as concept—to the development of the modern era of secular nation-states. Thus his importance; he is a problematic thinker because he, like many of the philosophers and legal scholars he cites, actually ends up erasing and concealing America in his account of the nomos of the earth.

Schmitt's key point in the first sections of *The Nomos of the Earth in the International Law of the Jus Publicum Europaeum* is that land appropriation is the primeval act of all possible law. It is the relationship between this assertion and the historical act of sixteenth-century land appropriation in America that I will examine in detail; but first, a brief outline of Schmitt's overall project in *Nomos*. That project takes the form of a historical and philosophical investigation into the origins and developments of the European concept of international law, yet it also serves the function of a eulogy for the passing of that order in the wake of two world wars. Schmitt believes the "bracketing of war" within the European order of nation-states to be the chief, heroic accomplishment of international law and global politics in the modern era; the disintegration of that system and the seeming vacuum (in the late 1940s, but still visible today) it left represent, consequently, the most significant challenge to the maintenance of world peace since the religious and civil wars that plagued Europe during the medieval period. Schmitt's text has four major sections. The first advances the centrality of land appropriation as the ontological, historical, and legal ground for any political/social ordering of human life. The second section argues for the centrality of the sixteenth-century land appropriation of the Americas as the foundational and defining moment of what will develop into the jus publicum Europaeum, or the European concept of international law based on the "bracketing" of war. The third section details the functioning of that particular nomos, both in legal and philosophical terms. The final section documents the disintegration of the European spatial order and imagines what possible nomos could take its place.

As Schmitt argues that any spatial order has at its root a division of land, the priority he gives to the act of enclosure is understandable. Indeed, Schmitt opens his text with a direct appeal to the mythological foundation of law and justice in the land itself. Justice and law arise from the earth in a threefold fashion, he states. First, the law within the earth—the earth's inner measure—is the justice of growth and harvest. Second, the natural demarcation of human cultivation—the tilled soil, the rotated crops—is the law manifest upon the earth. Finally, fences visualize human power and domination: Fence is the law sustained above the earth.[2]

Yet Schmitt does not settle on the mythical invocation of original appropriation, nor does he posit a "state of nature" as an intellectual construct. Instead, he declares, appropriation is a historical event: "Not only logically, but also historically, land-appropriation precedes the order that follows from it. It constitutes the original spatial order, the source of all further concrete order and all further law. It is the reproductive root in the normative order of history."[3] Thus appropriation is at once the primeval source of order and, in any given circumstance, the particular historical event and legal fact that gives rise to radical legal title:

> Nomos is the immediate form in which the political and social order of a people becomes spatially visible—the initial measure and division of pasture-land, i.e., the land-appropriation as well as the concrete order contained in it and following from it. In Kant's words, it

is the "distributive law of mine and thine," or, to use an English term that expresses it so well, it is the "radical title." *Nomos* is the *measure* by which the land in a particular order is divided and situated; it is also the form of political, social, and religious order determined by this process. Here, measure, order, and form constitute a spatially concrete unity. The *nomos* by which a tribe, a retinue, or a people becomes settled, i.e., by which it becomes historically situated and turns a part of the earth's surface into the force-field of a particular order, becomes visible in the appropriation of land and in the founding of a city or a colony.[4]

To the logical, legal, and historical primacy of Fence, we might add the ontological priority that Schmitt affords it. In short, Schmitt's answer to the question we have posed is clear: Fence absolutely precedes political community. So, then: what was before Fence?

Given Schmitt's dual interest in land appropriation—as mythological origin and the root of the normative order of history—it is not surprising that he turns to the conquest of the Americas as the prime example of originary appropriation. For it is the European conquest of the Americas that makes a truly global spatial order possible: "The originally terrestrial world was altered in the Age of Discovery, when the earth first was encompassed and measured by the global consciousness of European peoples."[5] The emergence of America in European consciousness allows for a planetary concept of a spatial order based on scientific measurement; in fact, scientific measurement will prove to be the most powerful justification in Schmitt's argument for the European conquest itself.

Schmitt's invocation of the European conquest of the Americas as the key moment in the shift from a medieval-mythological to a modern-scientific consciousness is not a claim uniquely his own; Alexandre Koyre's thesis of the shift from a closed world to an infinite universe presents a popular version of that same argument.[6] Yet for Schmitt, there is a particular and uniquely European link between discovery, conquest, and measurement that, when they are combined, results in a just land appropriation capable of sustaining a new nomos. As Bruno Bosteels points out, when Schmitt posits the European conquest of the New World as the legendary, unrepeatable historic event that stands as the paragon of authentic land appropriation, his only justification lies in the assertion of the empirical success of European conquest.[7]

When reduced to its core, Schmitt's argument sounds rather brutish and banal: Europe conquered and measured America, while America neither conquered Europe nor measured its own continent to the standards of the nascently modern field of European science.[8] Therefore America could never have conquered Europe or measured its own land. Since land *must* be conquered and measured (how else to understand appropriation?), in order to establish any nomos whatsoever, the ex post facto empirical European superiority justifies European conquest and enclosure itself. In his own words: "It is a ludicrous anachronism to suggest that [the Indians] could have made cartographical surveys of Europe as accurate as those Europeans made of America. The intellectual advantage was entirely on the European side, so much so that the New World simply could be "taken," whereas, in the non-Christian Old World of Asia and Islamic Africa, it was possible only to establish subjugated regimes and European extraterritoriality."[9]

That is not to say Schmitt *dismisses* the complex problem of justification and reciprocity; on the contrary, he dedicates a substantial section of *Nomos* to Francisco de Vitoria, one of the key Spanish participants in the sixteenth-century debate over the justification of the conquest and the ontological status of the Amerindians. Schmitt argues that Vitoria is a key transitional figure, a theologian who represents medieval Christianity's final attempt to found international law in *justa causa* doctrine. For Schmitt, the shift from justa causa—just cause—to *justus hostis*—just enemy—is the seed that flowers into the European spatial order.[10] Only when the European powers worry about the ontological status of the *enemy*, as opposed to the theological and/or moral reasons for war, can war itself be "bracketed" within Europe.

Vitoria fascinates Schmitt because the Spanish theologian sketches out a preliminary theory of universal reciprocity that gestures toward a justus hostis concept of war, but he does so from within the medieval framework of justa causa. Schmitt describes this strange intermediary position as Vitoria's "scholastic objectivity." Christians and non-Christians, Vitoria argues, are equals in legal terms, and thus there is no direct right to appropriate the non-Christian lands of the New World. But Vitoria, according to Schmitt, goes even further: there is no ontological *newness* in the New World: Vitoria's "ahistorical objectivity goes so far that he ignores completely . . . the humanitarian concept of 'discovery' so laden with history in the modern view. From a moral standpoint, the New World for him was not new, and the moral problems it entailed could be handled by the immutable concepts and standards of his scholastic system of thought."[11] In other words: Vitoria arrives at true humanistic universality only by denying the *event* of the New World.[12]

Schmitt takes the opposite position: the conquest is a truly singular event that inaugurates a new nomos. For Schmitt, reciprocity and objectivity are tied inextricably to Vitoria's scholastic position, and this blinds Vitoria to the newness of the New World. Yet Schmitt sacrifices Vitoria's attractive concept of universality, and thus Schmitt finds himself in the awkward position of consistently advancing claims for a "European" international order, that is, an international order that does not recognize reciprocity between European nations and non-European nations (and thus is dubious in its claim to be truly *inter*national). As Schmitt himself argues, legal claims based on discovery "lay in a higher legitimacy";[13] Schmitt rather cryptically suggests that said legitimacy lies in Europe's superiority, whether technological, religious, moral, or some combination of the three.

Discovery or Enclosure?

Schmitt dismisses Vitoria's concept of reciprocity as a ludicrous anachronism; instead of proposing the hypothetical of an Amerindian "discovery" of Europe, Schmitt instead insists on the historic particularities of the "only discovery that ever was": the "unrepeatable historical event" of the Americas. In this view, it is *discovery* as political-technological fact that grants the common European title of acquisition in the New World; Schmitt, against any form of "reciprocal" thinking—whether scholastic like Vitoria or modern/relativistic—asserts the "common European origin" of American land-appropriation.

Yet it is here that Schmitt stumbles as a historical thinker. As Patricia Seed has argued, Europeans established colonial rule in the New World through a series of distinct ceremonial practices that carried enormous and varied political meaning, even within the emerging European international order. Seed contrasts the Iberian logic of "discovery" with the English logic of improvement;[14] Schmitt strategically ignores this distinction in order to focus on the transition in juridical and legal logic from a scholastic concept of justa causa to a modern concept of justi hostes. This transition in the ways European colonial powers formalized their claims of possession in the New World has implications for Schmitt's own argument, and any other theorization of the process of enclosure and appropriation in the Americas.

Seed outlines a general development in the ceremonies of possession that moves from the earliest Spanish claims based on the Requerimiento (a scholastic juridical exercise that had its origins in the Spanish Reconquista of the Iberian peninsula from Moorish occupation) through Portuguese claims based on navigational technology and up to English arguments based on the enclosure and improvement of "waste" lands.[15] It is the English concept of "improvement" that will come to dominate—over and above the Iberian claims of "discovery" that Schmitt seeks to emphasize—the legal register in which appropriation is understood in international law.

According to Seed, "sixteenth- and early-seventeenth-century Englishmen usually constructed their right to occupy the New World on far more historically and culturally familiar grounds: building houses and fences and planting gardens."[16] That is to say: "Englishmen shared a unique understanding that fencing legitimately created exclusive private property ownership in the New World."[17] "Fencing" was synonymous with "improving"; both terms implied a process of the private enclosure of land for the purpose of sedentary agriculture.[18]

The very concept of "improvement," which will become the backbone of John Locke's theory of property, rests on the logic of the American blank slate available for unlimited appropriation. More specifically, it rests on the early modern visions of the New World as a "localized" state of nature where man acted as wolf to man (according to Thomas Hobbes), or as a living relic of the prehistory of society (as in John Locke's theory of property). In Locke's *Second Treatise*, particularly, America exists as a prepolitical wasteland to be enclosed and improved; it is in this spirit that Locke famously and enigmatically affirms: "In the beginning, all the world was America." As with Thomas More's *Utopia*, America appears as a blank slate to be enclosed and cultivated.[19] Yet the temporality of Locke's utopian "state of nature" is quite distinct from More's perfect nonplace.

More, in his 1516 book that will come to name a genre, presents his island as a parallel world; this parallel structure frames More's entire text.[20] On the European side, corresponding to part 1 of *Utopia*, More sketches a satire of English enclosure; on the American side—part 2—he erects a perfect contemporary society. These two worlds exist in the same historical instant: one of More's primary contributions is bringing the myth of a lost golden age of humanity into a politically and historically contemporary moment. John Locke, writing a century and a half later, returns to a mythical invocation of a past state of humanity in the construction of his theory of property and politics. Locke, like More, leans heavily on the New World as an empirical fact in the construction of his argument. For Locke, Amerindians do not represent a parallel model of human organization, nor does the "discovery" of America serve as a heuristic tool to clear the philosophical slate and present a perfectly just commonwealth. Instead, Locke looks to the descriptions of pre-Columbian American societies as a historical relic, as a petrified record of the prehistory of Europe. Unlike More, Locke's utopia, which he calls the "state of nature," is not satirical. On the contrary, Locke uses the idea of a prepolitical America as a justification for European enclosure, at once justifying European appropriation in the New World and grounding the liberal theory of property on an invisible process of primitive accumulation.

In the fifth chapter of his *Second Treatise*, commonly called "On Property," Locke purports to show how individuals can justly divide up what "God gave to mankind in common" without any express contract.[21] That is to say, he must demonstrate a method of individual appropriation that historically predates organized/political society (which, for Locke, is based on an expressed contract). He begins by affirming, following various biblical passages, that "every man has a property in his own person." This implies that each person owns his/her own labor, and thus, "whatsoever then he removes out of the state that nature hath provided, and left it in, he hath mixed his labor with, and joined to it something that is his own, and thereby makes it his property. It being by him removed from the common state nature placed it in, it hath by this labor something annexed to it that excludes the common right of other men. For this labor being the unquestionable property of the laborer, no man but he can have a right to what that is once joined to, at least where there is enough, and as good, left in common for others."[22]

Locke elaborates that the hunter-gatherer appropriates through the labor of hunting/gathering: "That labor put a distinction between them and common: that added something to them more than nature, the common mother of all, had done; and so they became his private right"; and "the labor that was mine, removing them out of that common state they were in, hath fixed my property in them."[23] This becomes his most primitive model for justifying private property: the appropriation of naturally occurring things through human labor. Whenever he invokes the "primitive" hunter/gatherer model, he has been implicitly referring to America. He quickly makes this reference explicit: "Thus this law of reason makes the deer that Indian's [Amerindian's] who hath killed it; it is allowed to be his goods who hath bestowed his labor upon it, though before it was the common right of everyone."[24]

He then moves on to the more complex model of land appropriation. Man can appropriate the land itself through *improvement*, that is, agriculture;[25] Locke names this process of agricultural appropriation *enclosure*: "He by his labor does, as it were, enclose it from the common."[26] Enclosure via improvement continues as long as there is sufficient wasteland to be appropriated, and the model of wasteland is, again, America. He categorically states: "Thus in the beginning all the world was America."[27] Even in John Locke's present, America continued to be "wasteland" available for improvement and appropriation. Indeed, Locke's entire theory of land appropriation through agricultural improvement rests upon the existence of a vast "wasteland" called America, sparsely populated by prepolitical savages and available for almost unlimited appropriation by political—read: European—individuals.

James Tully has described in detail the use Locke makes of America in the *Second Treatise*. The process is twofold: first, Locke delegitimizes the existing forms of Amerindian political organization by positing a "so-called natural system of individual self-government." Instead of a recognizable polity, Locke sees atomized hunter-gatherer individuals living in nature. This move, according to Tully, dispossesses Amerindian governments of their political authority, which in turn effectively preempts any attempt to negotiate land appropriations through treaties with sovereign nations. After Locke has delegitimized Amerindian political organization, he uses a similar strategy to delegitimize Amerindian claims to American land: "The Amerindian system of property over their traditional territory is denied and it is replaced by a so-called natural system of individual, labor-based property, thereby dispossessing Amerindians of their traditional lands and positing a vacancy which Europeans could and should use without the consent of the first nations."[28]

In effect, Locke's argument takes the form of a strange inversion of More's *Utopia*: the Amerindians live without private property in a primitive, prepolitical utopia, and they actively *need* political European societies to colonize and enclose American lands in order to make politics a *possibility*.[29] America may represent a savage utopia to Locke, but only in so far as utopia is equivalent to an apolitical wasteland.

Yet is America solely a wasteland to be colonized? It is not exactly clear what Locke means when he invokes *America*, nor is it clear if he is consistent in his own understanding of the word. In "On Property," Locke relies heavily on a vision of hunter-gatherer and nonsedentary agricultural societies in North America in his description of the originary "American" state of nature. But elsewhere, Locke makes direct references to Inca Garcilaso de la Vega's *Comentarios reales* in response to the rhetorical question "Where are or ever were there any men in such a state of nature?"[30] One can find examples of contemporary states of nature, Locke suggests, in the Peru that Garcilaso so thoroughly describes. Locke does not mention the imperial civilization that flourished in the Andes prior to Spanish contact as a counter-example to the apolitical nature of Amerindian peoples. It is not only the Incan voice that Locke silences. In fact, a quick scan of the catalogue of Locke's library reveals that Locke had, in either English or French translations, copies of Gómara's *History of the Conquest of New Spain* and *General History of the West Indies*, Acosta's *Natural and Moral History of the Indies*, and Las Casas's *History of the West Indies*, along with Inca Garcilaso's *Royal Commentaries* and *History of Florida*.[31]

It is not ignorance, then, that leads Locke to ignore the significant pre-Columbian civil and political societies organized in Mesoamerica and the Andean region in his assertion (quoted earlier) that "thus in the beginning all the world was America."[32] According to Barbara Arneil, Locke makes deliberate omissions of relevant information from his source material. She argues, "Locke's descriptions of natural man, while drawn from accounts of Amerindians, were forced into a theoretical framework demanded by both the needs of his political philosophy and his moral judgment of civil man; what did not fit was ignored."[33] Locke's theory of property, founded upon a particularly English style of agricultural labor, at once excludes the Amerindian hunter-gatherer and the Spanish miner from any defensible claim to improvement, enclosure, or property.[34] For Locke, then, only enclosure of wasteland is capable of producing political space; this happens by appropriating a prepolitical and utopian state of nature. The prepolitical state of nature, in turn, exists in the Americas.[35] But Locke's own sources do not agree with his assessment of America as a prepolitical, propertyless state of nature. In fact, the very sources Locke employed have been mobilized to create an entirely opposite American utopia that insist on a space that precedes European enclosure.

Alberto Flores Galindo's *In Search of an Inca* is the most comprehensive critical study of this counter-colonial utopian tendency in the Andes.[36] According to Flores Galindo, the Andean utopian tradition is connected to an identity that finds its basis in an idealized concept of the Inca; as such, the Incan utopia breaks with More's pun of the utopian nonplace, as the Andean utopia is localized spatially and historically in a past golden age. Flores Galindo explains: "The Andean utopia was the project—or, better yet, projects—that confronted [Andean] reality, an attempt to reverse dependency and fragmentation, to search for an alternative path in the encounter between memory and the imaginary: the rebuilding of Inca society and the return of the Inca ruler. It was an effort to find in the reconstruction of the past a solution to their identity problems."[37] Far from Thomas More's pun about a perfect and nonexistent place, the Incan utopia became ever more locatable: it resided in the historical memory of Tahuantinsuyo, the pre-Columbian name for the Incan Empire. Flores Galindo elaborates:

> Andean people previously reconstructed the past and transformed it into an alternative to the present. This was and is a distinctive feature of the Andean utopia; the ideal city did not exist outside history or at the remote beginning of time. On the contrary, it was a real historic fact that had a name (Tahuantinsuyo); a ruling class (the Incas); and a capital (Cuzco). Andean people changed the particulars of this construction to imagine a kingdom without hunger, without exploitation, and where they ruled once again. It represented the end of disorder and darkness. Inca became an organizing idea or principle. [38]

In reaction to the nightmare of conquest and colonization, an inverted dreamworld emerged, and it was a world that preceded European enclosure. The imperial and expansionist policies of the brief pre-Columbian Incan hegemony became, in the popular imagination, a period of abundance, equity, equality, and health.[39] This vision of an empirical historical golden age represents an imaginary response to a real conquest; one effect of which has been to put into high relief the political and ideological nature of interpretations of Incan and pre-Columbian history.

The heterodox Peruvian Marxist José Carlos Mariátegui made one of the more subtle and exciting uses of this myth of an Incan golden age in defining a decolonial American tradition. Mariátegui's thought, if anything, was grounded in the concrete historical situation of early twentieth-century Peru. Yet he realized the centrality of myth in the discourse of political and social change. In his 1925 essay "Man and Myth," Mariátegui reveals what he believes to be the universal consensus of any investigation into the "world crisis": "Bourgeois civilization suffers from a lack of myth, of faith, of hope. That lack is the expression of its material bankruptcy."[40] Furthermore, it is only myth that can animate "man" in a historical sense: "Myth moves man in history. Without myth, man's existence lacks historical meaning. History possesses man and illuminates him with a higher belief, with a superhuman hope; the rest of humanity is the anonymous chorus of this drama."[41]

So, in Mariátegui's view, it is only a *myth* that can give human beings the orientation and strength necessary to follow a path of historical change; that is, to make history. And, for Mariátegui, "making history" had a clear and unambiguous meaning in his contemporary Peru: the inauguration of Peruvian socialism.

Mariátegui constructed this myth throughout his extensive writings in registers as diverse as correspondent columns in periodicals, addresses to labor and political organizations, and editorials in his own publication, *Amauta*. His thought is eminently dialectical, combining his animating vision from the past with a revolutionary vision for the future. He conjugated a Marxist-based interpretation of Peruvian reality with a Sorelean-inflected promise of a coming revolution, while drawing inspiration from a golden age myth, and always keeping open a pathway between materialism and an Andean spiritual-magical sensibility.

And yet, this golden age acts as ballast, lending gravity and equilibrium to his demands for Peruvian socialism. In perhaps his most famous revolutionary slogan, Mariátegui affirms: "We certainly do not want socialism in Latin America to be a copy or imitation. It should be a heroic creation. We have to give life to Indo-American socialism with our own reality, in our own language. Here is a mission worthy of a new generation." Immediately preceding this expression of revolutionary independence and fidelity to the Peruvian situation (and not often included in the quotable aphorism), Mariátegui states: "The most advanced primitive communist organization that history records is that of the Incas."[42] It is this mythical past, that of the world's first and most advanced communist society that gives weight to the twentieth-century Andean revolutionaries. Incan communism, however, is not to be a model; it is rather a guiding force that propels Peruvians forward in the knowledge that communism has already reigned in the Andes. Accordingly, the Peruvian intellectual Antonio Cornejo Polar describes the inter-action between revolution and historical tradition in Mariátegui's thought: "Only from a revolutionary position is it possible to vindicate tradition and convert it, not into a museum piece, but rather into living history."[43]

If Incan communism acts as a useful myth, Mariátegui turns a more critical eye to the colonial encounter and the racially charged feudalism it entailed. It is the stubborn persistence of conquest and feudalism that continues to mark his contemporary Peru; thus, Mariátegui's famed *Siete ensayos de interpretación de la realidad peruana*, dedicated as it was to the em-pirical situation in interwar Peru, presented a developed criticism of Peru's persistent and anachronistic feudal economy and society. The overarch-ing problem, Mariátegui states, is the latifundio; but the solution is not the liberal-democratic one of breaking up the latifundios into small lots. The division of the large landholdings into smaller individual lots, to be culti-vated and managed by a new class of small landholders, is *not* "utopian, nor heretical, nor revolutionary, nor Bolshevik, nor vanguardist, but orthodox, constitutional, democratic, capitalist, and bourgeois." Mariátegui rejects this liberal-individualist solution as antiquated given the global conditions of social and political revolution. Peru, furthermore, holds a distinct ad-vantage over other colonial nations submerged in the feudal remnants of a neocolonial situation: "the survival of the *comunidades* and elements of practical socialism in Indigenous agriculture and life."[44]

The survival of the comunidad offers a provisional answer to the ques-tion Carl Schmitt was incapable of asking and John Locke was successful in distorting: what preceded European enclosure of the New World? Mariáte-gui turns to Luís Valcárcel—one of the founders of the Peruvian *indigen-ismo* movement—to sketch an account of the Incan commons: "The land, in native tradition, is the common mother: not only food but man himself comes from her womb. Land provides all wealth. The cult of the Mama Pacha, Mother Earth, is on par with the worship of the sun, and such as the sun does not belong to anyone in particular, neither does the planet."[45] Mariátegui separates the authoritarian aspect of Tahuantinsuyo from the socioeconomic aspect. The authoritarian aspect of Incan rule is offensive to liberal sensibilities, Mariátegui concedes. But then, he adds, why should a Marxist worry about offending liberal sensibilities? "To view the abstract idea of freedom," he reminds his readers, "as consubstantial with a specific, concrete image of freedom with a Phrygian cap—daughter of Protestantism and the Renaissance and the French Revolution—is to fall into an illusion that rests upon the slight, although not disinterested, philosophical astigmatism of the bourgeoisie and its democracy."[46] Incan communism was indeed authoritarian, but it was also communism. And just as the contemporary socialist is capable of embracing bourgeois liberalism's authentic contributions to the cause of human liberation while simultaneously rejecting those liberal-bourgeois elements hostile to socialism, so too, Mariátegui argues, can the contemporary socialist draw from the Incan experience in crafting a truly modern, truly Peruvian social order.

And Mariátegui clearly explicates those elements of liberal-bourgeois society that must be overcome. In fact, the nominal liberalism of the Peruvian Republic does not even represent a threat to the neofeudal order. The specific constellation of Peruvian liberalism during the Republic (inaugurated after the successful conclusion of the early 1820s struggle for independence from Spain) had neither the political power nor the will to confront the persistent feudal organization of society, yet the Republic could easily expropriate the indigent members of the comunidades. This is Mariátegui's critique of the liberal Republic: impotent against the large landowners, it turned its attention to agrarian reform of the indigenous comunidades. Yet this so-called land reform merely enclosed commonly held lands, redistributed those lands into the hands of the propertied class, and converted the indigenous residents into de facto serfs.[47] It is Schmitt and Locke's appropriation through historical enclosure, repeated this time as farce.

Thus the major problem of Mariátegui's contemporary Peru is a *land* problem. The cause of the misery and wretchedness of Peru's indigenous population is, concretely, a continuous and unabated act of land appropriation. Mariátegui systematically rejects any other "exclusive and unilateral criteria," any "administrative, juridical, ethnic, moral, educational, ecclesiastical" explanation, because the "Indian problem" reduces fundamentally to an economic injustice. That injustice goes by the name "appropriation," which is synonymous with the existence of feudalism in contemporary Peru. The persistence of comunidades and communal practices within indigenous spheres only highlights that *things could be otherwise*. It is not that Mariátegui advocates a return to this pre-Columbian golden age (he says so explicitly throughout his writings) but rather that he seeks to mobilize the already-existing structures of a community-oriented, anticapitalist practice (for instance, the *ayllu* form of social organization) in order to further his goal of an autochthonous Peruvian/Andean socialism.

The comunidades, then, stand against the Lockean idea of an American wasteland. Mariátegui can speak of an indigenous agrarian *revindication*, realizing the mythical register in which the golden age of Incan communism must resonate. The myth, whatever its historical accuracy, also has the pragmatic and expedient value of, as Cornejo Polar argues, destroying the oppositions between on the one hand the blunt cosmopolitanism of the Comintern and the nativism of the Peruvian indigenismo tradition and on the other hand between an indigenous traditionalism and a program of modernization.[48] The myth gives direction and purpose to the Peruvian struggle. And, finally, it counters what Antony Anghie calls the European sequence of improvised colonial encounters with a sovereignty grounded in Peruvian reality.

According to Cornejo, Mariátegui's insistence on an Andean modernity is his primary contribution to political and social thought; furthermore, his thesis can be extrapolated to posit the existence of multiple modernities, each modernity developing from and responding to a dialectic between local and global conditions.[49]

Cornejo believes the identity of Mariátegui's modern (or modernizing) subject to be open and in construction. But in answering the Lockean/ Schmittian question of *what precedes enclosure*, Mariátegui falls into an identitarian trap. For, if what preceded enclosure was a commons, it must be understood as an Incan commons. As much as Mariátegui tries to ground himself, literally, in the land, his vision of Peru's socialist future is profoundly marked by the problem of indigenous identity. He justifies the legitimacy of the unenclosed commons through an appeal to a specific mythical construct; as Peruvian history attests, even Mariátegui's carefully constructed appeal to an Incan golden age can quickly collapse into a closed and reactionary identity that only serves to exacerbate conflicts and further fracture an already heterogeneous order.

The problem of land and the problem of identity are never too far apart. As Flores Galindo reminds us, the Incan utopia—in whatever iteration—is always fundamentally an identity-based utopia. When Mariátegui orients this Incan utopia toward a defense of a pre-Conquest commons, he substitutes the enclosure of land for the enclosure of a particular subject. If socialism and community precede *latifundismo* and enclosure, that unenclosed community is nonetheless a particular community based upon a specific identity: hence, the descriptor "Incan" communism.

In other words, Mariátegui's appeal to an open commons collapses upon itself, and that collapse has its inevitable origin in his identitarian move to enclose the Incan commons within one set identity. In insisting on an agrarian commons that precedes the imperial enclosure of so-called wasteland, Mariátegui answers our original question: What precedes Fence? His answer, however, relies on a common subject under the banner of a mythological Inca. This rhetorical move merely shifts the question to a subjective register: can there be a truly common subject without Fence, without the foundation of an already-constituted identity? Is Cornejo's heterotopia of multiple modernities with their respective subjects-in-construction an impossibility? Or do we see in Mariátegui's work the early stirrings of some future communal subject-to-come?

Far from having any definitive resolution, these questions resonate across the Andes today. *How to articulate a demand for the commons that at once remains open to multiple and heterogeneous subjects, and grounded in the material realities of whatever local situation?* These conditions suggest a very particular kind of universalism: a universalism that does not demand a stable, homogeneous subject; or a central, essential identity. What is clear, however, is that any viable notion of the commons—be it material, subjective, biopolitical, or digital—cannot come from a mere inversion or enclosure of a previously appropriated nomos. Not "the world turned upside down," then, but rather: the world—nomos—turned inside out.

NOTES

1. Quoted in Carl Schmitt, *The Nomos of the Earth in the International Law of the Jus publicum Europaeum*, trans. G. L. Ulmen (New York: Telos Press, 2006), 74.

2. See "Law as a Unity of Order and Orientation," in Schmitt, *Nomos*, 42–49.

3. Schmitt, *Nomos*, 48.

4. Schmitt, *Nomos*, 70.

5. Schmitt, *Nomos*, 49.

6. See Alexandre Koyre, *From the Closed World to the Infinite Universe* (Baltimore: Johns Hopkins University Press, 1968). See also J. H. Elliot, *The Old World and the New* (Cambridge: Cambridge University Press, 1992), and Edmundo O'Gorman's classic *La invención de América* [The invention of America] (Mexico City: Fondo de Cultura Económica, 2006), for a critique much more attuned to American historical reality.

7. Bruno Bosteels, "The Obscure Subject: Sovereignty and Geopolitics in Carl Schmitt's *The Nomos of the Earth*" in William Rasch, ed., "World Orders: Confronting Carl Schmitt's *The Nomos of the Earth*," special issue, *South Atlantic Quarterly* 104, no. 2 (Spring 2005): 302.

8. Schmitt, *Nomos*, 49

9. Schmitt, *Nomos*, 132.

10. Schmitt, *Nomos*, 52.

11. Schmitt, *Nomos*, 106.

12. In this point, Vitoria finds an unexpected ally in Guaman Poma, who famously proclaimed "There was no conquest."

13. Schmitt, *Nomos*, 132.

14. Ellen Meiksins Wood's *Liberty and Property* (New York: Verso, 2012) also distinguishes between the Spanish tradition of natural rights invoked as the Crown's defense of imperial conquest (best represented by Vitoria) and the English tradition of natural rights invoked as individual landholder's defense of private property (best represented by Locke); see 96–97.

15. See her *Ceremonies of Possession in Europe's Conquest of the New World, 1492–1640* (Cambridge: Cambridge University Press, 1995). In addition to the sections on the Spanish, Portuguese, and English examples discussed above, Seed dedicates a chapter to French colonial possession that focuses on ceremony and performance, as well as a chapter to Dutch navigational techniques that develop from and ultimately replace Portuguese possession claims based on scientific superiority.

16. Seed, *Ceremonies*, 18.

17. Seed, *Ceremonies*, 20.

18. Seed, *Ceremonies*, 30.

19. See Fredric Jameson, "Of Islands and Trenches: Naturalization and the Production of Utopian Discourse." *Diacritics* (June 1977): 2–21.

20. Thomas More, *Utopia*, in *The Complete Works of St. Thomas More*, vol. 4, ed. Edward Surtz and J. H. Hexter (New Haven, CT: Yale University Press, 1965).

21. John Locke, "Second Treatise of Government," in *The Selected Political Writings of John Locke*, ed. Paul E. Sigmund (New York: Norton, 2005), sec. 25.

22. Locke, "Second Treatise," sec. 27.

23. Locke, "Second Treatise," sec. 28.

24. Locke, "Second Treatise," sec. 30.

25. Locke, "Second Treatise," sec. 33.

26. Locke, "Second Treatise," sec. 32.

27. Locke, "Second Treatise," sec. 49.

28. James Tully, *A Discourse on Property: John Locke and His Adversaries* (Cambridge: Cambridge University Press, 1980), 151.

29. Tully, *Discourse on Property*, 152.

30. Locke, "Second Treatise," sec. 14.

31. See John Harrison and Peter Laslett, eds., *The Library of John Locke* (Oxford: Clarendon Press, 1971).

32. Locke, "Second Treatise," 49.

33. Barbara Arneil, *John Locke and America: The Defense of English Colonialism* (New York: Oxford University Press, 1996), 33. Arneil details the example of Locke's use of Acosta; Locke, arguing against Filmer's elevation of hereditary monarchy to the best form of political organization, cites Acosta to argue that governments

naturally evolve toward consent and election. Yet Acosta actually chronicles many examples of American monarchy that arose from previous democracy. See Arneil, *John Locke*, 33–43. Vicki Hsueh, in a recent series of articles, compares Locke's vision of the Amerindian as expressed in the *Second Treatise* with the image sketched his notebooks and correspondence in his capacity as proprietary administrator of colonial affairs. See Vicki Hsueh, "Giving Orders: Theory and Practice in the *Fundamental Constitutions of Carolina*," *Journal of the History of Ideas* 63.3 (July 2002): 425–46; "Cultivating and Challenging the Common: Lockean Property, Indigenous Traditionalisms, and the Problem of Exclusion," *Contemporary Political Theory* 5.2 (May 2006): 193–214; "Unsettling Colonies: Locke, 'Atlantis,' and New World Knowledges," *History of Political Thought* 29.2 (summer 2008): 295–319.

34. Arneil, *John Locke and America*, 102–3.

35. Jimmy Klausen, in "Room Enough: America, Natural Liberty, and Consent in Locke's *Second Treatise*," *Journal of Politics* 69, no. 3 (August 2007), has expanded this positions to its ultimate consequences: "Lockean liberalism not only thus enables and justifies settler-initiated colonialism; it ideologically requires it insofar as natural liberty relies on the availability of open space for full actualization" (762).

36. Alberto Flores Galindo, *In Search of an Inca: Identity and Utopia in the Andes*, trans. Carlos Aguirre, Charles F. Walker, and Willie Hiatt (New York: Cambridge University Press, 2010).

37. Galindo, *In Search*, 5.

38. Galindo, *In Search*, 27.

39. Galindo, *In Search*, 53.

40. Mariátegui, "Man and Myth," in *José Carlos Mariátegui: An Anthology*, ed. and trans. Harry E. Vanden and Marc Becker (New York: Monthly Review Press, 2011), 383. Translation slightly modified.

41. Mariátegui, "Man and Myth," 384. Translation slightly modified.

42. Mariátegui, "Anniversary and Balance Sheet," in *Mariátegui: An Anthology*, 130.

43. Antonio Cornejo Polar, *Escribir en el aire: Ensayo sobre la heterogeneidad socio-cultural en las literaturas andinas* (Lima Peru: Editorial Horizonte, 1994), 187. Jorge Coronado, in *The Andes Imagined: Indigenismo, Society, and Modernity* (Pittsburgh: University of Pittsburgh Press, 2009), also describes a similar operation in Mariátegui's thought: "For Mariátegui, Amauta described a project that distanced itself from the remote past at the same time that it renewed and deployed the forms it found therein. Thus the journal would take Incan history as a point of departure, but the past would not be its destination. In a move that characterizes Mariátegui's political positioning of culture, his choice of this title culls from the ashes of an old civilization the kindling necessary to ignite a new one" (28). The resonances with Walter Benjamin's theory of history and the dialectical image have not gone uncommented. See, for instance, Quijano's introduction to José Carlos Mariátegui, *Textos básicos* (Mexico City: Fondo de Cultura Económica, 1995), vii-xvi.

44. Mariátegui, "The Land Problem," in *Mariátegui: An Anthology*, 71.

45. Mariátegui, "Land Problem," 73.

46. Mariátegui, "Land Problem," 94. Translation slightly modified.
47. Mariátegui, "Land Problem," 90.
48. Polar, *Escribir en el aire*, 189–90.
49. Polar, *Escribir en el aire*, 190.

PART III Forms of Life

7

Decontainment The Collapse of the Katechon & the End of Hegemony

GARETH WILLIAMS

In *Walled States, Waning Sovereignty* (2010) Wendy Brown examines the contemporary proliferation of border walls designed and erected in recent years with a view to closing off territories, controlling cross-border interactions, and limiting population and migrant flows. Brown observes that the "post-Westphalian" political architecture of these divisions is iconographic of the predicament of contemporary state power, since constructions such as the U.S.-Mexico border wall, to name just one example she examines, denote a "theatricalized and spectacularized performance of sovereign power . . . a wish that recalls the theological dimensions of political sovereignty."[1] The post-Westphalian order—as an order of desire—is predicated at least in part on the attempt (and of course on the failure) to contain the real and symbolic movements and symptoms of contemporary unfettered capital; that is, to produce administrative and often militarized architectural solutions to the demographic and political realities of the contemporary world's territorial "decontainment." Within the new world order of unfettered capital, Brown points to the historical desuturing of the conceptual and institutional relation between territory, theology, and the political, which is now part and parcel of the ongoing collapse of modern political space—the nation—understood as a functional force of restraint or effective geometry of social containment. In the emergence of new forms of immediate mediation between territory and the vagrancies of surplus value (forms for which we have no stable or fully trustworthy vocabulary—and for which there appears to be no affirmative biopolitics, immunization, or theory of political actuality) the conceptual legacy of Carl Schmitt certainly comes to mind. However, in Brown's work, Schmitt is irrelevant for explaining the effective truths of a present dominated by the waning sovereignty of a post-Westphalian redistribution of space and jurisdiction. In this regard, Brown notes that contemporary barriers "are not built as defense against potential attacks by other sovereigns, as fortresses against invading armies, or even as shields against weapons launched in interstate wars. . . . Rather, they take shape apart from conventions of Westphalian international order in which sovereign nation-states are the dominant political actors. As such, they appear as signs of a post-Westphalian world."[2]

My intention is to supplement Brown's important insights into the paradoxical theological and politico-economic narratives that lead to the desire for post-Westphalian "bordering." In order to do this I will define further what we can understand, conceptually and historically, by the term "post-Westphalian decontainment" and what consequences this might have for thinking the political. Ultimately, my argument is that post-Westphalian decontainment—or globalization—inaugurates the invalidation of hegemony theory and requires a posthegemonic reevaluation of the political.

By now it is clear that globalization is at least in part the new *nomos* of deterritorialized—unfettered and financialized—capital. As evidenced in the meteoric rise of Chinese capital in recent decades, as well as in the collapse of the U.S. economy and overall financial debacle of the Eurozone after 2008, what Carl Schmitt defined as the Western "Nomos of the Earth"—that is, the political, legal, and spatial configuration of a Euro-Atlantic modern imperial order initiated in the sixteenth century (which he refers to as the jus publicum Europaeum)—is giving way under the weight of intense endogenous and exogenous forces. Let me begin my approach to decontainment, then, by first grasping the conceptual grounds of containment.

For this, I revisit the Schmittian critical vocabulary of *katechon, nomos,* and *anomie*. My definition of these terms allows me to move toward the emerging nomos called *globalization* and to the critique of hegemony theory within the framework of post-Westphalian decontainment. On the way, I take into consideration the end of imperial and, indeed, of national restraint. Finally, I consider what the collapse of restraint—the dissolution of specific geometries of containment—implies for the thought of the political today, at a time in which "the old categories of politics—theology, identity, war, justice—do not have explicative effectiveness when they are taken from modern space and applied to global nonspace."[3]

Ultimately, my thesis is that contemporary political philosophy must undertake what Carlo Galli refers to as the radical deconstruction of its own foundational concepts. Both Schmitt and hegemony theory must be held to account in this process, but perhaps they should be abandoned in the accounting, for Schmitt's notes on empire and hegemony's decisionist politics of containment, as evidenced in particular in the work of Ernesto Laclau and Chantal Mouffe, cannot address the effective truth of the political for the contemporary age of capital. They have been rendered obsolete (which, of course, is not the same as saying they were wrong or should no longer be read).

The Katechon and the Anomie of the Earth

Like Hobbes—who considered that for a Christian sovereign "there can be no contradiction between the Laws of God and the Laws of a Christian Commonwealth"—Schmitt was a thinker of the ancient (Paulist) katechon. He was a thinker of the force that restrains the coming of the lawlessness of the Antichrist.[4] The need to delay the end of empire—and therefore to restrain the history of its ultimate demise—predetermines and conditions the need for a strong decisionist concept of sovereignty. The political and legal territorialization of the Euro-Atlantic imperial order, initiated in the sixteenth century by the empire of Spain, was the post-Romanic nomos that restrained the coming of the Antichrist. As Schmitt notes toward the end of *The Nomos of the Earth*, the word *a-nomia* refers to a zone of exception to nomos. Following Hobbes, Schmitt viewed anomie as that which lies beyond the line of demarcation that divides the sovereign realm from a state of nature, which he views as an empty space just waiting for European imperial land appropriation, division, and distribution. Anomie is thus a zone external to the legal norms of land appropriation, division, distribution, and production. In addition, Schmitt viewed anomie as being internal to the sovereign realm itself, in such a way that one form of anomie cannot exist without the other. Anomie internal to sovereign force is the sovereign exception that is always measured from within nomos and that is subject to it. Anomie therefore is the exception to the *nomic* world of the law that nevertheless anchors the law to the social geometry of sovereign power; it is the outside *of* the nomos and the outside *within* the nomos that allows for nomic extension, either by the strong political decisionism of sovereign exceptionality or by the decision for land appropriation, or by the combination of both.

The restraining order of the bourgeois nation-state, the modern katechon of the territorialization of capital within specific geometries and jurisdictions of regional, national, and imperial containment, was fully consummated by the beginning of the twentieth century. With the ongoing dissolution of the bourgeois imperial katechon, of national capitals sutured to the discourses of economic and societal development, underdevelopment, and dependency; of discrete centers and equally discrete peripheries, and therefore of specific insides and outsides, the wars that used to appear as the sovereign *extension of the imperial Westphalian nomos* (that is, as episodes in the territorialization of the bourgeois integral state) now appear as the *post-Westphalian extension of deterritorialized capital, demographic mobility, and resource extraction.* With the end of the ideological-territorial conflicts of the Cold War, war now seems to adopt prior forms, though now of course with far greater techno-destructive power than their predecessors.

It could be said that the deterritorialization of capital has initiated the breakdown of the very measure and subjection of normlessness, or of anomic exceptionality, to the nomic world of the law. If *anomie*, in Schmitt, is measured by nomos and if it remains always subject to it, then anomie is mediated by legislative restraint. Sovereign decisionism—the sovereign's ability to decide on the state of exception—is what mediates the relation between nomos (law) and anomie (lawlessness). The latter, though, remains at all times central to the exercise of sovereign command. Anomie is internal to the sovereign's ability to suspend the law in the name of the sovereign order, and is therefore internal to the imperium of sovereign territorial authority.

The deterritorialization of capital we now refer to as globalization, however, shows something far more intense, profound, and problematic. We are now experiencing the collapse of restraint; the decontainment of many (though not necessarily all) historical and spatial forms of mediation between territory, authority, culture, and economy, and perhaps even the disintegration of the nomos-anomie relation itself that is central to the organized sovereign monopoly on violence. Globalization—in which capital transgresses the territorial and legal boundaries of the state and extends across borders—inaugurates the possible dissolution of all geometries of restraint and containment; the exhaustion of the legal norms of land appropriation, division, and distribution; and the socialization of that exhaustion via the multiplication and corporatization of sovereign force. All forms of specifically sovereign control can now shift and confront the possibility of collapse, while sovereign decisionism becomes generalized, socialized, corporatized, franchised. The state wages war in order to regain the monopoly on violence and to resuture the nomos-anomie relation internal to the exercise of sovereign force (for example, through the War on Terror or the War on Drugs). But the state does not do so in the name of hegemony and the territorialization of capital. It does so in the name of domination passing itself off now as morality and security. The profitability of illicit deterritorialized capital demonstrates with utmost clarity that the restraining mediation of the state—the state's ability to suture national territory to the law—can be, and in many occasions has been, overcome by the immediate mediation of corporate profit in either legal or illicit forms. The difference between legal and illicit capital can be purely cosmetic, as is our ability to decide on the relation between peace and war. The decision itself has become deterritorialized, and as a result infinitely more arbitrary, violent, spontaneous, and widespread.

In his reading of Carl Schmitt in *Political Spaces and Global War*, Galli notes: "We are seeing the end of the concrete and spatially determined concept of the enemy, brought about not (or at least not only) by technology, nor by a worldwide revolution, but because of globalization. This is the force that despatializes both politics and war, removing them from the logic of the friend and enemy and the categories of 'the partisan.'" "This means," he continues, "that the logical frontier of Schmittian thought, which surpassed itself in the moment it was reached, has become everyday life. The extreme has become normal, and the unthinkable, unplaceable in political space or modern political categories, is today the new figure of politics and war." As a result, "the political thought of Schmitt is dead," for "Global War commences only where Schmittian political theory is exhausted."[5] The problem now is that there is no territorial anomie of the earth. What we face now is the privatization and violent extension of the anomie of sovereign exceptionality applied to an earth and a humanity that is positioned as a standing-reserve for labor/resource extraction and surplus value.[6] The traditional nexus between hegemony, culture, and the subject is no longer of consequence. The rethinking of the political must begin in the wake of this reality.

Hegemony

The concept of hegemony emerged and developed in accordance with the historical consolidation and extension of the integral nation-state and its territorial logic of power at the end of the nineteenth century. It is directly related to the forging of the modern nation-state understood as "the directive force of historical impetus."[7] Hegemony distributes itself between leadership, domination, and consent, and can be deployed as both anomic and nomic in its arrangements, meaning that it can be utilized in reference to the transformational content and political autonomy of a certain Jacobin spirit, as much as in reference to the ethical content of a fully regulated society.[8] The reason that attaches to hegemony—the reason that conceives of itself as hegemonic, as the basis for its extension—can function in the name of revolution (anomie) as well as in the name of the extension of class domination through the forging of a specific state apparatus (the law, that is, as political dictatorship). Therefore, hegemony always raises the question of the relation between calculation, incalculability, spacing, and measurement. It can reference the experience of the incommensurability of freedom and equality in their relation to constituted power, law, and authority, or it can explain the systematization of freedom and indetermination in the name of the law and legislation of sovereign will.

In the wake of the exhaustion of the bourgeois revolutionary period and the ongoing crisis of the integral nation-state, Laclau and Mouffe set out in their 1985 book, *Hegemony and Socialist Strategy: Towards a Radical Democratic Politics*, to reevaluate and revitalize the notion and place of hegemony for contemporary political philosophy and practice.[9] On the way, they noted that what was at issue in the newly emergent neoliberal era was "the very articulation between liberalism and democracy which was performed during the course of the nineteenth century."[10]

In contrast to the classic Marxist reduction of the field of the political to the figure and agency of the proletarian class, the authors note that the 1980s signal "the displacement of the frontier of the social," insofar as in the neoliberal deterritorialization of capital "a series of subject positions that were accepted as *legitimate differences* in the hegemonic formation corresponding to the Welfare State are expelled from the field of social positivity and construed as negativity—the parasites on social security (Mrs. Thatcher's 'scroungers'), the inefficiency associated with union privileges, and state subsidies, and so on."[11]

As a result of the displacement of the frontier of the social inaugurated by the crisis of the territorial logic of state power, there is no longer a predetermined subject of hegemony, and class struggle no longer determines the form of hegemonic articulations. Gone are the dictatorship of the proletariat and the category of social class for the thought and practice of hegemony, even though hegemony for the authors remains at all times constitutive of the political.

What I am interested in highlighting is the way Laclau and Mouffe's theory is predicated on a not so covert decisionist thrust that, while not being furnished with a specific Schmittian vocabulary of its own, is nevertheless far from being disassociated from the Schmittian eschatological conception of the political.[12] In *The Origins of Totalitarianism* Hannah Arendt notes that Thomas Hobbes's Commonwealth "is a vacillating structure and must always provide itself with new props from outside; otherwise it would collapse overnight into the aimless, senseless chaos of the private interests from which it sprang."[13] Similarly, hegemony theory in Laclau and Mouffe is a Hobbesian katechontic discourse concerning the need to guard against the end of the world, which they now refer to as "the implosion of the social and an absence of any common point of reference."[14] For Schmitt the katechon guarded against the coming of the Antichrist and translated the theology of history into the times of empires.[15] For Laclau and Mouffe hegemony guards against the implosion of the social and translates the crisis of bourgeois capitalism into the time of "the People" (though the relations between leftism, populism, fascism, and indeed capital remain elusive and undefined).

It is hardly surprising, then, that Laclau and Mouffe's theory of hegemony should rest on the question of the decision in relation to undecidability, groundlessness, and incommensurability. In their 2001 preface to the second edition of *Hegemony and Socialist Strategy*, the authors characterize hegemony as a decisionist ontology designed to carry out expansive work on the terrain of undecidability: "If undecidables permeate the field which had previously been seen as governed by structural determination, one can see hegemony as a theory of the decision taken in an undecidable terrain."[16] Laclau and Mouffe's insistence on hegemony's ability to decide on what they call "the undecidable" clearly references the essential work of incommensurability that lies at the heart of any notion of freedom, of democratic politics, and of dual power.[17] However, hegemony in Laclau and Mouffe is a politics designed to displace indetermination in favor of intelligibility; measurelessness in favor of calculability; ambiguity in favor of certainty; incommensurability in favor of the decision as closure. In this work *against* incommensurability it is the category of "equivalence" that mediates between, and alleviates, the potentially ambivalent effects of dissymmetry and difference inaugurated by the aporetic.

What, then, is the logic of the articulating decision in its relation to any aporia in Laclau and Mouffe? The answer to this question is strikingly simple: the political thrust of hegemony is to decide on externality in order to guarantee the reduction and closure of the social field to a certain form of intelligibility articulated across a radically open or aporetic social sphere. The work of hegemony is to open up to externality, but to open up in order to close off undecidables—or aporiae—via the decision. When the authors describe hegemony as a theory of articulation what they mean is that it is a theory of political decisionism in a space that is no longer anchored—in a relation of fixity—to the social pact enforced by the sovereign will of Hobbes's Leviathan or by its katechontic surrogate: the bourgeois integral state.

Hegemony for Laclau and Mouffe is "a space in which bursts forth a whole conception of the social based upon an intelligibility which reduces its distinct moments to the interiority of a closed paradigm."[18] What does hegemony "burst forth" against and strive to reduce and close? Again, the answer is clear: "It is because there are no more assured foundations arising out of a transcendent order, because there is no longer a center which binds together power, law, and knowledge, that it becomes necessary to unify certain political spaces through hegemonic articulations."[19] Hegemony is a surrogate force working in the wake of the integral sovereign state to bind together power, law, and knowledge as an assured foundation for the political, across a social terrain in which transcendent sovereignty has been supplemented by societal unfixity (or by the aporiae of an emergent bio-capital power on a global scale). Hegemony, then, is grounded in an act of openness to the constitutive outside, but simultaneously in an act of closure and constraint, for openness or lack of unity—lack of all reference to unity in the wake of the end of the era of bourgeois revolution—is, they say, as dangerous as the restoration of authoritarian unity (closure). Hegemony constructs a bridge between eschatology and political thought in the wake of the integral nation-state.

Hegemony, as such, is the exercise of an unceasing protonomic decisionism; a never-ending and, as they say, an impossible nomic judgment on a world heterogeneous to hegemonic reason. The sole function of reason for Laclau and Mouffe is to constantly measure, calculate, and decide upon the incommensurable relation between what constitutes too much unity (authoritarianism) and what constitutes too little unity, which they refer to as "a lack of all reference to this unity." When, one might ask, is too much unity too much? When is too little unity too little? To decide on this is "impossible," but, they say, we must do so anyway because if we do not, hegemony will cease to exist, and we will succumb to the chaos and lawlessness of social implosion. Thus, in the wake of the bourgeois integral state, hegemony in Laclau and Mouffe is a katechontic decisionism designed "to prevent an implosion of the social and an absence of any common point of reference." For whom? For the hegemonizers and their constitutive outsides—for hegemony works katechontically for both "Left" and "Right." In this sense, the fear of social implosion is the law and template that conditions the value and functionality of *undecidables*, in the process rendering decisions conceivable as specifically hegemonic decisions, as the product of a specifically hegemonic exercise of reason.

The constant hazard for hegemony, of course, is that its essential antagonism lies in that which remains external to its own reason and intelligibility. Openness to the constitutive outside (anomie) and its subsequent domestication (nomos) is the theory's essential proposition. As such, the relation to openness, while necessary to guarantee closure, is fraught with problems: "The first problem concerns . . . the external moment which hegemony, like any articulatory relation, supposes."[20] The problem appears to be a question of measurement: How anomic can anomie actually be? This depends upon the level of acknowledgment there is in the relation between inside and outside. In Laclau and Mouffe's formulations, hegemony can be a friend to its real or potential enemy—that is, to its constitutive externality—only as long as that externality recognizes the legitimacy of the opposition: "A hegemonic formation embraces what opposes it, insofar as the opposing force accepts the system of basic articulations of that formation as something it negates."[21] Hegemony's constitutive outside is its anomic negation (its necessary enemy and therefore friend), a negation that remains at all times internal to hegemony's self-unfolding and extension. Hegemony in this sense is constitutive of a certain conception of the political in which there can be absolutely no event or disjunction, for an event occurs only at a distance from the symmetrical reasoning of the friend-enemy relation; at a distance, that is, from knowledge, reason, calculation, and truth.[22] Hegemony in relation to this constitutive (and therefore internal) externality is already, and only ever, a turn and a return to the self-constitution of hegemonic reason, of the sovereign One, whereupon the enemy is assigned a single place as a constitutive relation to the friend (hegemony). The anomic constitutive outside is only ever constitutive of nomos. Reason in this logic is always already immunized to any possible *alter*—to anything other than the law of hegemony, to any originary heterogeneity or to the unconditionality of the no-friend[23]—for difference here is only ever a function and extension of the selfsame, and the friend and enemy share fraternally in the self-legitimating acknowledgment of their mutual hegemonic negation and positive captivity.

Anything outside this fraternity—anything truly alter—is just not of the order of the political and is not addressed by Laclau and Mouffe. Hegemony, then, is clearly a question of pacifying and administering the negation of externality from within, in order for chaos and lawlessness—the implosion of the social—to not ensue. Indeed, this leads to the following question: From where are the terms of the oppositional relation to externality defined? The answer is by now predictable: "The *place of the negation* is defined by the internal parameters of the formation itself."[24] In other words, the constitutive outside that accepts and acknowledges the validity of the hegemonic articulation has no language other than that of the hegemonic formation itself, and there is no alter available at all because such a thing by definition does not respect the normal conditions of hegemony's articulation with the outside. The oppositional negation of hegemony—hegemony's necessarily external yet constitutive hostility—is in fact the closest, most familiar, and most intimate friend and brother.

Laclau and Mouffe state the following: "The theoretical determination of the conditions of extinction of the hegemonic form of politics, also explains the reasons for the constant expansion of this form in modern times."[25] As such, they indicate that the hegemonic articulation is a struggle against the death of the interiority of a closed paradigm (nomos) that is nevertheless open to its constitutive outside (anomie): "A formation manages *to signify itself* (that is, to constitute itself as such) only by transforming the limits into frontiers, by constituting a chain of equivalences which constructs what is beyond the limits at which it *is not*. It is only through negativity, a division and antagonism that a formation can constitute itself as a totalizing horizon."[26] Hegemony in Laclau and Mouffe strives to territorialize a will based on dedifferentiation, as a means of overseeing a fundamental bond between the social field and the scopic reason of subjective command: "*Veni, vidi, vici*—I came, I *oversaw*, and I conquered."[27] The expression of the discursive bond in question seems to go something like this: "I think and act hegemonically, therefore I am. You put me into question via your external negation, but you too can be my brother-in-reason. We can share a place, a home, a hearth, a territory, a familiarity, a kinship, a fraternity, a proximity, a gathering, if you acknowledge me and thereby help me exorcise the alter—the uncanny, the mad, the weird, the queer, the extraordinary, the expatriate, the disproportionate, the unsuitable, the singular, the incommensurate, the *whatever.*" Hegemony theory in Laclau and Mouffe is a reductive schema of self-familiarity; it is the extension of a phallogocentric sameness designed to exorcise from the social field all thought and practice grounded in alterity. Hegemony is the existential negation of the alter—the potentially infinite remove, which is the real enemy. In this sense Laclau and Mouffe's theory of hegemony is for the thought of the political what post-Westphalian *walling* is to the spatial debilitation of sovereignty. It is a prototheological quest for katechontic restraint against the threat of lawlessness, chaos, or the potentially infinite remove.

Clearly, there is no room here for the *experience* of the incommensurable relation between freedom and equality at the heart of revolution (as seen, for example, in the weak force of Lenin's "dual power") and no room for the nonfriend who underlies all democratic thought and practice, for such things are synonymous with the potential implosion of the social—katechontic lawlessness—that hegemony works to restrain and contain. Laclau and Mouffe's theory of hegemony is a reason grounded in anxiety, unleashed against alterity in an attempt to suppress all that is heterogeneous to the reductive reasoning of the hegemony-externality, nomos-anomie relation that remains internal to the hegemonic articulation. It is, as in the Schmittian apparatus, a conceptual framework designed katechontically to restrain and contain categorical and practical uncertainty, incalculability, and incommensurability, and it is extended in the name of subjective, sovereign decisionism now inflected toward what the authors call "a radical democratic politics." But it is katechontic thought in action, in which the decision for hegemony restrains the coming of the lawlessness of so-called social implosion.

However, in the wake of the reductive reasoning extended by hegemony's nomos-anomie, friend-enemy binarisms, a posthegemonic form of thought might raise the following question in reference to the thought and practice of conceptual and political freedom: "How can one imagine a political act whose primary determination is to move beyond phillocentrism, beyond community, beyond translation, and not against an enemy but toward the nonmilitant region from which all militancy and every partisan modality emerges? Not toward neutrality or pacifism, but against all enemy partisanship, which is also the impossible preventive partisanship of the friend, or of he who feigns to be so (for there are no friends)."[28] Many on both sides of the left-right divide will respond that the questions raised here are invalid because they are nihilistic or impossible to implement as either policy or politics, curtailing affective investments in specific nomenclatures such as communism, humanism, populism, or militancy. But the modern geometries of containment, such as the nation-state, "the people," or "the Party," no longer do the work they did even a few years ago, and the nomenclatures themselves appear increasingly to be the melancholic symptoms of a postimperialist political order more interested in rescuing the validity of prior forms than in examining the material conditions of the current conjuncture.

The question is how to create the postmodern conceptual tools and institutions capable of circumnavigating globalization and orienting us toward the image "of a free humanity no longer miserably crushed in the coils of chaos."[29] The easy answer is to err on the side of fidelity to the reterritorialization of modern legislative (that is, hegemonic or katechontic) consciousness, as the only progressive or conservative horizon available to us in deterritorializing times. Like the forces and relations of production we inherit and experience, the concepts we use "do not develop out of *nothing*, nor drop from the sky, nor from the womb of the self-positing Idea."[30] Rather, they emerge from within and sometimes in antithesis to the material conditions available to us and to the limitations imposed by the history of capital. While hegemony emerged and developed in response to the historical extension of the integral nation-state and its territorial logic of power in the years following the Paris Commune, Wendy Brown and others strive to signal the possibility of a thought that emerges from within, and in antithesis to, the limitations of the history of modern legislative consciousness and its regimes of regulatory representation, mediated subordination, and biopolitical subsumption.

Globalization has not developed out of *nothing*. It has developed out of the definitive rupture in the bond between the territorialization of power, the history of that power's legislative consciousness (including the phallogocentric history of the modern subject) and modernity's relations of property legislated on the terrain of juridically mediated interstate modalities of war. The need to delay the end of the time of Euro-Atlantic Empire—and therefore to restrain the history of its ultimate demise—has conditioned the desire for a strong decisionist concept of the political, which is what we see more or less camouflaged in Laclau and Mouffe's theory of hegemony.

But the time is here for the *deconstruction* of the conceptual apparatus contained by the ideologies of the integral nation-state and the imperial jus publicum Europaeum of the beginning of the twentieth century. This, it seems to me, is *posthegemonic* work that remains to be done, for posthegemony posits a historical and conceptual question regarding the boundaries and potentialities of the political in the epoch of decontainment. It traverses the question of the political while striving to guarantee that any thought of singularity, of the encounter, or of the coming of an event not succumb to the instinctive, nostalgic, or anxiety-laden recuperation and reiteration of modernity's regimes of regulatory representation, mediated subordination, and biopolitical subsumption. It posits theory and practice in light of the alter.

NOTES

1. Wendy Brown, *Walled States, Waning Sovereignty* (New York, Zone Books, 2010), 26.

2. Brown, *Walled States*, 21.

3. Carlo Galli, *Political Spaces and Global War*, ed. Adam Sitze, trans. Elisabeth Fay (Minneapolis, University of Minnesota Press, 2010), 183.

4. It is well known that the idea of the katechon originates in the second letter of the apostle Paul to the community in Thessalonica. The apostle Paul explains why the Lord has not come yet. As Michael Hoelzl explains, "among biblical scholars, it has been agreed that verses 6–7 are the central part of the letter. These two verses, in their wider context, read as follows: 5) Do you not remember that I told you these things when I was still with you? 6) And you know what is now restraining him, so that he may be revealed when his time comes. 7) For the mystery of lawlessness is already at work, but only until the one who now restrains it is removed. 8) And then the lawless one will be revealed, whom the Lord Jesus will destroy with the breath of his mouth, annihilating him by the manifestation of his coming. What precedes the second coming of the Lord? According to the apostle Paul, the 'lawless one,' *o anomos* [original text uses the Greek form], has to be revealed and this is the precondition for the second coming of the Lord." Michael Hoelzl, "Before the Anti-Christ Is Revealed: On the Katechontic Structure of Messianic Time," in Hoelzl, *The Politics to Come: Power, Modernity, and the Messianic*, ed. Paul Fetcher and Arthur Bradley (London, Continuum Books, 2010), 99–100. The comparison of St. Paul to Lenin drawn by Sebastian Budgen, Stathis Kouvelakis, and Slavoj Žižek in their introduction to *Lenin Reloaded: Toward a Politics of Truth* (Durham, NC: Duke University Press, 2007), fails to address the question and legacy of the Paulist katechon—that is, the question of political theology—for the history of the communist Left: "In the same way that St. Paul and Lacan reinscribed original teachings into different contexts (St. Paul reinterpreting Christ's crucifixion as his triumph; Lacan reading Freud through mirror-stage Saussure), Lenin violently displaces

Marx, tearing his theory out of its original context, planting it in another historical moment, and thus effectively universalizing it" (2–3). What the editors of *Lenin Reloaded* indicate through their language of violence and tearing is that Lenin was a very good reader and strategist.

5. Carlo Galli, *Political Spaces and Global War*, ed. Adam Sitze, trans. Elisabeth Fay (Minneapolis: University of Minnesota Press, 2010), 182.

6. Standing-reserve: "Everywhere everything is ordered to stand by, to be immediately at hand, indeed to stand there just so it may be on call for a further ordering. Whatever is ordered about in this way has its own standing. We call it the standing-reserve." Martin Heidegger, "The Question Concerning Technology," in *The Question Concerning Technology and Other Essays* (New York: Harper and Row, 1977), 17.

7. Antonio Gramsci, *Prison Notebooks*, vol. 2, notebook 7, no. 9, ed. Joseph A. Buttigieg (New York: Columbia University Press, 1992), 161.

8. For the question of translation and slippage in Gramsci's definition of hegemony as both *direzione* and *dominazione*, see Antonio Gramsci, *Selections from the Prison Notebooks*, ed. Quintin Hoare and Geoffrey Nowell Smith (New York: International, 1971), 55.

9. My reading of Laclau and Mouffe's *Hegemony and Socialist Strategy: Towards a Radical Democratic Politics*, New York: Verso, 2001, supplements the substantive reading of hegemony theory's relation to populism developed by Jon Beasley-Murray, *Posthegemony: Political Theory and Latin America* (Minneapolis: University of Minnesota Press, 2010), 15–67.

10. Laclau and Mouffe, *Hegemony*, 171.

11. Laclau and Mouffe, *Hegemony*, 176.

12. It is not by chance, in other words, that since 1985 Chantal Mouffe herself has become a faithful follower of Schmitt.

13. Hannah Arendt, *The Origins of Totalitarianism* (New York: Meridian Books, 1958), 142.

14. Laclau and Mouffe, *Hegemony*, 188.

15. Julia Hell, "*Katechon*: Carl Schmitt's Imperial Theology and the Ruins of the Future," *Germanic Review* 84, no. 4 (2009): 284.

16. Laclau and Mouffe, *Hegemony*, xi.

17. Vladimir I. Lenin, "The Dual Power," in *Lenin Collected Works*, vol. 24 (Moscow: Progress Publishers, 1964), 38–41.

18. Laclau and Mouffe, *Hegemony*, 93.

19. Laclau and Mouffe, *Hegemony*, 187.

20. Laclau and Mouffe, *Hegemony*, 138.

21. Laclau and Mouffe, *Hegemony*, 139.

22. Jacques Derrida, *Politics of Friendship*, trans. George Collins (New York: Verso, 1997), 30.

23. Derrida, *Politics of Friendship*, 222.

24. Laclau and Mouffe, *Hegemony*, 139.

25. Laclau and Mouffe, *Hegemony*, 139.

26. Laclau and Mouffe, *Hegemony*, 143–144.

27. Martin Heidegger, *Parmenides*, trans. André Schuwer and Richard Rojewicz (Bloomington: Indiana University Press, 1992), 41.

28. Alberto Moreiras, *Línea de sombra: El no sujeto de lo político* (Santiago, Chile: Palinodia Editores, 2006), 84 (my translation).

29. Galli, *Political Spaces and Global War*, 189.

30. Karl Marx, *Grundrisse: Foundations of the Critique of Political Economy* (New York: Penguin Books, 1973), 278.

8

The Savage Ontology of Insurrection Negativity, Life, & Anarchy

BENJAMIN NOYS

The recently announced "anarchist turn" in contemporary political philosophy has laid claim to the possibility of a new "anarchist hypothesis" on the basis of the resurgence of anarchism as a political, or perhaps better antipolitical, practice, allied with "new" currents in political and critical theory.[1] This proposed synthesis between anarchism and contemporary theory was predated by the contested attempt of "postanarchism" to broker a liaison, forced or otherwise, between anarchism and poststructuralism.[2] The allure of anarchism lies, in part, in an assertion of autonomy from the state and capital, and from the usual forms of political organization. The suspension of the "arche" licenses a new self-determination, a new autonomy, beyond what are regarded as the stagnant and ineffective political forms of the present. It is exactly this alliance of anarchy and autonomy that I wish to question and problematize, especially as it formed through an appeal to the autonomy of "life." The desire to separate "life" from the misery of existent capitalist life is widespread, and by no means confined to explicitly anarchist currents. It is the multiplicity and dispersion that life seems to incarnate, the idea that life is everywhere, that licenses the multiple and plural theoretical and practical articulations of this life. The appeal to life, which cuts across many currents of autonomist and postautonomist movements of indigenous sovereignty, is an appeal to the insurgent and uncontrollable *force* of life.

My attention will focus particularly on the formulation of insurrectional anarchism and its convergence with vitalist theorizations. Insurrectional anarchism is that "strain" (to use an appropriately viral and violent term) of anarchist thought that dictates the rejection of existing organizations, uncompromising negation, and the immediate destruction of all external forms of power and control in violent insurrection.[3] This type of thought, I will argue, emerges from the same post-Hegelian legacy that also forms and structures many of the variants of contemporary theory: a legacy constituted by the rejection of Hegelian "synthesis," the valorization of the power of the negative, and a radicalized discourse of life. To be more precise, what is shared between insurrectional anarchism and certain neovitalist forms of contemporary theory is what Michel Foucault called, remarking on nineteenth-century biological thought, a "savage ontology of life," in which "life" exceeds and erodes all forms of constraint and representation.[4] The autonomy of "life" is posed in terms of this savage and corrosive power that resists all forms of subsumption and control. Therefore, the proximity of insurrectionalism to contemporary neovitalist theorizations is not a matter of serendipity or chance, but instead the result of a shared problematic, even if their responses to that problematic take divergent forms.

It is this ontologization of "life" as the condition of its autonomy that I wish to critique. Certainly, as I will demonstrate, in one sense it poses a coherent theoretical and political response to the limits of Hegelian thought, one anchored in the powers of life as excessive over all codifications and all instances of "state thought."[5] The motivational power of such thinking should not be underestimated, hence its persistent attraction. While focusing on a particular conjunction of insurrectional anarchism and vitalist theorizations, the "viral" spread of life goes much further into the constitution of what is claimed as autonomy—taking in postautonomist theorizations, post-Agambenian radicalism, and forms of ultraleftism. These discourses of excess and attack rely, I will argue, on a *disregard* for the forms of state and capitalist power, and it is this which gives them their revolutionary and theoretical élan. Such disregard, however, comes at a theoretical and political price. The invocation of the immediate autonomy of "life" is forced to engage in a constant labor to extract and separate this autonomy from its miring in the forms of power. In particular, hymning "life," qua destructive and excessive force, does not so much challenge the fundamental tenets of capitalism as risk replicating the molten core of capitalism's own contradictory ideology.

My focus here is on this "savage ontology" as a rupture *within* Western discourse. There is, of course, another savage ontology: the ontology of "savages," as Eduardo Viveiros de Castro has elaborated, that contests from the *outside* Western ontologies.[6] Here the appeal to "life" takes on a different form—pantheist and animist, to use Western terminology. While this mode of thinking contests Western ontology it also finds itself engaged in a difficult relation with contemporary global capitalism and the forms of the "developmental" state.[7] The difficulty here is while this ontology contests the self-image of capitalist modernity it has always been threatened with destruction by that self-same modernity. In particular the absorptive capacities of capital threatens to capture this form of savage thought within the usual forms of exoticization, tourism, banalization, and soft exterminism. The convergence of this ontology of "savages" with my argument here would be around the contestation of the productivist and developmentalist imaginary of capitalism, which even extends, as I will suggest, into the discourse of "savage ontology."[8]

Taking one path through this plural field, my analysis begins from Foucault's equivocal articulation of "savage ontology," which lies somewhere between an analysis and an endorsement. I then turn to post-Hegelian articulations of "classical" insurrectional anarchism, focusing particularly on the work of Mikhail Bakunin, Max Stirner, and the less well-known Italian insurrectionalist Renzo Novatore. Returning to the philosophical or metaphysical, I take Gilles Deleuze as the key point of theoretical articulation for contemporary insurrectional thought. My aim is then to develop a critique of this valorization of life as the moment of insurrection, or what we could call an "insurrectional imaginary." While these currents correctly point to the role of life in the contemporary forms of biopolitical power, I suggest that they overestimate the power of life to overturn the operations of the state and capital. In particular, capitalism operates on the very site of life as excess to produce value. Therefore what is required is a more careful attention to the role of life, including to the role of life as a consolatory ideological form of excess that claims to ground or guarantee an insurgent and insurrectional politics.

An Ontology of Annihilation

In *The Order of Things* (1966) Michel Foucault notes that in nineteenth-century biological thought "life becomes a fundamental force": one of movement opposed to immobility, time to space, and the secret wish to the visible expression. The power of this "savage ontology" lies in the fact that this force encompasses and folds within itself all that which would seem opposed to life. In this ontology being and nonbeing, life and death, positivity and negativity, are melded together. The pulsing force of life is not one that simply invigorates and instantiates forms, but also saps all forms from within, eroding and destroying them. Contrary to the usual alignment of life with growth and development, Foucault argues that an "ontology of annihilation" overturns and revolutionizes everything it confronts.[9] In particular, contrary to the thinking of political economy, this excess of life refuses and destroys any discourse of need, limit, and individuality. Life is an infinite duration, a ruptural intervention, the dissipation of consciousness, and so departs from a discourse of political economy. What we can see here is "life" opposed to all the illusions of consciousness, all the limits of economy, and all the reified and static moments of power (*potera*), in the name of the power of life (*potenza*).

We can note that this ontology of life incorporates negativity as a radical power of erosion. Life is not opposed to death, or to destruction or negativity, but already operates through *affirming* radicalized negativity.[10] What is difficult to judge is how far Foucault is posing this discourse as an analytic object, or endorsing it. This is particularly true as his characterization of this "savage ontology" carries unmistakable echoes of the work of his then friend Gilles Deleuze. Deleuze's project, framed in Nietzschean and Bergsonian forms, could be taken as a radicalization of this strain of nineteenth-century thought, or it may be that Foucault is surreptitiously disputing the originality of Deleuze's intervention. This ambivalent status of the "savage ontology" is further reinforced by Foucault's posing of it against the discourse of political economy. Again, is he endorsing this excess of the discourse of life over the limits of political economy, following from his remark in *The Order of Things* that "Marxism exists in nineteenth-century thought like a fish in water: that is, it is unable to breathe anywhere else," or is he merely offering an analytic reflection?[11]

Evidence for endorsement can be found in the fact, drawn out by Joan Copjec, that in his essay on Binswanger, "Dream, Imagination and Existence" (1954), Foucault endorsed Binswanger's disjunction of life and history.[12] Copjec goes on to point out that we can read Foucault's analysis of sexuality as the fatal operator of power that forces together and fuses life and history. Using the terms of Foucault's reworking of Binswanger, we can say that sexuality forms a "mirage"—an image of illegitimate fusion.[13] Therefore, the disjunction of life and history, explicit in this early work, implied in *The Order of Things* and the later analysis of sexuality, can be read as forming a central element in Foucault's work, and such a disjunction, I would add, empowers many contemporary political vitalisms by implying a potential autonomy of life. This is one reason why Foucault's "savage ontology" has such a fecund future.

To clarify the status of this nineteenth-century discourse of life I also want to turn to a brief note by Fredric Jameson in which, reflecting on Hegel's notion of "life" as central to his analysis of the working of spirit, Jameson states: "We might give Hegel credit for the first timid step in the direction of that vitalism which, a mighty stream from Nietzsche and Tolstoy through D. H. Lawrence to Deleuze, has been so energizing a worldview (which is to say, ideology) in contemporary thought."[14] There are three points I want to take from this suggestive note. The first is that the vitalism that we often take as anti-Hegelian—usually vectored (as it is in Deleuze) through the key anti-Hegelian figures of Spinoza, Nietzsche, and Bergson—is actually entwined with Hegelianism. This is a point that I will explore later through a tracing of post-Hegelian insurrectional anarchism. The second point, which is related, is that already this "vitalism" is entwined with negativity and the seeming antonyms of "life": death, destruction, and negativity. This is evident in the most famous passage in the preface to Hegel's *Phenomenology*, meditated on by George Bataille, in which the life of spirit is not opposed to death and negativity but is regarded as a "tarrying with the negative."[15] The third point is the notion of Hegelian vitalism as an "*energizing* worldview" (or ideology). To preempt my concluding arguments, I already want to suggest that this energizing function is a result of vitalism overrunning and exceeding the discourse of political economy. Vitalism offers the hope of a new creative ontology that resists and dissolves all representation, both philosophical and political.

Foucault's "savage ontology" resonates with this post-Hegelian moment of vitalism as a counter-discourse. This convergence occurs around vitalism as an energizing ideology of resistance and excess; it will also run, like a red thread, through the currents of insurrectionalism and contemporary theory that engage with the radicalization of the post-Hegelian legacy. The path to a radicalized negativity will also wind, as I will show, through the affirmative positivity of life. It is worth noting that, considering the well-attested difficulty of escaping from Hegel, it will be Hegel's own thought that provides the possibilities for the development of counter-Hegelian thinking. This counter-current will take up the excessive negativity of life against the political and philosophical compromises of Hegel and Hegelianism. It is something of an irony that Hegel—usually taken, incorrectly, as *the* state-philosopher—should also provide the elements of an anarchic vitalism.

The origins of insurrectional anarchism can be located within this space of post-Hegelian vitalism, and I will focus on the insurrectional anarchists Bakunin, Stirner, and Novatore. Of course, this form of anarchism is best known for its emphasis on radical *practice*—on the art of insurrection and the *attentat*.[16] Therefore, to locate it philosophically might seem a gesture of neutralization. In fact, however, the post-Hegelian lineage is obsessed with the *realization* of philosophy in practice, and with realizing the implicit wager of Hegel's own speculative identification of reason with actuality.[17] Therefore, this is not a rephilosophizing of insurrectionalism, but rather a locating of it within the attempt to break the constraints of the tendency of Hegel to identify negativity as encoded and embedded within the forms of the state, and to transit from his treatment of philosophy as retrospective justification to philosophy as living practice of revolt. There is no simple contrast here between theory and practice, as the aim of these articulations of "life" is to dissolve this antinomy, and to produce a radicalized practice. A second query could be raised about whether the instances I have chosen are "typically" or "really" insurrectionalist or anarchist, despite their own self-identification as such. Rather than become bogged down in the seemingly endless disputes concerning who is "really" anarchist, I want to suggest that the commitment of these thinkers to a fluid power of life, an encompassing negativity that erodes all reifications and all static identities (including "anarchist"), is what makes them "typically" anarchist.

To begin, let us take one of the most well-known anarchist statements, from Bakunin's early and still-Christian and -Hegelian text "The Reaction in Germany" (1842): "Let us therefore trust the eternal Spirit which destroys and annihilates only because it is the unfathomable and eternal source of all life. The passion for destruction is a creative passion, too!"[18] Here we find the coordinates of the savage ontology: radicalized destruction and negativity, the affirmation of life, and the affirmation of a superior creativity. In this text Bakunin emphasizes that the deepest sense of revolutionary agitation is negation, and that it is only by this passage through negation that we can reach the truth of a more just existence: "the spirit of revolution is not subdued, it has only sunk into itself in order soon to reveal itself again as an affirmative, creative principle, and right now it is burrowing—if I may avail myself of this expression of Hegel's—like a mole under the earth."[19] What we can see, as summarized in the more famous statement concerning destruction as the condition of creation, is the revelation of a force of negativity that serves a superior affirmation. The dialectic of the negative, which breaks with Hegelian "synthesis," finds itself rooted in a philosophy of life as the "affirmative, creative principle." It does not take much, already, to detect commonalities with the contemporary forms of "affirmationist" and vitalist theory.[20]

The same could easily be said of Stirner, who has proved to be a crucial figure in the articulation of postanarchism;[21] and who is also crucial to the genealogy of individualist and insurrectionist anarchism. Stirner's critique of all the ideological "spooks" of religion and state power was founded not only on a critical individualism of the "unique" but also on a discourse of life as dissolving and excessive force. In a formulation prefiguring Bataille, Stirner writes: "I am no longer afraid for my life, but 'squander' it."[22] This ontology of excess is paralleled in Stirner's thinking of insurrection as an activity that exceeds any social and political limits, and that refuses to be constrained by the mere negation of existent circumstances. Founded on an individual discontent, insurrection dictates no program or arrangements, but overturns all arrangements and institutions.[23] This individualist insurrection is predicated on the affirmation of a "true life" and the critique of the ideological "spooks" in the name of the concrete powers of life that exceed all capture.

Stirner, along with Bakunin, can then be placed within the field of the savage ontology of life that overturns and erodes *all* forms. The rehabilitation of Stirner for postanarchism also, without noting this point, demonstrates that his links to contemporary theory are actually well-founded in the legacy of post-Hegelianism and this ontology. The opposition of "life" and the concrete to the religious and ideological "spooks" of power, including the power of money, will find its resurgence in the neovitalism of the present, which takes a more explicitly anti-Hegelian, immanent, and anti-Idealist form. To indicate this commonality, we can also trace how close this post-Hegelian inflection of life and negativity is to that great self-declared antagonist of Hegel: Friedrich Nietzsche. Rather than simply taking the path from Nietzsche, key to contemporary theory, as the indubitable sign of having had done with Hegel, we can rather see it as part of an unfolding of life as the power of the negative with longer roots.

Before he was killed in an ambush by the Italian police on November 29, 1922, Renzo Novatore fused Stirner and Nietzsche in his insurrectional writings. His text *Toward the Creative Nothing* (*Verso il nulla creatore*) (1924), has a Stirnerite title.[24] Novatore's poetic formulations once again integrate vitalism, negativity, and creativity in an insurrectional "synthesis" that refuses all limits and constraints, in explicitly Nietzschean terms. The prophetic tone is one of radicalized destruction and negativity: "But our individual 'crimes' must be the fatal announcement of a great social storm. The great and dreadful storm that will smash all the structures of the conventional lies, that will unhinge the walls of all hypocrisy, that will reduce the old world to a heap of ruins and smoking rubble!"[25] This is linked to the affirmation of the excessive powers of life, in what might be taken as the most extreme instance of a "savage ontology":

> But the Antichrist—the spirit of the most mysterious and profound instinct—calls Life back to himself, shouting barbarically to her: Let's begin again!
> And Life begins again!
> Because it does not want to die.
> And if Christ symbolizes the weariness of life, the sunset of thought: the death of the idea!
> The Antichrist symbolizes the instinct of life.
> He symbolizes the resurrection of thought.
> The Antichrist is the symbol of a new dawn.[26]

The resurrection of life is the resurrection of barbaric negativity, and the new beginning that refuses Hegelian-Christian "synthesis," but that also takes up again the rending power of the negative in an explicitly affirmative direction: "We will take these unknown brothers by the hand to advance together against all the 'no' of denial, and to climb together toward all the 'yes' of affirmation."[27]

In Novatore's Nietzschean insurrectionalism we can see not only the connection with the "New Nietzsche" of contemporary theory but also the continuity of the radicalization emerging from the ruins of Hegelianism.[28] The Nietzschean tone that dominates in much contemporary theory and much contemporary insurrectionalist anarchism is drawn out of this more dispersed "savage ontology" that cuts across the post-Hegelian landscape. When the anonymous author or authors of the pamphlet *At Daggers Drawn* (1998) announce that "insurrection . . . [is] the *unknown* bursting into life [the] life of all" and that "subversion is a game of wild, barbarous forces,"[29] they stand in this lineage. This mode of thinking, predicated on a realization in the process of "life" as dissipation and excess, already prefigures neovitalist and other currents of contemporary theory, precisely because they operate in the same matrix of thought; therefore, any "synthesis" of the "postanarchist" kind is, strictly speaking, superfluous. Rather, it is more a matter of assessing and considering the persistence of this "energizing" ideology and, as I will suggest, its possible exhaustion.

Metaphysical Insurrections

The formations of insurrectionalism respond to similar problems that have dominated twentieth- and twenty-first-century theory: the endless agon with Hegel, the reworking of negativity, the turn to affirmation, the recourse to Nietzsche, the posing of negativity against synthesis, and the notion of the superior powers of life. To propose an exhaustive genealogy of these themes and links with insurrectional anarchism would take me far beyond the limits of a single essay. To keep things within reasonable limits I want to take the case of Deleuze—who is a useful synecdoche because of the influence of his work, and especially his work with Guattari, on contemporary radicalism. Also, in *Nietzsche and Philosophy* (1962), Deleuze explicitly recognizes the place of Stirner in the evacuation and opening of the dialectic: "Stirner is the dialectician who reveals nihilism as the truth of the dialectic."[30] It is Nietzsche, for Deleuze, who marks the passage beyond this dialectical limit and into the true savage ontology of life. In this way Nietzsche and Deleuze can be presented as the true radicalization of the discourse of life, finally detached from its embedding in the dialectic.

In his *Deleuze: The Clamor of Being* (1997) Badiou remarks that Deleuze's own self-identification with "crowned anarchy" implies an elitist thinking at odds with the usual identification of Deleuze's cowork with Guattari as the model for "anarcho-desirers."[31] In fact, if we place Deleuze within the framework I have traced of the savage ontology of insurrection, we could argue exactly the contrary. Deleuze's "anarchism" lies, precisely, in the individualist and insurrectionist refusal of constraint and representation that finds its key conceptualization in the radicalization of life that operates as an *aristocratic* critique of political and philosophical forms.[32] Deleuze's aristocratism is what makes him anarchist, not any "democratic" appeal. Of course, as I have already noted, Foucault's own characterization of the savage ontology of nineteenth-century thought seemed to draw on Deleuze's own rewritings of Bergson and Nietzsche. So, we have a complex arrangement of "influence," which tracks both backward and forward. Bearing this in mind, we can note how Deleuze's own particular "vitalism" incarnates the exemplary excess of life: "There are never any criteria other than the tenor of existence, the intensification of life."[33] To use the terms of Peter Hallward's critical discussion of Deleuze, the creative power of life always dissolves and erodes the confinements of the "creatural."[34]

Deleuze's articulation of this vitalism dissolves consciousness and representation into "molecular" processes, lines of flight, and movements of deterritorialization. Of course, he is renowned for his explicit hostility to Hegel, an "enemy" not deserving refutation, but his radicalized vitalism, which alchemizes negativity into superior affirmation, still equivocally belongs to the post-Hegelian moment I have traced.[35] Deleuze pursues his radicalization by very different means but arrives in a similar place. If the "classical" insurrectionalists pushed toward fusing philosophy with action, then we could say Deleuze provides a retooled metaphysics of life. Certainly, Deleuze, especially in his work with Guattari, reaffirms this politically. In fact he identifies ontology *with* politics. Certainly his formulations with Guattari have often constituted a lingua franca of contemporary radicalism ("lines of flight," "minor politics," "desirerevolution," etc.), often at the expense of their more nuanced articulations of these concepts.[36] This flattening-out and one-sided valorization of Deleuzoguattarian binaries is particularly inflected through the work of Antonio Negri and Michael Hardt.[37] Adding additional terms like "multitude" and "Empire" to the political, or antipolitical, lexicon, they have reinforced the vitalist elements of excess, rupture, and counter-power.

In the case of Negri, both in his own work and his work with Hardt, the inflection of this savage ontology is not so much toward an insurrectional imaginary—except perhaps in certain moments of his work from the 1970s[38]—but rather toward an insurgent constitutive power linked to life. Negri is insistent that this is not a vitalism, due to the fact he is referring to singularities and not life.[39] Despite this, however, his modeling of insurgent power that overflows the constituted grids of state and capitalist power still seems to operate within the ambit of this "savage ontology." For Negri this takes a more "classical" form of the insistence on the powers of the multitude merely being on loan to capital and, hence, capable of reappropriation. That said, we still have a dialectic of life at work here, at once fused with the abstractions of capitalist control and beyond those containments.[40] While Negri's work is resonant, it also risks further simplification and abstraction of the opposition of the powers of life, in the figure of the multitude, to capital and the state as power of death.

This situation is what accounts also for the resonance of the language of the multitude and empire, despite all the differences between positions, with the contemporary insurrectional imaginary. Again, I would insist that this is not to explain that insurrectionalism as a mere "expression" of theory, or as derivative from theory, but rather to suggest a convergence in conceptual structure. Although not *sensu stricto* "anarchist," the Invisible Committee's *The Coming Insurrection* (2007) codes insurrection in vitalist terms. They remark that "a real demonstration has to be 'wild'" and figure the origin of insurrectional desire in "a vital impulse."[41] The desert of the present is predicated on the biopolitical management of life that destroys or channels these "vital impulses," denying the disruptive and excessive effects of negativity that refuse all limits and constraints. Of course, two caveats are immediately required: first, these formulations are vectored philosophically primarily through the work of Giorgio Agamben, and second, they are not beholden to insurrectionalist anarchism. In answer to the first point, we could note not only the influence of Deleuze on Agamben's thinking but also that Agamben's thinking of "bare life" as site of destitution and power could easily be taken as another form of savage ontology, radically coordinating an extreme negativity with "life."[42] Second, we could say that while not explicitly adopting an anarchist insurrectionalism, we could still see commonalities, in terms of "immediacy," the posing of life against "Empire," and a discourse of the decomposition of all existent forms of power.

The persistence and convergence of these forms of thought lies precisely in the fact that they fuse theory and practice through the concept of a negativized "life," which is then affirmed as such. This brings into coincidence radicalized affirmation with radicalized negativity, a common strategy across the theoretical and political currents of "affirmationism." What I am stressing is that we cannot simply align the usual contradiction or antinomy between theory and practice as lying, in this case, between neovitalist theory and anarchist practice. Instead, the appeal of the "savage ontology" of life can be traced in its capacity to "bridge," "fuse," or perhaps better "dissolve," this antinomy. In line with the stress on dissolution and the resolute opposition to any or all reifications, conceptual or practical, this "line" of thought is defiantly promiscuous—cutting across political and theoretical oppositions. This is why I have stressed it as a widespread mode of writing and practice that does not simply remain confined to insurrectionalism but becomes a common language.

Under the Foucauldian sign of biopolitics, which unifies capital's extraction of value with the state's regulation of life, contemporary power everywhere seems to rest on life.[43] Whereas capitalism was classically taken as the subsumption of labor-power, now, it appears, the extension of labor to all elements of life and the penetration of power into life make life in its totality the site of subsumption.[44] To use a recent insurrectionalist formulation, "our own lives" are "the authentic *place* of the social war."[45] Hence it is not difficult to account for the persistence of the "savage ontology of life" as a counterdiscourse that stresses how life can overflow even the limits of contemporary capillary forms of power that penetrate and subsume the living body. It is difficult to dispute, therefore, the "energizing" power of this ontology. Even when power penetrates most deeply into life, down into the molecular level or out across all forms of life, this discourse promises a moment of escape, disruption, and revolt. This is why it is particularly difficult to critique, especially when the critique of such savage ontologies often takes for vices what it regards as virtues. The antistrategic immediacy of violent opposition, the stress on intermittent and unrepresentable forms of struggle, the unyielding hostility to all existent political forms, the voluntarism of combat, the reliance on processes of contagion and "resonance" of attacks, are all premised on the refusal of representational compromises and an unyielding binarism of life versus power. To chide these forms with a lack of strategy, of mediation, of structural awareness, of negotiation, and persistence, seems to miss the point. The anonymous pamphlet *At Daggers Drawn* notes that Bakunin's concept of rebellion as "*the unleashing of all evil passions*" is bound to make "the cold analysts of the historical movements of capital smile."[46]

To play that "cold analyst," I do want to suggest that there is some truth in these charges because of the particular forms of biopolitical power that capitalism and the state incarnate. In this savage ontology, "life" is located in a dualism with "power" as an antinomy or opposition. For this insurrectional ontology, "life" often plays the role of structural excess, which can be codified and canalized, but only temporarily, and which then overruns all limits. Remarking of Guy Debord, another figure who courts being read in such vitalist terms, Anselm Jappe points to his tendency to "reduce society to two opposing monolithic blocks, neither of which has any serious internal contradictions, and one of which may be either the proletariat, or simply the Situationists, or even just Debord himself."[47] We might say this too is the problem of the insurrectionalist ontology I have sketched, that plays "Life" with a capital *L* against "Power" with a capital *P*. In fact, we can also see the same tendency to locate this "Life" at different levels, from mass insurrection to the affinity group or the individual theorist or anarchist.[48]

I want to suggest that, in fact, "life" plays a more ambiguous role. Bringing together Marx and Foucault, we could argue that capitalism and the state incite the power of life as a resource, galvanizing a sense of life as structural "outside," all the better to extract value from it.[49] The very contradictory place of life—torn between passivity and activity, despair and joy, conformity and revolt—speaks not simply to a problem of political activation but to its contradictory place within the social order of capitalism. Marx notes, in the *Grundrisse*, that labor-power appears as both the source of wealth *and* the denuded experience of "*absolute poverty.*"[50] Rather than an antinomy or opposition we have the more complex siting of a productive contradiction, in which the capitalist and the state posit "life" as exterior power or source.[51] In this sense, the savage ontologies I have explored are certainly probing a neuralgic point, but too often they tend to suppose the resolution of this contradiction into the violent opposition of struggle, and a "magical," or better theological, reversal of terms, in which "Life" expels "Power." Even when the penetration of capitalist power into life is recognized—as in those formulations of Negri that state that capital unleashes life as a productive force it cannot finally control—despair is turned into revolt, misery to happiness, and control into liberation.

This dialectic is fundamentally Christological in passing from an experience of abjection and destitution to an experience of redemption and transcendence. Also, this dialectic is, slightly ironically, focused on the human as the site of transformed powers, even if this includes an augmentation by new technologies in a kind of Nietzschean cybercommunism.[52] The thought of life and autonomy proposed in currents of indigeneity and political ecology responds to neither of these moments. Instead it insists on a relational experience that refutes transcendence and relocates the human as one among others, especially in the articulation of "multinaturalism."[53] While this is a salutary and necessary deflation of a productivist savage ontology, it still confronts the tensions and violence by which capital and the state extract value. The insistence on other forms of living and relation still struggle with capital's own tendency to posit an outside from which to extract value.

The continuing vampiric extraction of value from life by capital does not, I am suggesting, imply a simple opposition between life and capital.

It is an irony that although the theorization of biopolitics depends on the work of Foucault, all too often it forgets his analysis of the capillary and molecular forms of domination. In the case of Marx, too, the notion of capitalism as "positing its presuppositions," including positing labor-power as the perpetual source of value, suggests that a simple reversal is not sufficient.[54] In fact, Marx remarks on the theological form of the error that valorizes the power of labor or life as exterior to capital: "Those who demonstrate that the productive force ascribed to capital is a *displacement*, a *transposition of the productive force* of labor, forget precisely that capital itself is essentially this *displacement, this transposition*, and that wage labor as such presupposes capital, so that, from its standpoint as well, capital is this *transubstantiation*; the necessary process of positing its own powers as *alien* to the worker."[55] The notion of capital as discardable integument, under which pulse the excessive and savage powers of life, is a result of affirming the very form of value that structures capitalism. In a period of crisis, when capital abandons its "surplus population"[56]—that is, those now no longer required for value production—such a discourse risks reproducing this situation as one of victory rather than defeat or as a terrain of struggle.

Certainly some contemporary theorizations of insurrectionalism, like those of Alfredo M. Bonanno, have tried to grapple with the difficulty of the new forms of capitalist dominance.[57] The result is a questioning of the "grounds" of resistance and insurrection in the face of the collapse of "workers' identity," capitalist abandonment of labor, and the reconfiguration of crisis capitalism in the new forms of austerity, sacrifice, and assault on the remaining elements of socialist or social democratic forms. In these formulations we can see the immense stress placed on the insurrectional problematic by the modes of capitalist despotism, which erode the capacities of "life" as site of resistance by constantly displacing it as an "outside." What are undermined are precisely the conditions that made possible an insurrectional discourse. Of course, it is always possible to answer that the dispersion of the "savage ontology" of insurrection is precisely what makes it capable of exceeding the constraints of the political economy of capitalism and of "traditional" leftism. Hence, the discourse can always be reconfigured or restated, due to its own protean excess. The difficulty here is that this lack of coalescence and political form cannot contest the forms of capitalist power, but instead tends to ratify them as merely "limits" that can always be overcome.[58]

The difficulty will then be to grasp, analyze, and act from and against these effects of abandonment to "wageless life," without simply valorizing them as the sites of "life" freed from the shibboleths of "leftism" and "labor."[59] The particular "freedom" is, in fact, another form of subjection, in which the reproduction of "life" is displaced into self-reproduction outside the "securities" of the state. What is important, I think, is not to mistranslate situations of relative powerlessness into situations of encrypted or hidden powers. Rather than this fundamentally Christological discourse of reversal and "saving"—in which the most extreme state of destitution is the path to glory—we need a more nuanced strategic thinking that does not simply repeat the mantra of the "excess" of life and the immanence and imminence of insurrection.

Certainly life is at stake, and not just human life but also the forms and diversity of planetary life. The moment of the Anthropocene or, as some prefer, the Capitalocene, reveals the human as the truly geopolitical agent of and against life.[60] The strategic thinking I am suggesting aims to engage with this situation, rather than offering the "energizing" certainties of insurrection and the solvent power of life as solutions. It is only by thinking the contradictory position of life, as agency and as mere agent of capital, that we can avoid the consolatory fantasy of dialectical, better pseudodialectical, reversals. Instead of a superior productivism this probing attends to the tensions of absorption, which is neither full immersion nor detached autonomy. The supposedly "old" problems of labor, the state, and capital have not been surpassed but need to be reconfigured to resist this perpetual swinging between hope and despair.

NOTES

1. Jacob Blumenfeld, Chiara Bottici, and Simon Critchley, eds., *The Anarchist Turn* (London: Pluto, 2013).

2. See Todd May, *The Political Philosophy of Poststructuralist Anarchism* (University Park: Pennsylvania State University Press, 1994); and Saul Newman, *From Bakunin to Lacan* (Lexington: Lexington Books, 2001), for classical statements of "postanarchism."

3. For a critical discussion of contemporary insurrectional anarchism see Leonard Williams and Brad Thomson, "The Allure of Insurrection," *Anarchist Developments in Cultural Studies* 1 (2011): 226–89.

4. Michel Foucault, *The Order of Things* (London: Tavistock/Routledge, 1974), 303 (translation modified by author). See also Davide Tarizzo, "The Untamed Ontology," trans. Alvise Sforza Tarabochia, *Angelaki* 16, no. 3 (2011): 53–61.

5. Gilles Deleuze and Félix Guattari, *A Thousand Plateaus*, trans. Brian Massumi (London: Continuum, 2004), 27.

6. Eduardo Viveiros de Castro, *The Inconstancy of the Indian Soul*, trans. Gregory Duff Morton (Chicago: University of Chicago Press, 2011).

7. Mario Blaser, *Storytelling Globalization from the Chaco and Beyond* (Durham, NC: Duke University Press, 2010).

8. Déborah Danowski and Eduardo Viveiros de Castro, "L'arrêt de monde," trans. Oiara Bonilla in *De L'Univers Clos Au Monde Fini* (Paris: Éditions Dehors, 2014), 222–39.

9. Foucault, *Order*, 303.

10. Scott Lash remarks: "In vitalism life is not at all counterposed to death. Instead death is part of life. Our future is always inorganic matter. Death is seen as entropic, and part of a recombinant life process." "Life (Vitalism)," *Theory, Culture & Society* 23, no. 2–3 (2006): 327.

11. Foucault, *Order*, 262.

12. Joan Copjec, "The Sexual Compact," *Angelaki* 17, no. 2 (2012): 39.

13. Copjec, "Sexual Compact," 40.

14. Fredric Jameson, *The Hegel Variations: On the "Phenomenology of Spirit"* (London: Verso, 2010), 2n2.

15. G. W. F. Hegel, *The Phenomenology of Spirit*, no. 32, trans. Terry Pinkard (Cambridge: Cambridge University Press, 2008), 29. See Georges Bataille, "Hegel, Death and Sacrifice," trans. Jonathan Strauss, in *On Bataille*, Yale French Studies 78 (New Haven, CT: Yale University Press, 1990), 9–28.

16. For a sympathetic discussion of the radical and violent *attentats* of anarchism, mostly predicated on the failure of mass insurrectional strategies, see Mike Davis, "Artisans of Terror," in *In Praise of Barbarians: Essays against Empire* (Chicago: Haymarket Books, 2007), 263–77.

17. See Stathis Kouvelakis, *Philosophy and Revolution: From Kant to Marx* (London: Verso, 2003).

18. Mikhail Bakunin, "The Reaction in Germany" from *Notebooks of a Frenchman*, October 1842, trans. and ed. Sam Dolgoff, Marxists Internet Archive. Last accessed: October 5, 2014. www.marxists.org/reference/archive/bakunin/works/1842/reaction-germany.htm.

19. Bakunin, "Reaction in Germany."

20. For a characterization of contemporary theory as affirmationist, see Benjamin Noys, *The Persistence of the Negative: A Critique of Contemporary Continental Theory* (Edinburgh: Edinburgh University Press, 2010).

21. See Saul Newman, *Power and Politics in Poststructuralist Thought: New Theories of the Political* (London: Routledge, 2005); and Newman, ed., *Max Stirner*, Critical Explorations in Contemporary Thought series (Basingstoke: Palgrave Macmillan, 2011).

22. Max Stirner, *The Ego and His Own*, trans. Steven T. Byington (London: Verso, 1907), 300.

23. Stirner, *Ego and His Own*, 295–96.

24. Renzo Novatore, *The Collected Writings of Renzo Novatore*, trans. Wolfi Landstreicher (Berkeley: Ardent Press, 2012), 24–58. See Stirner, *Ego and His Own*, xxiii.

25. Novatore, *Collected Writings*, 27.

26. Novatore, *Collected Writings*, 28.

27. Novatore, *Collected Writings*, 49.

28. On the "New Nietszche," see David B. Allison, ed., *The New Nietzsche* (Cambridge, MA: MIT Press, 1985).

29. Anon., *At Daggers Drawn with the Existent, Its Defenders and Its False Critics*, trans. Jean Weir with John Moore and Leigh Stracross (London: Elephant Editions, 2001). http://325.nostate.net/library/At%20Daggers%20Drawn.pdf. Accessed: October 5, 2014.

30. Gilles Deleuze, *Nietzsche and Philosophy* [1962], trans. Hugh Tomlinson (New York: Columbia University Press, 1983), 161.

31. Alain Badiou, *Deleuze: The Clamor of Being* [1997], trans. Louise Burchill (Minneapolis: University of Minnesota Press, 2000), 13.

32. See Jean Baudrillard, "When Bataille Attacked the Metaphysical Principle of Economy" [1976], in *Bataille: A Critical Reader*, ed. Fred Botting and Scott Wilson (Oxford: Blackwell, 1998), 139–45. Baudrillard's reference is to Bataille, and we could obviously extend this "savage ontology" to Bataille's work. For a consideration of the possible vitalism of Bataille, see Benjamin Noys, " 'Grey in Grey': Change, Crisis, Critique," *Journal of Critical Globalisation Studies* 4 (February 2011): 45–60. www.criticalglobalisation.com/Issue4/45_60_GREY_IN_GREY_JCGS4.pdf. Accessed October 5, 2014.

33. Gilles Deleuze and Félix Guattari, *What Is Philosophy?*, trans. Hugh Tomlinson and Graham Burchell (New York: Columbia University Press, 1994), 74.

34. Peter Hallward, *Out of This World: Deleuze and the Philosophy of Creation* (London: Verso, 2006), 55.

35. Peter Hallward refers to Hegel as Deleuze's "most dangerous *rival*" (*Out of This World*, 6), and we could argue that this is because of their close *proximity*.

36. See Rodrigo Nunes, "Politics in the Middle: For a Political Interpretation of the Dualisms in Deleuze and Guattari," in "Deleuze and Political Activism," ed. Marcelo Svirsky, special issue, *Deleuze Studies* 4 (2010): 104–26.

37. Michael Hardt and Antonio Negri, *Empire* (Cambridge, MA: Harvard University Press, 2000).

38. See Antonio Negri, "Domination and Sabotage: On the Marxist Method of Social Transformation" [1977], in Negri, *Books for Burning*, trans. Arianna Bove et al., ed. Timothy S. Murphy (London: Verso, 2005), 231–90.

39. Antonio Negri in Cesare Casarino and Antonio Negri, *In Praise of the Common: A Conversation on Philosophy and Politics* (Minneapolis: University of Minnesota Press, 2009), 149.

40. Antonio Negri, *Art and Multitude*, trans. E. Emery (Cambridge: Polity, 2011), 78–79.

41. The Invisible Committee, *The Coming Insurrection*, 2009, http://tarnac9.files.wordpress.com/2009/04/thecominsur_booklet.pdf, 84, 10. Accessed October 5, 2014.

42. For a nuanced identification and sophisticated analysis of Agamben as a sui generis vitalist see Lorenzo Chiesa and Frank Ruda, "The Event of Language as Force of Life: Agamben's Linguistic Vitalism," *Angelaki* 16.3 (2011): 163–80.

43. For a sympathetic account see Miguel Vatter, "Biopolitics: From Surplus Value to Surplus Life," *Theory & Event* 12, no. 2 (2009), DOI: 10.1353/tae.0.0062.

44. Stewart Martin, "Artistic Communism—A Sketch," *Third Text* 23.4 (2009): 494.

45. Anon., *At Daggers Drawn*, 5.

46. Anon., *At Daggers Drawn*, 10.

47. Anselm Jappe, *Guy Debord*, trans. Donald Nicholson-Smith (Berkeley: University of California Press, 1999), 114.

48. This also suggests another genealogy or form of what Alain Badiou refers to as "speculative leftism," which describes the tendency to abstractly oppose revolts to "Power"; see Alain Badiou, *Being and Event* [1988], trans. and intro. Oliver Feltham (London: Continuum, 2005), 210–11, and Bruno Bosteels, "The Speculative Left," *South Atlantic Quarterly* 104, no. 4 (Fall 2005): 751–67.

49. See, in particular, Karl Marx, *Grundrisse*, trans. Martin Nicolaus (London: Penguin, 1973), and Michel Foucault, *The Birth of Biopolitics: Lectures at the Collège de France, 1978–79*, trans. Graham Burchell (Basingstoke, UK: Palgrave, 2008).

50. Marx, *Grundrisse*, 296.

51. Gavin Walker, "On Marxism's Field of Operation: Badiou and the Critique of Political Economy," *Historical Materialism* 20, no. 2 (2012): 68–69.

52. Deleuze insisted on life as a "Superfold" that reached into the genetic code and into the potential of silicon; see Gilles Deleuze, *Foucault*, trans. Seán Hand (London: Athlone Press, 1988), 131. See also Hardt and Negri, *Empire*, 91.

53. Philippe Descola, *Beyond Nature and Culture*, trans. Janet Lloyd (Chicago: University of Chicago Press, 2013).

54. See Marx, *Grundrisse*, 298.

55. Marx, *Grundrisse*, 308.

56. See Aaron Benanav, "Misery and Debt: On the Logic and History of Surplus Populations and Surplus Capital," *Endnotes 2* (2010), http://endnotes.org.uk/articles/1.

57. See Alfredo M. Bonanno, *From Riot to Insurrection*, trans. Jean Weir (London: Elephant Editions, 2009).

58. On the necessity of forms of compact and directed agency for politics see Peter Hallward, "The Politics of Prescription," *South Atlantic Quarterly* 104 (2005): 769–89.

59. Michael Denning, "Wageless Life," *New Left Review* 66 (2010): 79–97.

60. Dipesh Chakrabarty, "The Climate of History: Four Theses," *Critical Inquiry* 35 (2009): 197–222.

9

Unreasonability, Style, and Pretiosity

FRANS-WILLEM KORSTEN

Unreasonability

For classical theorists who pondered the principles of the free market, rationality or rational choice was the basic principle. For many others since, as if by analogy, capitalism appears to be operating *reasonably*, that is: if it is given the necessary free hand (throughout its history the *Economist*, to name an important example, has been a staunch defender of this option). In contrast, partly beginning with Marx, others have come to diagnose capitalism as, basically, mad. Gilles Deleuze and Félix Guattari gave two studies, *Anti-Oedipus* and *A Thousand Plateaus*, the same telling subtitle: "Capitalism and Schizophrenia." Accordingly, they contended in an interview, published in 1995, that capitalism can be characterized as being in a state of delirium, and a very special one at that: "Something that hasn't been adequately discussed about Marx's *Capital* is the extent to which he is fascinated by capitalist mechanisms, precisely because the system is demented, yet works very well at the same time. . . . Capital, or money, is at such a level of insanity that psychiatry has but one clinical equivalent: the terminal stage."[1] Evidently, capitalism requires all sorts of rational behavior and mechanisms. Still, this rationality is also the veil for an underlying madness. The example Deleuze and Guattari provide is the stock market: understandable, logical, rational, yet mad. When they define the system as "demented" this is to indicate a "society for which it is proper to decode and deterritorialize all the flows: flow of production, flow of consumption."[2] To be sure, previous societies were not unaware of this possibility but resisted it or responded in panic. Now that capitalism has become dominant, panic and insanity have become constitutive.[3]

Capitalism has not been mad in the same way throughout its relatively short history, and the current capitalist delirium may be special in another sense than the one defined by Deleuze and Guattari. With respect to this, Fredric Jameson appears to be in accordance with their analysis when he suggests that capitalism answers to the nature of the *average* delirium: "every delirium is first of all the investment of a field that is social, economic, political, cultural, racial and racist, pedagogical and religious ... overreaching on all sides."[4] Yet in this very definition, Jameson's notion of "overreaching" hints at another possibility. The current "overreaching" does not concern the shift from regional or national contexts to the entire globe. This was predicted already by Marx. It is not even a matter of speed, of capitalism's general mode of acceleration, leading to ever faster cycles of crisis. The current overreaching is special, as Melinda Cooper argues, *in* that it is "intimately and essentially concerned with the limits of life on earth and the regeneration of living futures—beyond the limits."[5] Many scholars have dealt with capitalism's tendency to cross limits, such as David Harvey in his *The Limits to Capital* or Deleuze and Guattari in their claim that capitalism will seek ever new lines of flight, but the crossing of the limit that Cooper is talking about is different with respect to this "regeneration of living futures." As a consequence of the coincidence of neoliberalism with biotechnology, the panic-driven delirium that corresponds to ever shorter periods of time between recurring crises is currently followed by something else: in its madness capitalism is now constantly *ahead of us*.

For those who oppose capitalism one question is, then, how to deal with a system that is in a lasting state of panic and yet vigorous (perhaps because of this panic) or that is both demented, insane, and successfully in operation and, as such, is incurably *unreasonable*. The other question has become, how a system that is constantly ahead of us can live up to the requirement of reasonability. Given the madness of capitalism, those who oppose it in terms of logic and reasonability find themselves on a dead-end street at this point, unable to respond to a new form of acceleration propelled by the coincidence of neoliberalism and biotechnology. As for those who support capitalism and who are being taken up by it (willingly or unwillingly), the question is not so much whether they would want to listen to reason as whether they can.

The tendency or desire to want capitalism to answer reasonably is a distinct heritage of Hegelian dialectics. Moreover, in accordance with the basically argumentative logic of dialectics (the very term is meaningfully derived from classical, Aristotelian dialectics), most forms of analysis and critique of capitalism have focused on *functional* relations within the dynamic of dialectical oppositions. Master and slave are not just dialectically bound opposites, they have a functional relationship with one another, just as the capitalist and the laborer have. The laborer does not belong to an altogether different species from the capitalist. Both occupy positions that are dialectically defined and that are functionally related to one another. In a sense it is their functional relation what makes history "function."

However, capitalism's selection mechanisms and current propulsion of biotechnology, in a radicalization of both biopower and biopolitics, is now on the verge of producing different forms of the self that are no longer comparable with, for instance, differing biological casts within one species, but that concern different *styles* of human beings. These styles can only in part be defined within a humanist framework, because they indicate different styles of being human. "Style," in the Deleuzian sense of the word, is both an expression of form and of content; it is a form of composition of disparate elements that acquire consistency through a process of individuation. As such, different styles may result in politically and aesthetically incompatible "parties." These parties, based on styles instead of programs, can live next to one another, they can mingle, they can talk with one another, but if they find themselves in a political conflict, on whatever level, they will be engaged in a *style struggle* that embodies incompatible, heterogeneous types of worlding.[6]

As Deleuze argues, style is beyond the false opposition of appearance and materiality, surface and depth. Style must be thought also beyond the binarism of immaterial and material labor, or even beyond the binary distinction between biopower and biopolitics. As for the issue of materiality, it is not for nothing that shortly before his death Deleuze was working on a study that should have been called *Grandeur de Marx*, or *The Greatness of Marx*. It would certainly have moved the study of Marx beyond binary dialectics. In fact it might have connected to what Harvey explains to be Marx's reworking of Hegelian dialectics so that it could "take account of 'every historically developed form as being in a fluid state, in motion.' Marx had, therefore, to reconfigure dialectics so that it could grasp the 'transient aspect' of a society as well. Dialectics has to, in short, be able to understand and represent processes of motion, change and transformation."[7] In order to make dialectics capable of dealing with "fluid" historical conditions, it had to become fluid itself. As for biopower and biopolitics, which in postautonomia thinking have been distinguished as conceptually different, the very distinction becomes complicated when different styles are operative within *both*. Moreover, different styles may be operative between different beings or within one being in different forms of intensity, and on the different planes of potential and power. This means that, in terms of power and potential, styles are not restricted to one of the latter two domains, as class would be.

Styles are not of *the* surface, of deception, pastiche, or parody, they are of *surfaces* and folds in connection, material through and through. With respect to this, style has nothing to do with stylistic postmodernism either, since styles may define both individuals and collectives, both small-scale *groupuscules* and masses of beings, each endowed with a specific form of reasonability. Consequently, a style struggle can only be analyzed in terms of reasonability if one sticks to one particular style. Or, taken in their multiplicity, styles do not fall under the rubric of a unified, or in the end universal, form of reasonability. To put this differently, if style struggle is the current metamorphosis of class struggle, it cannot be brought to a conclusion by reason, synthesis, or *Aufhebung* or by being brought under the umbrella of an overarching horizon.[8]

The conceptualization of style I am concerned with here is comparable to, but still different from, Giorgio Agamben's or Tiqqun's notions of forms of life, and is radically different from any marketable lifestyle in the context of capitalism. Agamben's "happy life" concerns a form of life in general, in which *bios* and *zoe* would no longer be separate.[9] For the French collective Tiqqun, working between 1999 and 2001 and searching for a new community, forms of life came into existence because of an "intimate polarization" that permitted the constitution of a community or a party that might operate in conflict with others.[10] For Tiqqun, *thought* converts a form of life "into a *force*, into a sensible effectivity." This comes close to what I have in mind, with the important distinction that thought, which would be at the basis of a political program, is not constitutive in my analysis. Style is not something that can be brought back to a ground or that can be *thought*, nor is it something that is simply definable as a *common*.[11]

When styles are able to exist next to one another, and sometimes *in* one another, any opposition to capitalism as the primary form of conflict loses its primacy. The goal is not necessarily a battle against capitalism because the battle itself could exhaust us, bind us dialectically to capitalism, which in turn could propel it forward while leading us away from what we would like to *practice*. A good example of an alternative, following the logic of style and style struggle with relation to the *social autonomy and self-determination of groups*, is what Pierre Clastres would call "primitive war." This is not a strategic war and it would not even need to be an armed one, as maintained by Bernard Aspe. It concerns "a practice of irreconcilability" that has received perhaps too little scholarly attention in the past two centuries.[12]

Practicing Pretiosity

Styles operate by means of heterogeneous sets of rationality and empathy. It is style that defines a being and defines what it finds precious, what a being will stubbornly persist in holding on to. To quote Aspe again, in a section tellingly titled "Le trésor perdu" ("The lost treasure"), this may concern, for instance, all those forms of existence that are threatened by an irrevocable loss: "Forms of a communal life, living forms and their environments, forms of sensibility and its transindividual resonances."[13] The loss that Aspe is referring to is the result of the *socius* being decoded in order to free the flows of capitalism. In practice, this decoding must take, at one moment or another, the form of dispossession. With respect to this, Rosa Luxemburg was right in pointing out that primitive accumulation is not something that defines the *prehistory* of capitalism but remains *intrinsic* to it, which is what David Harvey defines as accumulation through dispossession.[14] It is through different forms of dispossession that capitalism takes away what is precious to people, as it is through different forms of dispossession that people are being brought into a precarious state. Dispossession, then, brings together the precious and the precarious.

Although *precious* and *precarious* appear to be related terms, they are etymologically distinct. The *pre-* of precarious is derived from *prex/precis*: prayer; the *pre-* or precious from *preti*: back—as if it concerns some form of exchange, or something lost that one wants to get back. Dispossession relates to the precious in that it concerns that which one will defend at all costs, and to the precarious in that it concerns that which one will beg or pray for in despair. Dispossession relates to the precarious in that it implies the loss of what one was clinging to, and to the precious as what one was clinging to because it was dear.[15]

The counterpart of precarity (understood as insecurity and vulnerability) may *seem* to be security and, by implication, stability. Or it may seem to be invulnerability and, by implication, some form of sovereignty. Yet these dialectical opposites do not do justice to the sociocultural and ecological damage involved when people and nature are thrown into a state of precariousness. Nor do these opposites allow for a positive revalorization of the precarious, or for a viable alternative to it. Precarity can be better understood affectively, in relation to what I want to call *pretiosity*, a word current in English in the seventeenth and eighteenth centuries and now no longer in use. Pretiosity is both related to and distinctly different from the precious. Pretiosity concerns what we hold dearly *and* what is our real other: the thing that we value but can never possess or own. We can never possess or own our *relationship* with the ones we love and respect; with the land; with plants, trees, animals, or machines, for that matter. The car that people own and possess may be precious, but their relationship with the car is a matter of pretiosity. Tellingly, people will be at a loss for words when they want to define pretiosity. It may escape the logic of representation.

If a relationship cannot be owned, the tempting question for capitalism would be how it can be given a value. Social relationships are what capitalism needs for its processes of valorization, and, as a consequence, the pretiosity of relationships is what capitalism will ultimately seek to capitalize.[16] Think, for example, of the capitalist evaluation of land, which in effect asks: "How much do you want me to pay for your loving this piece of land, which, apparently, to you does not seem to be just a piece of land?" In contrast, for those who oppose dispossession through capitalism, the question is how their relationships can be sustained and furthered. The simple answer is that they need to be practiced, which is what makes it very difficult. With respect to this, the later work of Michel Foucault might not be of direct help. Whereas in previous studies Foucault had focused on practices of power, his focus in the end came to be on how we can practice the care of self, as in *The Courage of Truth: The Government of Self and Others II*. However, in this study Foucault was still aiming for an understanding of truth that would preside over a relatively homogeneous world. Pretiosity is not a matter of defining what is precious "in truth" but of practicing the relationships that define one form of pretiosity as opposed to radically different ones.

The emphasis on relationships, and by consequence alliance, is key to what one can call the anthropological turn in the domain of the critical analysis of capitalism that has taken place in the last two decades. I am thinking of the work by the Colectivo Situaciones, the *Precarias a la Deriva*, but also of the work done by John Pickles and his team;[17] David Graeber's anthropological studies that culminated in his influential *Debt*; Stevphen Shukaitis's work on the Colectivo Situaciones and his *Imaginal Machines: Autonomy and Self-Organization in the Revolutions of Everyday Life*; or the work done by Keith Hart, Jean-Louis Laville, and Antonio David Cattani.[18] For all of them capitalism is what happens in relation to people's daily lives, to the spaces they inhabit, the movements they can make, the cares that they have or are allowed to have.

With respect to this, the alternatives to capitalism have to be found in both other relationships and in radically different definitions of relationship. These could be defined in terms of the "savage," as I already hinted at by referring to Clastres. They would require what Eugene Holland, in his reading of Deleuze and Guattari's *Anti-Oedipus*, calls "a return to alliance-based social relations in order to re-establish the mobility and social value of death and expenditure."[19] The recoding that would have to take place for this would indeed have to lead to a situation in which, for instance, death is no longer the culmination of fear in relation to (unpaid) debt, but, again, the socially inscribed end of life. Such recoding would have to be realized on the basis of alliances, contemporary forms of kinship structures, which for Deleuze and Guattari as well were "a practice, a praxis, a method and even a strategy."[20]

Both collectively and individually, the question is whether pretiosity can be an ethical guiding thread in battles that are already here and demand a long-term determination. This is a difficult question because pretiosity cannot be defined logically or grasped permanently. In the context of capitalism it requires a code and therefore recoding, and this can be sensed best when one considers how practicing pretiosity is distinct from work and labor in terms of the organization of time. As for labor, it is time that "measures labor insofar as it reduces it to homogenous substance, but also determines its productive power in the same form: through the multiplication of average temporal units."[21] To be sure the practice of pretiosity takes time as well. We cannot just *state* that we have a relationship with the land we cultivate, for instance, we have to *practice* cultivating it. The time invested in this practice cannot be measured, however, in terms of marketable temporal units. The time spent on this practice needs to be coded, as opposed to a time that sticks to no code but only answers to the law of economic measurability.

One aspect of the battles already begun and those to come concerns the struggle over different and incompatible modes of organizing time. In this sense, people will set aside a certain amount of time to practice pretiosity. A second aspect concerns the public or nonpublic definition and inscription of our pretiosity, which is essential in the effort to link the individual and the collective. A third aspect, linked to the second one, concerns the preservation of pretiosity for a longer period of time. Such preservation requires resistance and persistency, although at the same time it is important not to essentialize the practice of pretiosity. Pretiosity is pivotal, here, for the forms of autonomy we want to realize. A fourth aspect of the battles that are already here and to come concerns the use of practices of attacking or fleeing, retreating, hiding from the forces that try to decode or damage our pretiosity.

The fifth and last aspect is the ability to wait consciously and see what kind of world will open up as a result of the savage battles and retreats that concern people's practicing pretiosity. These battles concern a world that is here and now, and people's practicing pretiosity concerns a distinct form of worlding. Their goal is not a utopia. Savage citizens, in choosing their alliances, have enough imagination to envision alternative worlds as opposed to a world that threatens them. There is a chance that they may find what pretiosity meant for them too late. They may also find that the thing that they did not value explicitly and practiced nevertheless, will, in the end, open up the door to a new world. And there is the chance that in the explicit, political, continuous practice of pretiosity and in a battle for this practice, a new world will open up.

NOTES

1. Gilles Deleuze and Félix Guattari, "Capitalism: A Very Special Delirium," in *Chaosophy*, ed. Sylvere Lothringer, Autonomedia/Semiotexte, 1995. Accessed October 2014. www.generation-online.org/p/fpdeleuze7.htm.

2. Deleuze and Guattari, "Capitalism."

3. Gilles Deleuze, "Capitalism, Flows, the Decoding of Flows, Capitalism and Schizophrenia, Psychoanalysis, Spinoza," Cours Vincennes, November 16, 1971. Accessed October 2014. www.webdeleuze.com/php/texte.php?cle=116&groupe=Anti+O edipe+et+Mille+Plateaux&langue=2.

4. Fredric Jameson, "Marxism and Dualism in Deleuze," *South Atlantic Quarterly* 96(3) (1997): 393–417.

5. Melinda Cooper, *Life as Surplus: Biotechnology and Capitalism in the Neoliberal Era*. (Washington: University of Washington Press, 2008), 20.

6. Though Deleuze was clearly inspired by Nietzsche, this is distinctly not "like" Nietzsche's idea of style: "One thing is needful—to 'give style' to one's character—a great and rare art. It is practiced by those who survey all the strengths and weaknesses of their nature and then fit them into an artistic plan until every one of them appears as art and reason and even weaknesses delight the eye." Nietzsche, *The Gay*

Science, trans. Walter Kaufman (New York: Vintage Books, 1974), par. 290. In fact Deleuze's idea of style fit in better with what Pauline Westerman defined as the best understanding of divine law in Aquinas, which was nothing that we would understand under the rubric of law but can be called a *style*, a distinct and specific form of order and proportion that defines a world. See Westerman, *The Disintegration of Natural Law Theory: Aquinas to Finnis* (Leiden: Brill, 1998).

7. David Harvey, *A Companion to Marx's "Capital"* (London: Verso, 2010), 11.

8. I am referring, here, to Jodi Dean's passionate plea in *Communist Horizon* (London: Verso, 2012) for the revitalization of a communist party that would orchestrate the political battle against capitalism.

9. Giorgio Agamben, *Means without End: Notes on Politics*, trans. Vincenzo Binetti and Cesare Casarino (Minneapolis: University of Minnesota Press, 2000), 13–116.

10. Tiqqun, *Introduction to Civil War*, trans. Alexander R. Galloway and Jason E. Smith (Los Angeles: Semiotext(e), 2010), 20.

11. This groundlessness of style is also crucial in the analysis of scientific arguments and thought by Ian Hacking, "Styles of Scientific Reasoning," in J. Rajchman and C. West, eds., *Post-analytic Philosophy* (New York: Columbia University Press, 1985), 145–65, which was based predominantly on Alistair Crombie's massive, three-volume study *Styles of Scientific Thinking in the European Tradition: The History of Argument and Explanation Especially in the Mathematical and Biomedical Sciences and Arts* (Ann Arbor: University of Michigan Press, 1994), which, in turn, was the major source of inspiration for Chunglin Kwa's *Styles of Knowing: A New History of Science from Ancient Times to the Present* (Pittsburgh, PA: University of Pittsburgh Press, 2011).

12. Bernard Aspe, *Les mots et les actes* (Caen, France: NOUS, 2012), 243; my translation.

13. Aspe, *Les mots et les actes*, 248; my translation.

14. See David Harvey, *Reading Marx's Capital*, http://davidharvey.org/2008/06/marxs-capital-class-01/. Accessed October 2014; *A Companion to Marx's "Capital"* (London: Verso, 2010); and *The New Imperialism* (Oxford: Oxford University Press, 2003).

15. "Precious" is derived from *pretiosus*: costly, valuable; which in turn is derived from *pretium*: value, worth, price. "Price" is directly derived from pretium, and this is in accordance with its root of "back" in the sense of a recompense. As may be clear, the term "precious" also has acquired other, even principally other, connotations.

16. The capitalization of even intimate relationships was at the core of Ayn Rand's not so idiosyncratic form of capitalism defined as "Objectivism." See her novels *The Fountainhead* and especially *Atlas Shrugged*, later followed by nonfiction such as *The Virtue of Selfishness* (1964) and *Capitalism; The Unknown Ideal* (1967). In the context of my argument it is telling that for Rand reasonability is key, since, basically, for her man is an individual and as such a trader. Her utopian project concerned, as any utopian project will, the destruction of this world first in order to get to the New. In this sense her project was aimed at destroying existing relationships, not only human ones, but all those relations connected to human beings. It is no coinci-

dence, both philosophically or historically speaking, that Rand's ideas proved to be decisively influential for the Chicago School of Economics, specifically, and for neoliberalism in general. The essential features of all forms of utopian thought were defined by Hans Achterhuis in several studies (1995, 1998); see e.g. Hans Achterhuis, "La responsabilita tra il timore e l'utopia," in G. Hottois and M. G. Pinsart, eds., *Hans Jonas: Natura e responsabilita* (Lecce, Italy: Edizioni Milella, 1996), 99–110. Recently he published *De utopie van de vrije markt* [The utopia of the free market] (2010), which deals with the utopian nature of neoliberalism. One key characteristic of utopian thinking, according to Achterhuis, is that *this* world, any current world, needs to be *gone* first, thus to be destroyed first. Because of its overreaching desire, capitalism will try to capitalize intimate relationships, then. This was at the center of several books by Arlie Hochschild, to begin with *The Managed Heart: Commercialization of Human Feeling* (1979), and then more recently with *The Outsourced Self: Intimate Life in Market Times* (2012). The pivotal issue that Hochschild appears to miss, however, is that in order to analyze this problem, we need to distinguish sharply between labor and work on the one hand and practice on the other.

17. The latest contributions to date are John Pickles, Sebastian Cobarrubias, and Maribel Casas-Cortes, "Le regard cartographique, les nouvelles cartographies des frontiers, et les responsabilites du cartographe" [The cartographic gaze, new cartographies of the border, and the responsibility of mapping], in Aliocha Imhoff and Kantuta Quiros, eds., *Géoesthétique*, coproduced by the Parc Saint Leger [art center], the High School of Fine Arts of Clermont-Ferrand, the National Center for Books, and the National Center for Contemporary Art (Paris: B42, 2014), 37–53; or John Pickles, Maribel Casas Cortes, and Sebastian Cobarrubias, "Commons," in D. Nonini, ed., *A Companion to Urban Anthropology* (New York: Wiley, 2014); or again Maribel Casas Cortes, Sebastian Cobarrubias, and John Pickles, "Re-Bordering the Neighbourhood: Europe's Emerging Geographies of Non-Accession Integration," *Journal of European Urban and Regional Studies* 20, no. 1 (January 2013): 37–58.

18. See Keith Hart, Jean-Louis Laville and Antonio David Cattani, eds., *The Human Economy: A Citizen's Guide* (London: Polity Press, 2010).

19. Eugene W. Holland, *Deleuze and Guattari's "Anti-Oedipus": Introduction to Schizoanalysis* (London: Routledge, 1999), 96.

20. Deleuze and Guattari, *Anti-Oedipus: Capitalism and Schizophrenia I*, trans. Robert Hurley, Mark Seem, and Helen R. Lane (London: Continuum, 2004), 147.

21. Antonio Negri, "The Constitution of Time," in Negri, *Time for Revolution*, trans. Matteo Mandarini (London: Continuum, 2003), 24. Quoted in Matteo Mandarini, "Antagonism, Contradiction, Time: Conflict and Organization in Antonio Negri," 202.

10

Re-enchanting the World Technology, the Body & the Construction of the Commons SILVIA FEDERICI

Almost a century has passed since Max Weber, in "Science as a Vocation" (1918–1919), argued that "the fate of our times is characterized, above all, by the disenchantment of the world," a phenomenon he attributed to the intellectualization and rationalization produced by the scientific and scientifically oriented technological organization of knowledge and society. By "disenchantment" Weber referred to the vanishing of the magical—the mysterious, the incalculable—from the world.[1] But we can interpret his warning in a more political sense, as the emergence of a world in which our capacity to recognize the existence of any logic other than that of capitalist development is in question. This "blockage" has many sources combining to prevent the misery we experience in everyday life from turning into transformative action. The restructuring of production, which the globalization of the world economy has activated, has dismantled working-class communities and forms of organization, products of a century of struggle, and deepened the divisions that capitalism has planted in the body of the world proletariat. There is, however, something else at work that we must acknowledge and demystify.

I propose that what prevents our suffering from becoming productive of alternatives to capitalism is also the seduction that the products of capitalist "technology" exert on us, as they appear to give us powers without which it would seem impossible to live. It is the main purpose of my article to challenge this myth. This is not to engage in a sterile attack against technology, yearning for an impossible return to a primitivist paradise, but to acknowledge the cost of the technological innovations by which we are mesmerized and, above all, remind us of the knowledges, powers, and reasons that we have lost in the process of their production and acquisition. It is the discovery of other logics than that of capitalist development and the reconstitution of these powers and reasons that I refer to when I speak of "re-enchanting" the world, a practice, I believe, that is central to today's most antisystemic movements and a precondition for resistance to domination. For if all we know and value is what capitalism has produced, then any hope of truly revolutionary change is doomed. Any society not prepared to scale down the use of industrial technology must face ecological catastrophes;[2] competition for diminishing resources; and a growing sense of despair about the future of the earth and our presence in it. In this context, struggles aiming to reinstitute a closer relation with the natural world and revalorize the work required for our reproduction are crucial for our future. They are not only necessary for our physical survival but are the paths to a "re-enchantment" of our world, as they enable us to reconnect what capitalism has divided in our lives and restore a sense of wholeness to our existence that is essential for effective social change.

Technology, the Body, and Autonomy

The attraction that modern technology exerts on us is in great part attributable to the impoverishment—economic, ecological, cultural—that five centuries of capitalist development and technological innovation have produced in our lives. This impoverishment has many dimensions, exceeding the misery produced by the capitalist appropriation of the wealth we produce. As Marx relentlessly acknowledged, the history of capitalist production has been that of a constant expropriation and transfer of skills and knowledges from the workers to the machine. Like the worker, the earth too has been depleted. As he wrote, with reference to the development of industrial agriculture,

> All progress in capitalist agriculture is a progress in the art not only of robbing the worker, but of robbing the soil; all progress in increasing the fertility of the soil for a given time is a progress towards ruining the more long term sources of that fertility. The more a country proceeds from large-scale industry as a background of its development, as in the case of the United States, the more rapid is this process of destruction. Capitalist production, therefore, only develops the techniques and the degree of combination of the social process of

production by simultaneously undermining the original source of all wealth—the soil and the workers.[3]

Today the industrial theft of the earth's wealth that Marx so precisely observed has reached a critical stage, as injections of chemical fertilizers are used to squeeze crops from depleted soils. There is, however, another kind of impoverishment, less visible but equally destructive, that the Marxist tradition has largely ignored. This is the loss produced by the long history of capitalism's attack on our autonomous powers, through our separation from the land, from our own bodies, as well as the regimentation of our work and reproduction. By "autonomous powers" I refer to the complex of needs, desires, and capacities that millions of years of evolutionary development in close relation with the natural world have sedimented in us, and that constitute one of the main sources of resistance to exploitation. I refer to the need for the sun, the winds, the sky, the need for touching, smelling, sleeping, making love, being in the open air, instead of being surrounded by closed walls. (Keeping children enclosed within four walls is still one of the main challenges that teachers encounter in many parts of the world.) Insistence on the discursive construction of the body has made us lose sight of this reality. Yet, this accumulated structure of needs and desires, that has been the precondition of our reproduction, has been a powerful limit to the exploitation of labor, which is why, from the earliest phase of its development, capitalism had to wage a war against our body, making of it a signifier of all that is limited, material, opposed to reason.[4] Foucault's intuition of the ontological primacy of resistance and our capacity to produce liberating practices, can be explained on this ground.[5] That is, it can be explained on the basis of our bodies' constitutive interaction with an "outside"—which we can call the cosmos or the "world of nature"—that has been immensely productive of capacities and collective visions and imaginations, although obviously mediated through social/cultural relations. All the cultures of the South Asian region—Vandana Shiva has reminded us—have originated from societies living in close contact with the forests.[6] Also some of the most important scientific discoveries have originated in precapitalist societies where people's lives were profoundly shaped by a daily interaction with nature. Four thousand years ago Babylonians and Mayan sky-watchers discovered and mapped the main constellations and the cyclical motions of heavenly bodies.[7] Polynesian sailors navigated the high seas in the darkest nights, finding their way to the shore by reading the ocean swells, so knowledgeable were their bodies of the changes in the undulations and surges of the waves.[8] Preconquest native American populations produced many of the crops that now feed the world, with a mastery unsurpassed by any agricultural innovations introduced over the last five hundred years, generating an abundance and diversity that no agricultural revolution has matched.[9] I turn to this history, so little reflected upon, to dispel the idea that capitalism has brought knowledge and *techne* into the world, and to highlight the impoverishment that we have undergone, in the course of capitalist development, and for which no technological device has compensated. Indeed, parallel to the history of capitalist technological innovation we could write a history of the disaccumulation of our precapitalist knowledges and capacities, which is the premise on which capitalism has developed our capacity to work. This is not accidental. The capacity to read the natural elements, discover the medical properties of plants and flowers, gain sustenance from the earth, live in woods, forests, and mountainous regions, be guided by the stars and winds on the roads and the seas has been a source of "autonomy" that has had to be destroyed—"autonomy" here understood not as self-reliance and isolation from others, of the kind Rousseau and liberal political theory have imagined and celebrated as constitutive of the individual in the "state of nature," but as social/collective capacity for self-activity, self-movement, and independence from external power. The history of mountainous and forested regions is instructive in this context, as they have been the privileged sites of communities of rebels, heretics, masterless men, Maroons. The development of industrial technology has been built on the loss of this autonomy and has amplified it, by capturing and incorporating the most creative aspects of the living labor used in the production process.

Of Computers and Commons

It is important here to remember that technologies are not reducible to material devices, but incorporate and produce specific systems of social relations, starting with specific disciplinary and cognitive regimes that "worm their way in every aspect of our lives and tolerate no alternatives."[10] "With them," Otto Ullrich writes, "typically comes an infrastructural network of technical, social, psychological conditions without which the machines and [their] products do not work." Exemplary have been the redefinition of industrial production and urban space/time that the automobile has produced and the militarization of the social environment imposed by the development

of nuclear plants. Digital technology as well carries a specific social and political program as a further step in the transfer of work skills to the machine
and depersonalization of the worker. Mental labor was once seen as the last
bastion of creativity and uniqueness, but with the introduction of the Turing
machine to the analysis of the labor process this last wall has been broken
down.[11] Consider the case (mentioned by Franco Berardi) of recombinant
productive circuits that fractalize and reassemble fragments of work-time
performed in the global cyborg space by a variety of isolated workers, only
connected to it by their mobile phones, or the "man-computer symbiosis"
idealized by current cognitive/work and military systems.[12] With digitalization, the abstraction and domination of labor have reached their comple-
tion, bringing to fulfillment La Mettrie's idea of the "man-machine," and
so has our sense of alienation and desocialization. What levels of stress the
digitalization of work and social relations is producing can be measured
by the epidemics of mental illnesses—depression, panic, anxiety, attention
deficit, dyslexia—that are now becoming typical of most technologically
advanced countries—epidemics that, not alone, I read as forms of passive
resistance to being assimilated to the machine, to becoming machine-like
and making capital's plans our own.[13] Add that rather than reducing our
work week or the burden of physical and mental labor, the promise of all
technotopias since the 1950s, digital work and computerization have inten-
sified them. Japan, the motherland of digital technology, leads the world
in the new phenomenon of "death by work." Computerization has also immensely increased the military capacity of the capitalist class, and its sur-
veillance of our work and lives. Thanks to the computer, millions of us now
work in situations where every move we make is monitored and registered
and every mistake or transgression is punished. Not last, an account of what
it takes to produce a computer preempts any optimistic view of the social
consequences of the Internet and the information revolution. As Saral
Sarkar reminds us, just to produce one computer requires on average fifteen
to nineteen tons of materials and 33,000 liters of pure water, obviously to
be taken from our commonwealth, plausibly the common lands and waters
of communities in Africa, Asia, and Latin America that in many cases do
not even have electricity available to them.[14] These communities, nevertheless, also supply the labor needed to excavate from their lands the materials
needed for the computers. Indeed, we can apply to computerization what
Raphael Samuel has written about industrialization in general: "If one looks
at [industrial] technology from the point of view of labour rather than that

of capital, it is a cruel caricature to present machinery as dispensing with toil . . . quite apart from the demands which machinery itself imposed there was a huge army of labour engaged in supplying it with raw material."[15]

Measured against these developments, the benefits we can draw from our personal computers pale.[16] Behind the appearance of interconnectivity, the computer has produced new forms of isolation. Social interaction is shrinking, as millions spend their days in front of their screens forfeiting the pleasure of physical contact and eye-to-eye conversation; communication becomes more superficial since the attraction of an immediate response replaces pondered letters with quick exchanges. It has also been noted that the fast rhythms to which computers habituate us generate a growing impatience in our daily interactions with other people, as they cannot match the velocity of the machine.[17] Nevertheless it is difficult to disabuse ourselves of the assumption that the introduction of the Internet and the computer in our work space and daily life has improved the quality of our existence, reduced socially necessary labor, and increased our capacity for communication and cooperation. An axiom prevalent in the mainstream media, but present also in radical circles, is that the new communicative technologies (Twitter, Facebook) have a major political potential, as conveyor belts of global revolution, at times described as the triggers of the "Arab Spring" and the movement of the squares. This, however, is an untenable assumption. Twitter and Facebook can bring thousands to the streets and have facilitated the formation of new forms of sociality. As Paolo Carpignano has pointed out, with reference to the experience of the Occupy movement in the United States: "It would be a mistake to think . . . that the new media are only the form of expression of a pre-constituted subjectivity, [and] just an instrument to circulate 'alternative' information generated by the movement. This instrumental vision of the new media does not grasp the constitutive element they have in the new subjectivities, which . . . they articulate."[18]

Nevertheless, the communal and creative ways that have characterized relations in the encampments cannot be attributed to the new technologies, issuing rather from a desire for body-to-body communication and a shared process of reproduction. Genuine transformative activity—for example, how to confront unequal power relations—is not triggered by online communication, which can potentially create new forms of discrimination. It is by camping in the same space, solving problems together, cooking together, organizing a cleaning team, confronting the police, all revelatory experiences for thousands of young people raised in front of their computer screens. Not accidentally, one of the most cherished practices in the Occupy movement in New York was the "mic check" of the "human microphone," which was invented because of the police ban on the use of the technological ones, now symbolic of independence from the state and the machine, and a signifier of the collective voice and desire. [19] "Mic check!" people now say on many occasions, even when it is not needed, rejoicing in this affirmation of collective power, the power to make our voices heard regardless of permissions from capital and the state. "Mic check is more powerful than a sword," stated a graphic applied to the pavement of New York's Union Square on the occasion of the May Day mobilization of 2012.

These considerations fly in the face of arguments attributing to the new digital technologies an expansion of our autonomy, and the parallel assumption that those who work at the highest levels of technological development are in the best position to promote revolutionary change. In reality, it is not among the populations that are most technologically advanced from a capitalist viewpoint that we find today the highest level of struggle and confidence in the possibility of transformative action. As Gustavo Esteva's contribution to this book, and Michael Hardt's and Alvaro Reyes's interview with Raúl Zibechi in a special issue of the *South Atlantic Quarterly* indicate, the main examples of "autonomy" come from the struggles and autonomous spaces constructed by the peasant and indigenous communities of South America, which despite centuries of colonization have maintained a close contact with nature and communal organization of reproduction.[20] The material foundations of this world are presently under attack as never before, being the target of an incessant process of enclosures conducted by mining, agribusiness, biofuel, oil companies. That even "progressive" Latin American governments cannot overcome the logic of extractivism is a sign of the depth of the problem. The ongoing assault on lands and waters is compounded by the equally pernicious attempt by the World Bank and a plethora of NGOs to bring all the subsistence-oriented activities that women have created to escape the dominance of the market under the control of monetary relations, through the politics of rural credit and microfinance, which turns multitudes of self-subsistent traders, farmers, and food and care providers into debtors.[21] But despite this attack, this world, which some have called "rurban" to stress its simultaneous reliance on town and country, refuses to wither away. Witness the multiplication of land squatting movements, water wars, and the persistence of communal practices built on relations of reciprocity, like the *tequio*, that continue even among immigrants abroad.[22] Contrary to what the World Bank would tell us, the "farmer"— rural or urban—is a social category not yet destined for the dustbins of history. Some, like the Zimbabwean sociologist Sam Moyo, speak of a process of "re-peasantization," arguing that rural movements presently constitute "the most important source of democratic transformation in national and international politics," and that the drive for land reappropriation, sweeping from Asia to Africa, is possibly the most decisive anticapitalist struggle on earth. In turn, Raúl Zibechi speaks of "societies in movement," stressing that in some South American regions the struggle for land has been replaced by the struggle for "territorial control," a first embryonal forms of self-government.[23]

Other Reasons

What we are witnessing, then, is the beginning of a "transvaluation" of political and cultural values, most visible in the programs and visions of the ecological, indigenous, and feminist movements but more subterraneously operating also in popular culture. Its main political manifestation is the changed identification of the "revolutionary subjects." Whereas the Marxian road to revolution would have factory workers lead the way to communism, increasingly the new paradigms come from those who, working in the fields, kitchens, and fishing villages of the planet, are struggling to disentangle our reproduction from the hold of corporate power and preserve our access to the first, most essential elements of our "commonwealth": the land on which we walk, the seas, the forests that are the material basis of our life. From the Fiat workers to the Zapatistas—from Detroit, world capital of carmaking, to Detroit, center of urban gardening—a realignment of political of actors, objectives, and desires that was unthinkable only two decades ago, among them the importance of land and the reproduction of our material life in the revolutionary process stand out. The novelty, however, is that these questions are no longer only confined to the "Third World" but are now becoming central also in the "North"; witness the "solidarity economies" and movements that have developed out of the ruins of the welfare state and wage labor. Land, here understood as in the culture of the native populations of the Americas, is not only an economic factor, but is also a source of sociality, of new knowledges and spirituality. Another novelty is the decentering of work as a terrain of self-identification, even when it remains an important terrain of struggle. Only in part can this be attributed to the fact that in a regime of precarity work can no longer be a way of life and source of identity-formation. As Chris Carlsson has argued in his *Nowtopia* (2008), his journey through the "other America," the refusal to center one's life on work is also rooted in the search for alternatives to the regimentation of the nine-to-five existence and the need to be more creative.[24] Along the same lines, social struggles today follow a different pattern from that of the traditional strike, reflecting a search for new models of social relations and new relations between human beings and nature. More frequently they spill from the "workplace" into the community, are sparked off by ecological concerns, and seek not only monetary gain but to institute forms of self-management. We see this same trend in the new interest for the discourse and practice of the "commons" that is already spawning new initiatives, like "knowledge commons," time-banks, and accountability structures. We see it also in the growing rejection of the sexual division of labor, as expressed in the preference for *androgynous* models of gender identity, the rise of the Transexual and Intersex movements, and the queer rejection of gender specification. We must also mention the global diffusion of the passion for tattoos and the art of body decoration, which are creating new and imagined communities across sex, race, and class boundaries.[25] All these developments point not only to a breakdown of disciplinary mechanisms, but to a profound desire for a remolding of our humanity in ways very different from, in fact the opposite of, those that centuries of capitalist industrial discipline have tried to impose on us. How profound is the desire for a humanity not shaped by capitalist relations and the industrial organization of our reproduction can be gauged by the popularity achieved in recent years by the movie *Avatar*, iconic in its anti-Cartesian celebration of "savage life," with its complete interpenetration of body and mind, the human, the natural, and the animal, and its celebration of communalism.[26]

Women's struggles over reproductive work play a crucial role in this process. Whether in the form of subsistence farming, or education, or child-raising and domestic labor, there is something unique about this work that makes it especially apt to regenerate our conception of work and its relation to technology, and make us rethink what it could be in a nonexploitative society. Producing crops for subsistence or human beings is in fact a qualitatively different experience from producing cars, as it requires a constant interaction with living processes whose modalities and timing we do not control. As such it potentially generates a deeper understanding of the natural constraints and limits within which we operate, which is essential to the re-enchantment of the world that I propose. It also reminds us that much of the work necessary for the reproduction of human beings cannot be automated, mechanized, industrialized, although communication technologies can make an important contribution to it. For care work does not consist only of physical tasks, but is emotional and affective labor that machines cannot replace.[27] Not accidentally, the attempt to force reproductive work within the parameters of an industrialized organization of work has had especially pernicious effects. Witness the consequences of the industrialization of childbirth, which has turned this potentially magical event into an alienating and even frightening experience, as women now, in most hospitals, give birth on a sort of assembly line, with a uniformly defined time-allotment for delivery, stretched on their backs, in a completely passive position, hooked to several machines, unable to gain strength by listening to the rhythms of their bodies.[28] Not surprisingly, in the wake of the women's liberation movement of the 1970s, movements have emerged demanding a return to more "natural" methods of childbirth, often quickly dismissed as "apolitical," yet on a continuum, in my view, with the logic of the ecological movements and all the movements that today are struggling for control over the means of our reproduction and against the devaluation it has undergone in capitalist society.

In different ways, through these movements, we glimpse the emergence of another rationality, another reason, not only opposed to social and economic injustice but reconnecting with nature, reinventing life as a process of experimentation and in this process redefining what it means to be a human being. This new culture is only on the horizon, for the hold of the capitalist logic on our subjectivity, as I stated at the beginning of this essay, remains very strong. It is sufficient to observe—in the street, on the subway, in the classroom—the compulsion with which younger generations consult their iPhones and iPads to realize how physically and psychologically bonded we still are to the products of the capitalist machine regardless of its ecological and human cost. I am also concerned that many feminists cooperate with the capitalist devaluation of reproduction. Witness the widespread fear of admitting that women can play a special role in the reorganization of reproductive work, evidence of the acceptance of the capitalist conception of what constitutes creative work and an inability to conceive reproductive activities as anything other than drudgery, not only in their present form but also in any possible reorganization of this work. This, in my view, is a mistake. For insofar as it is the material basis of our life and the first terrain on which we can practice our capacity for self-government, reproductive work, whether applied to the maintenance of the ecosystem or the production of human beings, is the "ground zero of revolution."

NOTES

An earlier version of this essay was published in Angela Miles, ed., *Women in a Globalizing World: Transforming Equality, Development, Diversity and Peace* (Toronto, Canada: Inanna, 2013).

1. Max Weber, "Science as a Vocation" [1918–1919], in H. H. Gerth and C. Wright Mills, eds., *For Max Weber: Essays in Sociology*, New York: Oxford University Press, 1946. As he wrote, "[disenchantment] means that principally there are no mysterious incalculable forces that come into play, but rather that one can, in principle, master all things by calculation. This means that the world is disenchanted. One need no longer have recourse to magical means in order to master or implore the spirits, as did the savage, for whom such mysterious powers existed. Technical means and calculations perform the service" (155).

2. See on this matter Saral Sarkar, who argues that "logically, then, a sustainable economy cannot be an industrial one . . . for an industrial economy is based mainly on non-renewable resources." *Eco-Socialism or Eco-Capitalism?: A Critical Analysis of Humanity's Fundamental Choices* (London: Zed Books, 1999), 137.

3. Karl Marx, *Capital*, vol. 1, chap. 15, "Machinery and Large Scale Industry," (London: Penguin 1976), 638, last paragraph.

4. On this matter see Silvia Federici, *Caliban and the Witch: Women, The Body, and Primitive Accumulation* (New York: Autonomedia, 2004), especially chap. 3.

5. This intution of Foucault is referred to in Michael Hardt and Antonio Negri, *Commonwealth* (Cambridge, MA: Harvard University Press, 2009), 31.

6. Vandana Shiva, *Staying Alive: Women, Ecology and Development* (London: Zed Books, 1989).

7. Clifford D. Conner, *A People's History of Science: Miners, Midwives and Low Mechanics* (New York: Nation Books, 2005), 63–64.

8. Conner, *People's History of Science*, 55. Conner also reports that it was from native sailors that European navigators gained the knowledge about winds and currents that enabled them to cross the Atlantic Ocean, 190–92.

9. Jack Weatherford, *Indian Givers: How the Indians of the Americas Transformed the World* (New York: Fawcett Columbine, 1988).

10. Otto Ullrich, "Technology," in Wolfgang Sachs, ed., *The Development Dictionary: A Guide of Knowledge as Power* (London: Zed Books, 1992), 275–87.

11. George Caffentzis, *In Letters of Blood and Fire: Work, Machines and the Crisis of Capitalism* (Oakland: PM Press, 2013), 168–69.

12. Franco "Bifo" Berardi, *Precarious Rhapsody* (New York: Autonomedia, 2009), 32–33. An excellent analysis of this symbiosis as realized in both education and the

military is found in Les Levidow and Kevin Robins, *Cyborg World: The Military Information Society*, London: Free Association Books, 1989.

13. Berardi, *Precarious Rhapsody*. See also, from the same author, *The Soul at Work: From Alienation to Autonomy*, New York: Semiotext(e)/Foreign Agents, 2009. As Jason Smith writes in the preface to this work, "depression starts to look less like a drying up of desire than a stubborn, if painful, libidinal slowdown or sabotage, a demobilization. The 'soul is on strike.'" (12).

14. See Sarkar, *Eco-Socialism or Eco-Capitalism*, 126–27; see also Tricia Shapiro, *Mountain Justice: Homegrown Resistance to Mountain Top Removal for the Future of Us All* (Baltimore: AK Press, 2010).

15. Raphael Samuel, "Mechanization and Hand Labour in Industrializing Britain," in Lenard Berlanstein, ed., *The Industrial Revolution and Work in Nineteenth Century Europe* (London: Routledge, 1992), 26–40.

16. Jerry Mander, *In the Absence of the Sacred: The Failure of Technology and the Survival of the Indian Nations* (San Francisco: Sierra Club Books, 1991), especially chap. 4, "Seven Negative Points about Computers."

17. Renata Salecl, *On Anxiety* (New York: Routledge, 2004).

18. See Paolo Carpignano, "ows: Occupy Everything," in Anna Curcio and Gigi Roggero, eds., *occupy! I movimenti nella crisi globale* (Verona, Italy: Ombre Corte, 2012), 135.

19. See George Caffentzis and Silvia Federici, "Go to Global Revolution," 2011, http://www.edu-factory.org/wp/go-to-global-revolution-report-on-visiting-the-wall-street-occupation/ (link no longer valid). Also Caffentzis, "In the Desert of Cities," in Kate Khatib et al., eds., *We Are Many: Reflections on Movement Strategy from Occupation to Liberation* (Oakland: AK Press, 2012), 389–97.

20. Gustavo Esteva, "Enclosing the Encloser: Autonomous Experiences from the Grassroots beyond Development, Globalization and Postmodernity," paper presented at conference "The Anomie of the Earth," University of North Carolina, Chapel Hill, May 3–5, 2012. Michael Hardt and Alvaro Reyes, "'New Ways of Doing': The Construction of Another World in Latin America: An Interview with Raúl Zibechi," *South Atlantic Quarterly* 111, no. 1 (Spring) 2012: 165–91.

21. See (among others) Graciela Toro Ibanez, *La Pobreza: Un gran negocio*, La Paz, Bolivia: Mujeres Creando, 2006; and Lamia Karim, *Microfinance and Its Discontents: Women in Debt in Bangladesh* (Minneapolis: University of Minnesota Press), 2011.

22. *Tequio* is describe by Wikipedia as a form of collective work, dating back from precolonial Mesoamerica, in which members of a community join their forces and resources for a community project, like a school, a well, a road.

23. Sam Moyo and Paris Yeros, eds., *Reclaiming the Land: The Resurgence of Rural Movements in Africa, Asia and Latin America* (London: Zed Books, 2005), 23, 27.

24. Chris Carlsson, *Nowtopia* (Baltimore, MD: AK Press, 2008).

25. The new passion for tattoos has been described in various ways, as a desire for rituals marking important events, as a means of reappropriating, reclaiming, one's body and a desire to "go primitive," play the "savage," and create tribal forms of identity. What these different functions have in common is a cultural revolt against

the alienation, anomie, loss of agencies experienced in everyday life and the control that the state and other institutions exercise over our bodies.

26. Written and directed by James Cameron, released in 2009, *Avatar* is a science fiction story of a tribal population whose land is threatened by an American mining company but prevails, thanks to the tribe's extraordinary powers, beginning with their neurological connection with the animal and vegetable world, and intense communalism.

27. Federici, "The Reproduction of Labor Power in the Global Economy," in *Revolution at Point Zero* (Oakland: PM Press, 2012), 107.

28. See Robbie Pfeufer Kahn, "Women and Time in Childbirth and Lactation," in Frieda Johles Forman with Caoran Sowton, eds., *Taking Our Time: Feminist Perspectives on Temporality*, New York: Pergamon Press, 1989.

Resonances of the Common

SANDRO MEZZADRA

The attempt to foster a "conceptual dialogue between contemporary movements of dewesternization and the resistance against capitalist labor and biopower coming from workerism and postautonomia," as the editors put it in their introduction, is an important enterprise in itself. This book sets the stage for a dialogue that has already started in recent years in Europe as well as in the Americas and that will hopefully continue in the future. Nevertheless, I must admit that my position in this dialogue is quite ambivalent. Sure, I am Italian and my participation in the autonomist movements in that country was crucial for me both politically and intellectually. I definitely continue to be influenced by the tradition of workerism in my writings and in my practices. But I am also very much interested in the attempt to "provincialize" that tradition, be it through the work I have been doing for many years on migration, through my interest in postcolonial criticism, or through the development of exchanges and relations with people based in many parts of the world (including Latin America).

This is the reason why I will not discuss the chapters of this book, most of which deal with "decolonial" struggles in Latin America, from the point of view of the concept of autonomy as developed within autonomist movements since the 1970s in Italy and other European countries. In fact I will say something about these movements in this afterword, but what interests me more is the broader set of questions underlying the project of this book. Let's list some of them. What are the conditions that make the "geophilosophical" interferences mentioned by the editors possible—and above all productive? Once we acknowledge the relevance of the "location," especially in attempts to "think from and with lived struggles" (Catherine E. Walsh), what is the aim of such interferences and dialogues? I can definitely learn a lot from accounts of indigenous struggles in Canada or in Ecuador, but I do not want to consider the authors of such accounts as a kind of benevolent "native informant" on the particular conditions they describe. So, is there something more at stake here, are there theoretical moments that can resonate well beyond those conditions? And even more generally: is the production of a shared language for the critique of capitalism a valuable goal to be pursued in the present? It is easy to see that such questions, which could be easily multiplied, raise crucial and at the same time vexed topics: simply put, that of universalism in theoretical terms and that of internationalism in political terms.

IF THERE IS something really important I learned from the work of "decolonial" scholars such as Aníbal Quijano and Walter Mignolo, it is precisely the deep implication of the coloniality of power in the production and circulation of knowledge and in the framing of its "geopolitics." It is a question that can productively be articulated in terms of borders (as particularly Mignolo himself has done in recent years). Reading together Carl Schmitt's *The Nomos of the Earth* and Karl Marx's analysis of "the so-called primitive accumulation" in *Capital*, Gavin Walker has for instance recently shown how the "global lines" described by Schmitt corresponded to the tracing of an epistemic border separating Europe (later the West) and "the rest" of the world.[1] This epistemic border has been constantly retraced and reorganized in subsequent centuries, but it has remained a distinctive feature both of international politics and law and of historical capitalism. In a way, to pick up the terms employed in a book I recently published with Brett Neilson (*Border as Method, or, the Multiplication of Labor*, 2013), this epistemic border has played the role of a crucial juncture in the relationship between the expansion of the "frontiers of capital" and the multifarious territorial boundaries upon which the frame of the modern world was politically constructed through conquest, colonialism, and imperialism.[2]

Notwithstanding many attempts to challenge it, this epistemic border has remained relatively stable, and it has infiltrated even into the concepts and the theoretical paradigms of critical and revolutionary thought. I did not mention by accident universalism and internationalism in the same sentence earlier. I think it would be interesting to reconstruct the history of international solidarity within and without the established communist movement from the point of view of the epistemic border between the West and the rest. Powerful tensions and clashes around that border would emerge, crisscrossing the universal language of internationalism itself. I think there is a lot to learn from the archives of internationalism, but I am fully aware that its history is over. Nevertheless it is useful to remember that it was no one less than Jacques Derrida who pointed to the importance of the political invention of internationalism, urging us to think and act within the empty space it has left. "No organized political movement in the history of humanity," Derrida writes in *Specters of Marx*, "had ever yet presented itself as geopolitical, thereby inaugurating the space that is now ours and that today is reaching its limits, the limits of the earth and the limits of the political."[3]

I am not primarily interested here in discussing the perspectives of a new internationalism conceived of as a systematic political project. One could say that something like that is already emerging from within struggles and movements in many parts of the world, and that it will probably bear a new name and definitely speak a new language. But both this name and this language will have to address common characteristics in the profoundly heterogeneous conditions of exploited and dominated subjects living across diverse geographical scales. I am convinced that the production of such a common language, capable of articulating a common desire of liberation, can only be the outcome of a labor of translation, more in the metaphorical (which means, political) than in the literal sense of the word.[4] A critique of the coloniality of power and of the resulting geopolitics of knowledge clearly needs to be part and parcel of any attempt to move in such direction.

Historical internationalism forged a set of conceptual and rhetorical tools that allowed making sense of struggles developing in different geopolitical contexts. The language of solidarity was key to this achievement. At the same time, as I already stated, it reproduced the epistemic as well as the geopolitical borders between the "first" and the "third world," or "center" and "periphery," without challenging their implicit Eurocentric blueprint. Showing solidarity in Italy with the resistance of the Vietnamese people or with the Nicaraguan revolution, to mention two relatively recent examples, definitely meant to "participate" in those struggles. But this "participation" took for granted the "qualitative" difference—and the kind of "metaborder" (to elaborate on Schmitt's *nomos*)—between the European and Western space where the initiatives of solidarity took place and the "other" spaces within which the actual struggles took place. Even crossing the "metaborder," for instance going to Nicaragua for many of my generation was a validation of what I called the "qualitative" difference between the space of origin and the space of destination. Sure, we admired the passion and the resolution of the Sandinistas, we worked hard with the campesinos, we shared their pain and hopes, but the only tool we had to make sense of their experiences and struggles was precisely the language of an abstract solidarity. "Our" experiences and struggles (as well as, in Italy in the early 1980s, our defeat) were of a totally different nature: no doubt on that.

Then, at some time in the 1990s, the political landscape suddenly changed. We started to "participate" in the struggles of the unemployed in Argentina, in the movements of the poor in South Africa and India, discovering that we could learn something useful for organizing "precarious" young people and migrants in Rome and in Milan. We livelily followed the development of peasants' struggles in Latin America, the related debates surrounding the topic of food sovereignty, and the critique of "developmentalism" to take inspiration for our action within environmental struggles in Europe. And these are just a couple of examples. The background of this change was of course the rise of the alterglobalization movement, uprisings against neoliberalism in many parts of the world, demonstrations in Seattle and Genoa, the world social forum in Porto Alegre in Argentina, and the multiplication of meetings as well as of platforms of communication and exchange. There would be a lot to learn from a critical reconstruction of this history, both from its successes and from its failures. But I am more interested here in the kind of lived experience I was evoking earlier, in a reflection on the meaning, the implications, and the challenges implied by the sudden change in the "geopolitical coordinates" of my ("our") own perception of struggles and movements in the so-called global South. I have no full-fledged theoretical framework within which to make sense of that experience (which I have presented in quite personal terms but was not of course a merely personal experience). Nevertheless I am convinced that it is worth interrogating it both from the point of view of the new possibilities it opens and from the one of the meaning it acquires within the "current geopolitical shift," to quote again the editors of this book.

WHAT MAKES THIS book particularly timely is in fact the way in which it intervenes within the spatial disruption we are living through. In this sense I think it is crucial to pick up again the question asked by Arturo Escobar and mentioned by Gustavo Esteva in his chapter: what happens when Europe is "displaced from the center of the historical and epistemic imagination"? Both Escobar and Esteva explore against the background of this question the current Latin American conjuncture, focusing on the "postcapitalist, postliberal, and poststatist" potentialities that they see embodied by some social movements and political processes. "Latin America," Escobar writes, "can be fruitfully seen as a crossroads: a regional formation where critical theories arising from many trajectories (from Marxist political economy and post-structuralism to 'decolonial thought'), a multiplicity of histories and futures, and very diverse cultural and political projects all find a con-vergence space."[5] I find this idea of a multiple and open constitution of a "regional formation" really inspiring. It resonates with debates on "critical regionalism" taking place in other parts of the world and makes an impor-tant contribution to the exploration of the geopolitical potentialities loom-ing behind the "anomie of the earth."

At the same time there is a need to further interrogate from the point of view of the emerging global configurations of power the meaning of this anomie of the earth and the displacement of Europe and the West that we are currently experiencing. What I find intriguing in the image of the "ano-mie" is that it sheds light both on the potentialities (for an alternative po-litical and epistemic imagination) and on the risks enclosed in the current global conjuncture. At the same time, at least in my reading, this image also points to the novelty of this conjuncture from the point of view of what I was calling earlier the articulation between the expanding frontiers of capital and territorial boundaries—or, to put it in the terms employed by world system theorists like Giovanni Arrighi, between capitalism and "territorialism." Re-thinking the work done by Arrighi since *The Long Twentieth Century*, one has to acknowledge, even with a bit of self-criticism in my case, that he was able to grasp in the early days of "globalization" and amid idyllic prophecies of a "new American century" the signs of a decline of the U.S. hegemony.[6] We should analytically insist upon this decline, which is an important aspect of the displacement and provincialization of Europe. Needless to say I do not use the term *decline* with "civilizational" tones (as it was used by conserva-tive authors like Oswald Spengler in Europe during and after World War I). And I am not blind either to the persistent huge concentration of wealth and power in the West or to the epistemic continuities of Eurocentrism in the contemporary world. Nevertheless the scenario of a capitalist world sys-tem without a "Western" center is a concrete possibility for the twenty-first century. It would be quite a rupture within a five-centuries-long history, and there is a need to take stock of its meaning, again both in terms of its potentialities and in terms of its risks.

Arrighi's work allows us to add an important dimension to the history of the Schmittian nomos of the earth, focusing on a series of hegemonic cycles that articulated the European and then Western dominance on a world scale. The relevant question here is whether we are not experiencing a radical change also in this regard. What Gareth Williams writes in chapter 8 about the "invalidation of hegemony theory" inaugurated by what he calls "post-Westphalian decontainment, or globalization" is particularly important. For me the image of the "anomie of the earth" also conveys a sense of the new modalities of connection and disconnection between capitalism and "territorialism" with which we are currently confronted. To be clear, the importance of territory has not diminished in the contemporary world, quite the opposite is the case! But territory tends to "deborder" established legal and political notions of "territoriality."[7] This leads among other things to the multiplication of borders and legal orders that Brett Neilson and I analyze in *Border as Method*. And it also troubles any attempt to map in a stable way the proliferating hierarchical relations between center and periphery, whose geography tends to become more and more multiscalar and, to put it simply, messy. "Development" itself becomes friable under these conditions, the accumulation of wealth coexists with the reproduction of the "wasteland" of poverty and destitution.[8] More than looking for the next hegemonic power, there is a need to focus under these conditions on the emerging variable geometries of power and capitalist development, on the points of condensation of tensions and conflicts that characterize them, on the reproduction of domination, and on the opening up of new political fields of possibility they imply.

Behind this sketch of the current geopolitical shift there is an attempt to understand some of the distinctive features of contemporary capitalism in which readers will easily recognize the lasting influence of my workerist formation and of my participation in the Italian autonomist movement. Again, particularly in the work I do with Brett Neilson, we have tried to take stock of the debates surrounding the "great transformation" of capitalism over the last decades.[9] Without going into the details of such debates, what seems to me interesting here is the question regarding the unity of capitalism and its relation with difference and heterogeneity. Should we "pluralize" the very concept of capital as some critical scholars suggest?[10] Or should we participate in the effort to map "varieties of capitalism" across diverse geographical scales, taking the nation as the prevalent research unit?[11] Working with many sources, for instance with the theory of "variegated capitalism" developed by geographers such as Jamie Peck and Nick Theodore, Neilson and I have tried to follow a different path.[12] Focusing on processes of financialization, in particular, we have outlined an analytic framework for grasping the common features of contemporary capitalism on a global scale that emphasizes its *extractive* dimension. To roughly sum up our argument, looking for instance at the operations of finance, logistics, urban gentrification, extraction in the literal sense, and data mining, it is possible to shed light on a series of crucial moments in the working of contemporary capitalism in which value is "extracted" from nature and from a social cooperation not directly organized by that particular capital (and this is the crucial difference with regard to the operations of industrial capital).

It would be silly to contend that extraction is something new in the history of capital; it rather brings us back to its "primitive accumulation." But it seems to me that the roles currently played by extraction in the extensive sense I just sketched are indeed quite new. Moreover, such roles point to a pattern that really seems to be global, although its manifestations and intensity are clearly differentiated. At the same time, it is important to stress that contemporary capitalism is not to be reduced to its extractive operations. Taken together—this is the research hypothesis—they are nevertheless prevalent in shaping and "commanding" contemporary capitalism. Investigating the extractive operations of capital means to carefully analyze the multiple ways in which they hit the ground, which may seem rather obvious in the case of literal extraction but is no less important in the case of finance or logistics. Which production of space, which production of subjectivity is implied by these operations? Which conceptual tools do we need in order to politically read the struggles against them, to build bridges between different struggles and to multiply their power? These are some of the questions I try to ask. But more important here is to emphasize that the global scope of the extractive operations of capital does not correspond to any homogenization of living and laboring conditions. The opposite is the case: these operations do not merely tolerate, they incite and continuously reproduce a deep heterogeneity.

I KNOW THAT what I have just written may sound abstract and at the same time obscure. I declared that this is a research hypothesis, and only its future development will show whether it is productive or not. But it is important to me to mention it in order at least to evoke the way in which I try to make sense of the spatial disruption and of the continuous processes of rescaling that lie at the heart of contemporary capitalist globalization. New geographies of power and struggle are in the making; even the "epistemic border" between "the West and the rest" has come under duress, but no stable "world order" is in sight. The emerging assemblages of territory, power, law, and capital give rise to variable geometries of domination and interdependence, within which multiple criteria of hierarchization produce a geography far more complex than the one organized around stable center/periphery relations. To the global pressure of the "extractive" operations of capital a deep social, economic, cultural, and political heterogeneity corresponds, not merely between different regions and countries of the world but also, more important, within them.

It is at the forefront of these conditions that the questions I asked at the beginning of this postscript need to be tackled again. And my modest "lived experience" of interchanges across diverse spaces, beyond a mere language of abstract solidarity, acquires its full meaning as a kind of illumination of a new field of possibility, without being of course anything more than an illumination. I must say now that in the experience I was recounting earlier, my long-term relation of friendship and collaboration with the Colectivo Situaciones of Buenos Aires played an outstanding role. Writing soon after the December 2001 "insurrection of a new type" in Argentina, they introduced a concept that seems to me particularly productive not merely from a political but also from a theoretical point of view. It is the concept of "resonance." Resonances, Colectivo Situaciones writes, "presuppose shared epochal problems, certain common obstacles, which make certain knowledges, feelings, and declarations transferable by means of situational compositions."[13] The Colectivo Situaciones introduced the notion of "resonance" in order to foster an attempt to think of a "diffuse network" among experiments in what they called "new social protagonism" in Argentina and more generally in Latin America. What they had in mind was a process of "multiscalar" exchange and organization capable of taking the "multiplicity" (which is also to say the singularity) of struggles not as a "problem" but rather as a resource. Again, this idea of a commonality produced through "resonances" is not the grand theory that will solve all our problems. But it is definitely a powerful hint at the kind of new forms of knowledge production and political practice that are urgently needed in front of the current "anomie of the earth."

One could say that since 1994 this is the way the Zapatista experience and language have traveled through Europe and the Americas, inspiring activists and critical scholars confronted with living conditions and struggles quite different from those of Chiapas. The analysis of the "territorial aspects of the Zapatista conflict" provided here by Alvaro Reyes and Mara Kaufman is a good case in point. Simply put, when they write "the production of space lies at the very heart of contemporary social antagonism," this immediately "resonates" in my mind with the powerful struggles for the "right to the city" in Istanbul, Rio, and other Brazilian cities in May-June 2013. And the "autonomous territorialization" and "spatialization of struggle" Reyes and Kaufman describe in the case of the Zapatistas become for me potentially part of a common language of movements and critical thinking across diverse geographical scales, although it is at the same time absolutely clear that "translating" those phrases onto the material conditions of Istanbul, Rio, or for that matter Rome requires a good deal of labor—both conceptually and politically.

While I have used a couple of times the word "universalism," I am acutely aware of the pitfalls of what Gustavo Esteva calls in his chapter "conventional universalism." If I resist here the temptation to get rid of the very term "universalism," it is because—in its connection with the political notion of "internationalism" that I stressed earlier—it continues to point to a *problem* we have not yet been able to effectively tackle with a new language. And this is the problem of the production of common notions, capable of building a platform of communication and exchange between struggles, experiences of critical thought, counterformations of knowledge across profoundly heterogeneous spatial, political, and cultural coordinates. Breaking with the idea that "Europe" is the site of *humanitas* and thus of theory production, while the "rest" of the world is the realm of *anthropos* (of the "suppliers of raw data and factual information") can only mean, as Naoki Sakai has recently demonstrated, to disrupt the very binary of humanitas and anthropos.[14] Only through this disruption does the chance of a real commonality emerge. And only through this disruption does it become possible to work toward the articulation of a critique of contemporary capitalism that takes stock of the common moments in its operations and of the deep heterogeneity of conditions, experiences, and struggles that corresponds to them.

There are important theoretical and political sides to this task, some of which I have tried to highlight in this afterword. At the same time there is a need to imagine new modalities and above all new positionalities (one could even say a new ethics) of exchange while engaged in such a project. This is again a point I would like to frame in personal terms. While traveling across Latin America and Asia in the last few years I have often thought of a book that is not ostensibly related to these questions, *Democracy and the Foreigner*, by Bonnie Honig.[15] Describing the ways in which the "immigrant" has been historically constructed in the U.S.-American public discourse, she famously distinguishes a "xenophilic" (the immigrant as a "giver") and a "xenophobic" version (the immigrant as the "taker"). For somebody such as myself, living in Europe and with a background of several years of political engagement, this distinction nicely captures the two prevailing attitudes within experiences of "international solidarity" and exchange. One can go to a distant place convinced that one has something to give (the correct "line" in the extreme variant) or thinking that one has something to take, which means to learn. (And here you have a huge amount of possible political or existential variations on the vexed motif of "going native.") Needless to say, as many others have, "I have crossed between the poles" in my own experience, to quote from a famous song. But I have come to the conclusion that, as Bonnie Honig writes regarding the image of the immigrant, this is another binary we have to get rid of. And that, simply put, only when one has something to "give" within a political or intellectual relation is one really able to "take" something (and of course this statement also works the other way around).

ZAC ZIMMER ASKS in chapter 7 a crucial question: "How to articulate a demand for the commons that at once remains open to multiple and heterogeneous subjects, and grounded in the material realities of whatever local situation?" This is a question that troubles and decenters established notions of political subjectivity, while it challenges any idea of essential identity. Moreover it leads us to positively complicate the way in which we conceive of the "commons," a point Zimmer himself grasps when he writes that "any viable notion of the commons—be it material, subjective, biopolitical, or digital—cannot come from a mere inversion or enclosure of a previously appropriated *nomos*." This is a point where I tend to agree with Michael Hardt and Toni Negri.[16] What we need to emphasize is the importance of a reflection on "the common" in singular, which means on the complex and sophisticated processes of organization, on the web of powers and counterpowers, on the social relations and forms of production and reproduction of life that can make something (be it water or knowledge) "a" common "open to multiple and heterogeneous subjects." "Autonomy" is for me an important keyword precisely because it resonates within struggles and movements that try to tackle these problems in many parts of the world. A cartography of "autonomous politics of nature and society," such as the one that this book contributes to drawing, is thus extremely important, because it shows both the achievements of the last decades and the pitfalls and shortcomings of our own political imagination and practices.

Introducing the important collective book *The Politics of Autonomy: Indian Experiences*, Ranabir Samaddar wrote some years ago: "This word, 'autonomy', Michel Foucault, if asked about its mechanics, would probably have read as the signature of governmentality. In this essay, however, we would differ with Foucault to read 'autonomy' as the symbol for the emerging patterns of new spaces in politics, spaces that speak of rights, and justice, the plank for these rights."[17] Taking stock of a long history of aspirations, struggles, claims for justice that speak the language of (territorial as well "nonterritorial") autonomy in the Indian subcontinent, Samaddar is keen to highlight the resulting tensions and clashes with a history of governmentality that since the colonial times has employed the reference to the liberal notion of autonomy as one of its key resources. In each of these tensions and clashes, Samaddar shows, the limits of theories of (national) sovereignty and rights are tested, while in many of them a powerful "principle of innovation" emerges and pushes toward the expansive horizon of "autonomy of autonomies."[18]

What is at stake here, as well as in the debates on commons and the common, is the very constitution of political subjectivity. The intensity of struggles and claims for autonomy that "refuse to be bound by governmental rules of a stable policy" can give way to very different political "translations."[19] These range from the "disconnection" described in several chapters of this book to negotiations, which, in turn, can result in a "recuperation" of the struggles or in the establishment of varying systems of "dualism of power." What counts more for me is not to praise one "model" over the others, but rather to keep the space open for a theoretical interrogation of the multifarious ways in which, "in the material realities of whatever local situation" (Zimmer), the political "intensity" of struggles for autonomy can be developed toward a politics of the common. Intensifying this theoretical interrogation, multiplying "resonances" across diverse locations and heterogeneous experiences, is a crucial political task in front of the current "anomie of the earth."

NOTES

1. Gavin Walker, "Primitive Accumulation and the Formation of Difference: On Marx and Schmitt," *Rethinking Marxism* 23, no. 3 (2011): 384–404.

2. See Sandro Mezzadra and Brett Neilson, *Border as Method, or, the Multiplication of Labor* (Durham, NC: Duke University Press, 2013).

3. Jacques Derrida, *Specters of Marx: The State of the Debt, The Work of Mourning and the New International* (London: Routledge, 2006), 47.

4. See Mezzadra and Neilson, *Border as Method*, chap. 9.

5. Arturo Escobar, "Latin America at a Crossroads: Alternative Modernizations, Post-liberalism or Post-Development?," *Cultural Studies* 24, no. 1 (2010): 3.

6. See Giovanni Arrighi, *The Long Twentieth Century: Money, Power, and the Origins of Our Time* (London: Verso, 1994).

7. See Saskia Sassen, "When Territory Deborders Territoriality," *Territory, Politics, Governance* 1, no. 1 (2013): 21–45.

8. See Kalyan K. Sanyal, *Rethinking Capitalist Development: Primitive Accumulation, Governmentality and the Post-Colonial Capitalism* (London: Routledge, 2007).

9. See Sandro Mezzadra and Brett Neilson, "Extraction, Logistics, Finance: Global Crisis and the Politics of Operations," *Radical Philosophy* 178 (2013): 8–18.

10. John T. Chalcraft, "Pluralizing Capital, Challenging Eurocentrism: Toward Post-Marxist Historiography," *Radical History Review* 91 (2005): 13–39.

11. Peter A. Hall and David Soskice, eds., *Varieties of Capitalism: The Institutional Foundations of Comparative Advantage*, (Oxford: Oxford University Press, 2001).

12. See Jamie Peck and Nick Theodore, "Variegated Capitalism," *Progress in Human Geography* 31, no. 6 (2007): 731–72.

13. Colectivo Situaciones, *19&20: Notes for a New Social Protagonism* (Brooklyn, NY: Autonomedia, 2011), 198.

14. Naoki Sakai, "Theory and the West," in *Transeuropéennes, International Journal of Critical Thought*, August 2, 2011. Accessed October 2014. www.transeuropeennes.eu/en/articles/316/Theory_and_the_West.

15. Bonnie Honig, *Democracy and the Foreigner* (Princeton: Princeton University Press, 2001).

16. Michael Hardt and Toni Negri, *Commonwealth* (Cambridge, MA: Harvard University Press, 2009).

17. Ranabir Samaddar, Introduction to Samaddar, ed., in *The Politics of Autonomy: Indian Experiences* (London: Sage, 2005), 9.

18. Samaddar, Introduction, 24–25.

19. Sabyasachi Basu Ray Chaundhury, Samir Kumar Das, and Ranabir Samaddar, Introduction to Chaundhury et al., eds., *Indian Autonomies: Keywords and Key Texts* (London: Sampark, 2005), ix.

Abensour, Miguel, ed. *Pierre Clastres.* Paris: Sens & Tonka, 2011.

Achterhuis, Hans. "La responsabilita tra il timore e l'utopia." In G. Hottois and M. G. Pinsart, eds., *Hans Jonas: Natura e responsabilita.* Lecce: Edizioni Milella, 1996: 99–110.

Acosta, Alberto. "El retorno del Estado: Primeros pasos postneoliberales, mas no postcapitalistas." *Observatorio Económico de América Latina,* May 8, 2012. www .obela.org/contenido/retorno-del-estado-primeros-pasos-postneoliberales -mas-no-postcapitalistas, accessed Oct. 1, 2014.

Acosta, Alberto. "El uso de la justicia como mecanismo de terror." *El Universo,* February 8, 2011. http://www.eluniverso.com/2011/02/08/1/1363/uso-justicia-como -mecanismo-terror.html, accessed Oct. 15, 2014.

Acosta, Alberto. "Toward the Universal Declaration of Rights of Nature, Thoughts for Action." 2010. Latin America in Movement, http://alainet.org/images /Acosta%20DDNN_ingl.pdf, accessed Oct. 1, 2014.

Adorno, Rolena. *Polemics of Possession in Spanish American Narrative.* New Haven, CT: Yale University Press, 2007.

Agamben, Giorgio. *Homo Sacer: Sovereign Power and Bare Life.* Trans. Daniel Heller-Roazen. Palo Alto: Stanford University Press, 1998.

Agamben, Giorgio. *Means without End: Notes on Politics.* Trans. Vincenzo Binetti and Cesare Casarino. Minneapolis: University of Minnesota Press, 2000.

Agamben, Giorgio. *The Open: Man and Animal.* Trans. Kevin Attell. Stanford, CA: Stanford University Press, 2004.

Agamben, Giorgio. *The Signature of All Things.* Trans. Luca D'Isanto with Kevin Atell. New York: Zone Books, 2009.

Agamben, Giorgio. *The State of Exception.* Trans. Kevin Attell. Chicago: University of Chicago Press, 2005.

Allison, David B., ed. *The New Nietzsche.* Cambridge, MA: MIT Press, 1985.

Althusser, Louis. *Philosophy of the Encounter: Later Writings 1978–1987.* Trans. G. M. Goshgarian. London: Verso, 2006.

Anghie, Antony. *Imperialsim, Sovereignty and the Making of International Law.* Cambridge: Cambridge University Press, 2004.

Anon. *At Daggers Drawn with the Existent, Its Defenders and Its False Critics.* Trans. Jean Weir with John Moore and Leigh Stracross. London: Elephant Editions, 2001. http://alphabetthreat.co.uk/elephanteditions/pdf/atdaggersdrawn.pdf, accessed Oct. 1, 2014.

Arendt, Hannah. *The Origins of Totalitarianism.* New York: Meridian Books, 1958.

Aristotle. *The Politics.* Bk. 1. Trans. H. Rackham. New York: Putnam, 1934.

Arneil, Barbara. *John Locke and America: The Defense of English Colonialism*. New York: Oxford University Press, 1996.

Arrighi, Giovanni. *The Long Twentieth Century: Money, Power, and the Origins of Our Time*. London: Verso, 1994.

Aspe, Bernard. *Les mots et les actes*. Caen, France: NOUS, 2012.

Badiou, Alain. *Being and Event* [1988], Trans. and intro. Oliver Feltham. London: Continuum, 2005.

Badiou, Alain. *Deleuze: The Clamor of Being* [1997]. Trans. Louise Burchill. Minneapolis: University of Minnesota Press, 2000.

Bakunin, Mikhail. "The Reaction in Germany" [from *Notebooks of a Frenchman*, October 1842]. Trans. and ed. Sam Dolgoff. Marxists Internet Archive, www.marxists.org/reference/archive/bakunin/works/1842/reaction-germany.htm, accessed Oct. 1, 2014.

Balakrishnan, Gopal. "The Convolution of Capitalism." In Craig Calhoun and Georgi Derlugian, eds., *Business as Usual: The Roots of the Global Financial Meltdown*. New York: New York University Press, 2011, 211–30.

Barker, Joanne. "For Whom Sovereignty Matters." In Barker, *Sovereignty Matters: Locations of Contestation and Possibility in Indigenous Struggles for Self-Determination*. Lincoln: University of Nebraska Press, 2005.

Bataille, Georges. "Hegel, Death and Sacrifice." Trans. Jonathan Strauss. *Yale French Studies* 78, 1990: 9–28.

Baudrillard, Jean. "When Bataille Attacked the Metaphysical Principle of Economy" [1976]. In *Bataille: A Critical Reader*, ed. Fred Botting and Scott Wilson. Oxford: Blackwell, 1998: 139–45.

Beasley-Murray, Jon. *Posthegemony: Political Theory and Latin America*. Minneapolis: University of Minnesota Press, 2010

Becker, Marc. *Pachakutik: Indigenous Movements and Electoral Politics in Ecuador*. Lanham, MD: Rowman and Littlefield, 2011.

Bellida, Maria Soledad. "Interculturalidad y pluralismo jurídico." *Derecho: Revista de la Facultad de Derecho* (2008). www.unsa.edu.pe/escuelas/de/rev . . . /093–100_08_MBellidoA01.pdf, (link no longer valid).

Bellinghausen, Hermann. "La otra campaña, opción para agrupar a las organizaciones campesinas en lucha." *La Jornada* (Mexico City), March 1, 2007.

Benson, S. "Inscriptions of the Self: Reflections on Tattooing and Piercing in Contemporary Euro-America." In J. Caplan, ed., *Written on the Body: The Tattoo in European and American History*. Princeton, NJ: Princeton University Press, 2000: 234–54.

Berardi, Franco "Bifo." *Precarious Rhapsody*. New York: Autonomedia, 2009.

Berardi, Franco "Bifo." *The Soul at Work: From Alienation to Autonomy*. New York: Semiotext(e)/Foreign Agents, 2009.

Berger, John. *And Our Faces, My Heart, Brief as Photos*. New York: Pantheon Books, 1984.

Berlanstein, Lenard R., ed. *The Industrial Revolution and Work in Nineteenth-Century Europe*. London: Routledge, 1992.

Blaser, Mario. *Storytelling Globalization from the Chaco and Beyond.* Durham: Duke University Press, 2010.

Blumenfeld, Jacob, Chiara Bottici, and Simon Critchley, eds. *The Anarchist Turn.* London: Pluto, 2013.

Bonanno, Alfredo M. *From Riot to Insurrection.* Trans. Jean Weir. London: Elephant Editions, 2009.

Bosteels, Bruno. "The Speculative Left." *South Atlantic Quarterly* 104, no. 4 (Fall) 2005: 751–67.

Bosteels, Bruno. "The Obscure Subject: Sovereignty and Geopolitics in Carl Schmitt's The Nomos of the Earth." In William Rasch, ed., "World Orders: Confronting Carl Schmitt's *The Nomos of the Earth*," special issue, *South Atlantic Quarterly* 104, no. 2 (Spring 2005): 295–305.

Briceño, Hector. "Ejecutados 150 mil en 7 Años, alcaldes" [Mayors: 150,000 executed in 7 years]. *La Jornada* (Mexico City), April 9, 2012.

Brown, Wendy. *Walled States, Waning Sovereignty.* New York: Zone Books, 2010.

Budgen, Sebastian, Stathis Kouvelakis, and Slavoj Zizek. Introduction to *Lenin Reloaded: Toward a Politics of Truth.* Durham, NC: Duke University Press, 2007:

Caffentzis, George. "In the Desert of the Cities." In Kate Khatib et al., eds., *We Are Many: Reflections on Movement Strategy from Occupation to Liberation.* Oakland, CA: AK Press, 2012: 389–97.

Caffentzis, George. *In Letters of Blood and Fire: Work, Machines and the Crisis of Capitalism.* Oakland: PM Press, 2013.

Caffentzis, George, and Silvia Federici. "Go to Global Revolution—Report on Visiting the Wall Street Occupation." 2011. Edu-Factory, www.edu-factory.org/wp/go-to-global-revolution-report-on-visiting-the-wall-street-occupation/, (link no longer valid).

Caplan, J., ed. *Written on the Body: The Tattoo in European and American History.* Princeton, NJ: Princeton University Press.

Capuzzo, Paolo, and Sandro Mezzadra. "Provincializing the Italian Reading of Gramsci." In Neelam Srivastava and Baidik Bhattacharya, eds., *The Postcolonial Gramsci.* New York: Routledge, 2011: 34–54.

Carpignano, Paolo. "ows: Occupy Everything." In Anna Curcio and Gigi Roggero, eds., *OCCUPY! I movimenti nella crisi globale.* Verona: Ombre Corte, 2012: 129–35.

Casanova, Pablo Gonzalez. "Otra política, muy otra: Los Zapatistas del siglo XXI" [A very other politics: The Zapatistas of the 21st century], *La Jornada* (Mexico City), January 26, 2013: 2.

Casarino, Cesare and Antonio Negri, *In Praise of the Common: A Conversation on Philosophy and Politics.* Minneapolis: University of Minnesota Press, 2009.

Casas Cortes, Maribel, Sebastian Cobarrubias, and John Pickles. "Re-bordering the Neighbourhood: Europe's Emerging Geographies of Non-accession Integration." *Journal of European Urban and Regional Studies* 20, no. 1 (January 2013): 37–58.

Castellanos, Laura. *Corte de Caja: Una Entrevista al Subcomandante Marcos*. Neza-hualcoyotl, Mexico: Grupo Editorial Endira Mexico, 2008.

Castro, Gustavo, and Miguel Pickard. "Los Derechos Economicos y Sociales en Chiapas: Salud y Educación." Pt. 2. *CIEPAC Bulletin*, no. 163, July 25, 1999. www.ciepac.org/boletines/chiapasaldia.php?id=163, accessed Oct. 1, 2014.

Centro de Analisis Multidisciplinario. "Reporte Número108, Política Contra la Pobreza: 42 años de fracaso" [Report 108: Anti-poverty policy: 42 years of failure]. Mexico City: UNAM, April 2013.

Chakrabarty, Dipesh. "The Climate of History: Four Theses." *Critical Inquiry* 35, 2009: 197–222.

Chalcraft, John T. "Pluralizing Capital, Challenging Eurocentrism: Toward Post-Marxist Historiography." *Radical History Review* 91, 2005: 13–39.

Chaundhury, Sabyasachi Basu Ray, Samir Kumar Das, and Ranabir Samaddar, eds. *Indian Autonomies: Keywords and Key Texts*. Calcutta: Sampark, 2005.

"Chickasaw and Choctaw Nations File Motion for Partial Summary Judgment." Press release, Chickasaw Media Relations Office, February 14, 2012. Official website of the Chickasaw Nation, https://www.chickasaw.net/News/Press-Releases/2012-Press-Releases/Chickasaw-and-Choctaw-Nations-File-Motion-for-Part.aspx, accessed Oct. 1 2014.

Chiesa, Lorenzo, and Alberto Toscano. *The Italian Difference*. Melbourne, Australia: Re: Press, 2009.

Chiesa, Lorenzo, and Frank Ruda. "The Event of Language as Force of Life: Agamben's Linguistic Vitalism." *Angelaki* 16, no. 3 (2011): 163–80.

Chow, Rey. *Writing Diapsora: Tactics of Intervention in Contemporary Cultural Studies*. Bloomington: Indiana University Press, 1993.

Clastres, Pierre. *La Sociétié contre l'État*. Paris: Éditions de Minuit, 2011.

Clastres, Pierre. *Recherches d'anthropologie politique*. Paris: Éditions du Seuil, 1980.

Clastres, Pierre. *Society against the State: Essays in Political Anthropology*. New York: Zone Books, 1989.

Colectivo Situaciones. *19&20: Notes for a New Social Protagonism*. Brooklyn, NY: Autonomedia, 2011.

Conner, Clifford D. *A People's History of Science: Miners, Midwives and Low Mechanics*. New York: Nation Books, 2005.

Cooper, Melinda. *Life as Surplus: Biotechnology and Capitalism in the Neoliberal Era*. Seattle: University of Washington Press, 2008.

Copjec, Joan. "The Sexual Compact." *Angelaki* 17, no. 2 (2012): 31–48.

Cornejo Polar, Antonio. *Escribir en el aire: Ensayo sobre la heterogeneidad socio-cultural en las literaturas andinas*. Lima, Peru: Editorial Horizonte, 1994.

Coronado, Jorge. *The Andes Imagined: Indigenismo, Society, and Modernity*. Pittsburgh, PA: University of Pittsburgh Press, 2009.

Council of Good Government of Oventic. "Second Encounter between Zapatista Peoples and Peoples of the World." Oventic, Chiapas, Mexico: July 21, 2007.

Crespo, Carlos. "Tipnis y autonomía." Blog entry, December 10, 2012. http://anarquia cochabamba.blogspot.com/2012/12/tipnis-y-autonomia.html, accessed Oct. 1, 2014.

Crombie, Alistair. *Styles of Scientific Thinking in the European Tradition: The History of Argument and Explanation Especially in the Mathematical and Biomedical Sciences and Arts*. London: Duckworth,1994.

Cuevas, J. H. *Salud y Autonomía: El caso Chiapas*. Report for the Health Systems Knowledge Network. World Health Organization, March 2007. http://www.who .int/social_determinants/resources/csdh_media/autonomy_mexico_2007_es.pdf, accessed Oct. 1, 2014.

Curcio, Anna, and Gigi Roggero, eds. *OCCUPY! I movimenti nella crisi globale*. Verona, Italy: Ombre Corte, 2012.

Danowski, Déborah, and Eduardo Viveiros de Castro. *L'arrêt de monde*. Trans. Oiara Bonilla. Paris: Éditions Dehors, 2014.

Dávalos, Pablo. "La Democracia Disciplinaria: El Proyecto Posneoliberal Para América Latina" [Disciplinary democracy: The postneoliberal project for Latin America]. Quito, Ecuador: CODEU, 2011.

Davis, Mike. "Artisans of Terror." In *In Praise of Barbarians: Essays against Empire*. Chicago: Haymarket Books, 2007: 263–77.

Dean, Jodi. *Communist Horizon*. London: Verso, 2012.

Deleuze, Gilles. "Capitalism, Flows, the Decoding of Flows, Capitalism and Schizophrenia, Psychoanalysis, Spinoza." Cours Vincennes, November 16, 1971. www .webdeleuze.com/php/texte.php?cle=116&groupe=Anti+Oedipe+et+Mille+Plateau x&langue=2, accessed Oct. 1, 2014.

Deleuze, Gilles. *Foucault*. Trans. Seán Hand. London: Athlone Press, 1988.

Deleuze, Gilles. *Nietzsche and Philosophy* [1962]. Trans. Hugh Tomlinson. New York: Columbia University Press, 1983.

Deleuze, Gilles, and Félix Guattari. *Anti-Oedipus: Capitalism and Schizophrenia I*. Trans. Robert Hurley, Mark Seem, and Helen R. Lane. London: Continuum, 2004.

Deleuze, Gilles, and Félix Guattari. *A Thousand Plateaus*. Trans. Brian Massumi. London: Continuum, 2004.

Deleuze, Gilles, and Félix Guattari. "Capitalism: A Very Special Delirium." In *Chaosophy*, ed. Sylvere Lothringer. Los Angeles: Autonomedia/Semiotexte, 1995. Generation Online, www.generation-online.org/p/fpdeleuze7.htm, accessed Oct. 1, 2014.

Deleuze, Gilles, and Félix Guattari. *What Is Philosophy?* Trans. Hugh Tomlinson and Graham Burchell. New York: Columbia University Press, 1994.

Denning, Michael. "Wageless Life." *New Left Review* 66 (2010): 79–97.

Derrida, Jacques. *The Beast and the Sovereign*. Vol. 1. Trans. Geoffrey Bennington. Chicago: University of Chicago Press, 2009.

Derrida, Jacques. *Politics of Friendship*. Trans. George Collins. New York: Verso, 1997.

Derrida, Jacques. *Specters of Marx: The State of the Debt, the Work of Mourning and the New International*. London: Routledge, 2006.

Descola, Philippe. *Beyond Nature and Culture*. Trans. Janet Lloyd. Chicago: University of Chicago Press, 2013.

Duncan, Richard. *The New Depression: The Breakdown of the Paper Money Economy*. Hoboken, NJ: Wiley, 2012.

Ejército Zapatista de Liberación Nacional (EZLN). *Cronicas Intergalacticas: Primer Encuentro Intercontinental por la Humanidad y contra el Neoliberalismo.* Montañas del Sureste Mexicano: Planeta Tierra, 1997.

Ejército Zapatista de Liberación Nacional (EZLN). "Ellos Y Nosotros: Los Mas Pequeños" [Them and us: The smallest of them all]. Enlace Zapatista. www .enlacezapatista.ezln.org.mx, accessed Oct. 1, 2014.

Ejército Zapatista de Liberación Nacional (EZLN). "Escucharon?" [Did you hear that?]. Enlace Zapatista. www. enlacezapatista.ezln.org.mx/2012/12/21 /comunicado-del-comite-clandestino-revolucionario-indigena-comand ancia-general-del-ejercito-zapatista-de-liberacion-nacional-del-21-de-diciembre del-2012/, accessed Oct. 1, 2014.

Ejército Zapatista de Liberación Nacional (EZLN). "Informe de 1 año de la junta de buen gobierno corazón céntrico de los zapatistas delante del mundo." Episode of *Radio Insurgente: La voz de los sin voz,* broadcast September 24, 2004. www .radioinsurgente.org, accessed Oct. 1, 2014.

Ejército Zapatista de Liberación Nacional (EZLN). "To the Soldiers and Command- ers of the Popular Revolutionary Army." Communiqué. August 29, 1996. Flag. Blackened.Net. http://flag.blackened.net/revolt/mexico/ezln/ezln_epr_se96.html, accessed Oct. 1, 2014.

Elden, Stuart. "Missing the Point: Globalization, Deterritorialization and the Space of the World." *Transactions of the Institute of British Geographers* 30, no. 1 (2005): 8–19.

Elden, Stuart. "Reading Schmitt Geopolitically." *Radical Philosophy* 161 (May–June 2010), 18–26.

El Kilombo Intergaláctico. *Beyond Resistance, Everything: An Interview with Subco- mandante Insurgente Marcos.* Durham, NC: Paperboat Press, 2008.

Endnotes. "Misery and Debt: On the Logic and History of Surplus Populations and Surplus Capital." *Endnotes* 2 (2010). http://endnotes.org.uk/articles/1, accessed Oct. 1, 2014.

Escobar, Arturo. "Latin America at a Crossroads: Alternative Modernizations, Post- liberalism or Post-Development?" *Cultural Studies* 24, no. 1 (2010): 1–65.

Escobar, Arturo. "Whose Knowledge, Whose Nature? Biodiversity, Conservation and the Political Ecology of Social Movements." *Journal of Political Ecology* 5 (1998): 53–82.

Esteva, Gustavo. "A Celebration of Zapatismo." *Humboldt Journal of Social Relations* 29 (2005): 127–67.

Esteva, Gustavo. "Der laufende Aufstand." In Projectgruppe "Zivilisationspolitik," ed., *Kann es eine "neue Erde" geben? Zur "Kritischen Patriarchatstheorie" under der Praxis einer postpatriachalen Zivilisation.* Frankfurt: Peter Lang, 2012: 233–72.

Esteva, Gustavo. "Enclosing the Encloser: Autonomous Experiences from the Grass- roots beyond Development, Globalization and Postmodernity." Paper presented at conference "The Anomie of the Earth," University of North Carolina, Chapel Hill, May 3–5, 2012.

Esteva, Gustavo. "Enclosing the Enclosers." Turbulence Collective, *What Would It Mean to Win?* Oakland, CA: PM Press, June 2007.

Esteva, Gustavo. "From the Bottom-Up: New Institutional Arrangements in Latin America." *Development* 53, no. 1 (March 2010): 64–69.

Esteva, Gustavo. "La crisis como esperanza." *Bajo el volcán* 8, no. 1 (2009): 17–54.

Esteva, Gustavo. "Los quehaceres del día." In Gabriela Massuh, ed., *Renunciar al bien común: Extractivismo y (pos)desarrollo en América Latina*. Buenos Aires, Argentina: Mardulce, 2012: 237–82.

Fanon, Frantz. *The Wretched of the Earth*. Trans. Richard Philcox. New York: Grove Press, 2004.

Federici, Silvia. *Caliban and the Witch: Women, the Body, and Primitive Accumulation*. New York: Autonomedia, 2004.

Federici, Silvia. "The Reproduction of Labor Power in the Global Economy." In *Revolution at Point Zero, Housework, Reproduction and Feminist Struggle*. Oakland: PM Press, 2012.

Fixico, Donald, ed. *Treading with American Indians: An Encyclopedia of Rights, Conflicts, and Sovereignty*. Santa Barbara: ABC-CLIO, 2008.

Flores Galindo, Alberto. *In Search of an Inca: Identity and Utopia in the Andes*. Trans. Carlos Aguirre and Charles Walker. New York: Cambridge University Press, 2010.

Ford, Lisa. *Settler Sovereignty: Jurisdiction and Indigenous People in America and Australia, 1788–1836*. Cambridge, MA: Harvard University Press, 2011.

Foucault, Michel. *The Birth of Biopolitics: Lectures at the Collège de France, 1978–79*. Trans. Graham Burchell. Basingstoke, UK: Palgrave, 2008.

Foucault, Michel. *The Order of Things*. London: Tavistock/Routledge, 1974.

Foucault, Michel. *Society Must Be Defended; Lectures at the Collège de France, 1975–76*. Ed. Mauro Bertani and Alessandro Fontana. Trans. David Macey. New York: Picador, 1997.

Foucault, Michel. *"Society Must Be Defended": Lectures at the Collège de France, 1975–1976*. Trans. David Macey. New York: Picador, 2003.

Frank, Andre Gunder. *Re-Orient: Global Economy in the Asian Age*. Los Angeles: University of California Press, 1995.

Galeano, Eduardo. "Global Fear." https://groups.google.com/forum/#!topic/red-tulips/cdsVGZiID9g, accessed Oct. 1, 2014.

Galeano, Eduardo. "We Must Stop Playing Deaf to Nature" [2008]. In Galeano, *The Rights of Nature*. San Francisco: Council of Canadians, Fundación Pachamama, and Global Exchange, 2011: 68–70.

Galli, Carlo. *Political Spaces and Global War*. Ed. Adam Sitze. Trans. Elisabeth Fay. Minneapolis: University of Minnesota Press, 2010.

Gentili, Dario. *Italian Theory: Dall'operaismo alla biopolitica*. Bologna, Italy: Il Mulino, 2012.

Goldberg-Hiller, Jonathan, and Noenoe K. Silva. "Sharks and Pigs: Animating Hawaiian Sovereignty against the Anthropological Machine." *South Atlantic Quarterly* 110, no. 2 (Spring 2011): 429–46.

Goldstein, Alyosha. "Where the Nation Takes Place: Proprietary Regimes, Anti-statism, and U.S. Settler Colonialism." *South Atlantic Quarterly* 107, no. 4 (Fall 2008): 833–61.

Gonçalves, Carlos W. Porto. "Da geografia às geo-grafias—um mundo em busca de novas territorialidades." In Ana Esther Ceceña and Emir Sader, eds., *La guerra infinita—hegemonía y terror mundial*. Buenos Aires, Argentina: Clacso, 2002: 217–56.

Graeber, David. *Fragments of an Anarchist Anthropology*. Chicago: Prickly Paradigm Press, 2004.

Gramsci, Antonio. *Prison Notebooks*. 3 vols. Ed. Joseph A. Buttigieg. New York: Columbia University Press, 1992.

Gramsci, Antonio. *Selections from the Prison Notebooks*. Ed. Quintin Hoare and Geoffrey Nowell Smith. New York: International, 1971.

Green, Natalia. "The First Successful Case of the Rights of Nature Implementation in Ecuador." Global Alliance for the Rights of Nature, 2013. http://therightsofnature.org/first-ron-case-ecuador/, accessed Oct. 1, 2014.

Grosfoguel, Rámon. "Transmodernity, Border Thinking, and Global Coloniality: Decolonizing Political Economy and Postcolonial Studies," 2008. Eurozine, www.eurozine.com/articles/2008-07-04-grosfoguel-en.html, accessed Oct. 1, 2014.

Gudynas, Eduardo. "The New Extractivism of the 21st Century: Ten Urgent Thesis about Extractivism in Relation to Current South American Progressivism." In *Americas Program Report*. Washington, DC: Center for International Policy, January, 21, 2010. www.iadb.org/intal/intalcdi/PE/2010/04716.pdf, accessed Oct. 1, 2014.

Guéhenno, Jean-Marie. *The End of the Nation-State*. Trans. Victoria Elliott. Minneapolis: University of Minnesota Press, 1995.

Hacking, Ian. "Styles of Scientific Reasoning." In J. Rajchman and C. West, eds., *Post-analytic Philosophy*. New York: Columbia University Press, 1985: 145–65.

Hall, Peter A., and David Soskice, eds. *Varieties of Capitalism: The Institutional Foundations of Comparative Advantage*. Oxford: Oxford University Press, 2001.

Hall, Stuart. "Cultural Studies and Its Theoretical Legacies." In Lawrence Grossberg, Cary Nelson, and Paula Treichler, eds., *Cultural Studies*. New York: Routledge, 1992: 277–94.

Hallward, Peter. *Out of This World: Deleuze and the Philosophy of Creation*. London: Verso, 2006.

Hallward, Peter. "The Politics of Prescription." *South Atlantic Quarterly* 104 (2005): 769–89.

Hanke, Lewis. *Aristotle and the American Indians: A Study in Race Prejudice in the Modern World*. Bloomington: Indiana University Press, 1970.

Hardt, Michael, and Antonio Negri. *Commonwealth*. Cambridge, MA: Harvard University Press, 2009.

Hardt, Michael, and Antonio Negri. *Declaration*. New York: Argo Navis, 2012.

Hardt, Michael, and Antonio Negri. *Empire*. Cambridge, MA: Harvard University Press, 2000.

Hardt, Michael, and Antonio Negri. "The Fight for 'Real Democracy' at the Heart of Occupy Wall Street." *Foreign Affairs.* New York: Council on Foreign Affairs, Oct. 11, 2011. www.foreignaffairs.com/articles/136399/michael-hardt-and-antonio negri/the-fight-for-real-democracy-at-the-heart-of-occupy-wall-street, accessed Oct. 1, 2014.

Hardt, Michael, and Alvaro Reyes. "'New Ways of Doing': The Construction of Another World in Latin America: An Interview with Raúl Zibechi." *South Atlantic Quarterly* 111, no. 1 (Spring 2012): 165–91.

Harney, Stefano, and Fred Moten. *The Undercommons: Fugitive Planning and Black Study.* Brooklyn, NY: Autonomedia, 2013.

Harrison, John, and Peter Laslett, eds. *The Library of John Locke.* 2nd ed. Oxford: Clarendon Press, 1971.

Hart, Keith, Jean-Louis Laville, and Antonio David Cattani, eds. *The Human Economy: A Citizen's Guide.* London: Polity Press, 2010.

Harvey, David. "The Enigma of Capital and the Crisis This Time." In Craig Calhoun and Georgi Derlugian, eds., *Business as Usual: The Roots of the Global Financial Meltdown.* New York: New York University Press, 2011: 89–112.

Harvey, David. *The New Imperialism.* Oxford: Oxford University Press, 2003.

Harvey, David. *Reading Marx's Capital.* http://davidharvey.org/2008/06/marxs-capital -class-01/), accessed Oct. 1, 2014.

Harvey, David. *A Companion to Marx's "Capital."* London: Verso, 2010.

Hegel, Georg W. F. *The Phenomenology of Spirit.* Trans. Terry Pinkard. 2010. https:// dl.dropboxusercontent.com/u/21288399/Phenomenology%20translation%20En glish%20German.pdf, accessed Oct. 1, 2014.

Heidegger, Martin. *Parmenides.* Trans. André Schuwer and Richard Rojewicz. Blomington: Indiana University Press, 1992.

Heidegger, Martin. "The Question Concerning Technology." In Heidegger, *The Question Concerning Technology and Other Essays.* New York: Harper and Row, 1977: 3–35.

Hell, Julia. "*Katechon*: Carl Schmitt's Imperial Theology and the Ruins of the Future." *Germanic Review* 84, no. 4 (2009): 283–318.

Henríquez, Pablo Gonzalez Casanova. "El Zapatismo avanza ante el desastre." *La Jornada* (Mexico City), January 24, 2009.

Henríquez, Pablo Gonzalez Casanova, et al. "La Situación de la Nutrición de las y los niños preescolares en la selva, frontera y altos de Chiapas durante la crisis bélica y social de 1994." *Revista CIMECH* 6, no. 1–2 (1996): 1–32.

Hobbes, Thomas. *Leviathan.* Ed. Edwin Curley. Indianapolis, IN: Hackett, 1994.

Hobbes, Thomas. *On the Citizen.* Ed. Richard Tuck and Michael Silverthorne. New York: Cambridge University Press, 1998.

Hoelzl, Michael. "Before the Anti-Christ Is Revealed: On the Katechontic Structure of Messianic Time." *The Politics to Come: Power, Modernity, and the Messianic.* Ed. Paul Fetcher and Arthur Bradley. London: Continuum Books, 2010: 98–199.

Holland, Eugene W. *Deleuze and Guattari's "Anti-Oedipus": Introduction to Schizo-analysis.* London: Routledge, 1999.

Honig, Bonnie. *Democracy and the Foreigner*. Princeton: Princeton University Press, 2001.

Horswell, Michael. *Decolonizing the Sodomite*. Austin: University of Texas Press, 2005.

Illich, Ivan, Robert Fox, and Robert Theobald. "A Call to Celebration." In Illich, *Celebration of Awareness*. London: Marion Boyars, 1971: 13–18.

Invisible Committee. *The Coming Insurrection*. 2009. Tarnac 10. http://tarnac9.files .wordpress.com/2009/04/thecominsur_booklet.pdf, 84, accessed Oct. 1, 2014.

Hsueh, Vicki. "Cultivating and Challenging the Common: Lockean Property, Indigenous Traditionalisms, and the Problem of Exclusion." *Contemporary Political Theory* 5, no. 2 (May 2006): 193–214.

Hsueh, Vicki. "Giving Orders: Theory and Practice in the *Fundamental Constitutions of Carolina*." *Journal of the History of Ideas* 63, no. 3 (July 2002): 425–46.

Hsueh, Vicki. "Unsettling Colonies: Locke, 'Atlantis,' and New World Knowledges." *History of Political Thought* 29, no. 2 (Summer 2008): 295–319.

Jameson, Fredric. *The Hegel Variations: On the "Phenomenology of Spirit."* London: Verso, 2010.

Jameson, Fredric. "Marxism and Dualism in Deleuze." *South Atlantic Quarterly* 96, no. 3 (1997): 393–417.

Jameson, Fredric. "Notes on the 'Nomos.'" *South Atlantic Quarterly* 104, no. 2 (Spring 2005): 199–204.

Jameson, Fredric. "Of Islands and Trenches: Naturalization and the Production of Utopian Discourse." *Diacritics* (June 1977): 2–21.

Jappe, Anselm. *Crédit á Mort: La decomposition du capitalism et ses critiques* [Credit unto death: The decomposition of capital and its critiques]. Paris: Éditions Lignes, 2011.

Jappe, Anselm. *Guy Debord*. Trans. Donald Nicholson-Smith. Berkeley: University of California Press, 1999.

Johles Forman, Frieda, and Caoran Sowton, eds. *Taking Our Time: Feminist Perspectives on Temporality*. New York: Pergamon Press, 1989.

Kane, Adrian Taylor, ed. *The Natural World in Latin American Literatures*. Jefferson, NC: McFarland, 2010.

Karim, Lamia. *Microfinance and Its Discontents: Women in Debt in Bangladesh*. Minneapolis: University of Minnesota Press, 2011.

Khatib, Kate, et al., eds. *We Are Many: Reflections on Movement Strategy from Occupation to Liberation*. Oakland: AK Press, 2012.

Khatibi, Abdelkebir. "Maghreb Plural." In Walter Mignolo, ed., *Capitalismo y geopolítica del conocimiento: El eurocentrismo y la filosofía de la liberación en el debate intelectual contemporáneo*. Buenos Aires, Argentina: Ediciones del signo, 2001: 71–92.

Kishore, Mahbubani. *The New Asian Hemisphere: The Irreversible Shift to the East*. New York: Public Affairs, 2008.

Klausen, Jimmy Casas. "Room Enough: America, Natural Liberty, and Consent in Locke's *Second Treatise*." *Journal of Politics* 69, no. 3 (August 2007): 760–69.

Klein, Naomi. "The Most Important Thing in the World." In Sarah van Gelder et al. eds., *This Changes Everything*. San Francisco, CA: Berret-Koehler, 2011: 45–49.

Kohr, Leopold. "Size Cycles." *Fourth World Review* 54 (1992): 10–11.

Kojève, Alexandre. *Outline of a Phenomenology of Right.* Trans. Bryan-Paul Fox and Robert Howse. Lanham, MD: Rowman and Littlefield, 2007.

Kouvelakis, Stathis. *Philosophy and Revolution: From Kant to Marx.* London: Verso, 2003.

Koyré, Alexandre. *From the Closed World to the Infinite Universe.* Hideyo Noguchi Lecture. Baltimore, MD: Johns Hopkins University Press, 1968.

Kwa, Chunglin. *Styles of Knowing: A New History of Science from Ancient Times to the Present.* Pittsburgh, PA: University of Pittsburgh Press, 2011.

Laclau, Ernesto, and Chantal Mouffe. *Hegemony and Socialist Strategy: Towards a Radical Democratic Politics.* New York: Verso, 2001.

La Mettrie, Julien Offray de. *L'Homme Machine* [1748]. In La Mettrie, *Machine Man and Other Writings,* trans. and ed. Ann Thomson. Cambridge: Cambridge University Press, 1996: 1–40.

Lander, Edgardo. "Crisis civilizatorio: El tiempo se agota." In *Sumak Kawsay/ Buen Vivir y cambios civilizatorios,* coord. Irene León. Quito: Fedaeps, 2010: 27–40.

Larsen, Neil. "Indigenism, Cultural Nationalism, and the Problem of Universality." In Larsen, *Reading North by South: On Latin American Literature, Culture, and Politics.* Minneapolis: University of Minnesota Press, 1995: 132–39.

Lash, Scott. "Life (Vitalism)." *Theory, Culture & Society* 23, no. 2–3 (2006): 323–49.

Le Bot, Yvon, and Subcomandante Marcos. *El Sueno Zapatista: Entrevistas con el subcomandante Marcos, el mayor Moises y el comandante Tacho, del Ejercito Zapatista de Liberacion Nacional.* Barcelona: Plaza y Janes, 1997.

Lebovics, Herman. "The Uses of America in Locke's *Second Treatise of Government.*" *Journal of the History of Ideas* 47, no. 4 (October–December 1986): 567–81.

Lefebvre, Henri. *The Production of Space.* Trans. Donald Nicholson-Smith. Malden, MA: Blackwell, 1991.

Lenin, Vladimir I. "The Dual Power." In *Lenin Collected Works,* vol. 24. Moscow: Progress Publishers, 1964: 38–41. Marxists Internet Archive, www.marxists.org /archive/lenin/works/1917/apr/09.htm, accessed Oct. 1, 2014.

Levidow, Les, and Kevin Robins. *Cyborg World: The Military Information Society.* London: Free Association Books, 1989.

Lévi-Strauss, Claude. *The Savage Mind.* Trans. John and Doreen Weightman. London: Weidenfeld and Nicolson, 1972.

Locke, John. *Second Treatise of Civil Government* [1690]. Buffalo: Prometheus Books, 1986.

Locke, John. "Second Treatise of Government." In *The Selected Political Writings of John Locke.* Ed. Paul E. Sigmund. New York: Norton, 2005.

Locke, John. *Two Treatises of Government: Second Treatise.* Cambridge: Cambridge University Press, 2004.

López de Palacios Rubios, Juan, *El Requerimiento,* 1513, www.encyclopediavirginia.org /El_Requerimiento_by_Juan_Lopez_de_Palacios_Rubios_1513, accessed Oct. 15, 2014.

Lowe, Lisa. "The Intimacy of Four Continents." In Ann Laura Stoler, ed., *Haunted by Empire: Geographies of Intimacy in North American History*. Durham, NC: Duke University Press, 2006: 191–212.

Lucero, Jose Antonio. *Voices of Struggle: The Politics of Indigenous Representation in the Andes*. Pittsburgh, PA: University of Pittsburgh Press, 2008.

Luisetti, Federico. "The Savage Decolonialist: Notes on Critical Exoticism." *Comparative Studies in Modernism: Literature, Law, Philosophy and the Arts* 1 (2012): 49–53.

Luisetti, Federico. *Una vita: Pensiero selvaggio e filosofia dell'intensità*. Milan, Italy: Mimesis, 2011.

Macpherson, C. B. *The Political Theory of Possessive Individualism: Hobbes to Locke*. New York: Oxford University Press, 1962.

Macpherson, C. B. *Property: Critical and Mainstream Positions*. Toronto: University of Toronto Press, 1978.

Maldonado-Torres, Nelson. *Against War: Views from the Underside of Modernity*. Durham, NC: Duke University Press, 2008.

Mandarini, Matteo. "Antagonism, Contradiction, Time: Conflict and Organization in Antonio Negri." *The Sociological Review* 53, no. 1: 192–214.

Marcos, Sylvia. *Taken from the Lips: Gender and Eros in Mesoamerica*. Boston: Brill, 2006.

Mariátegui, José Carlos. *José Carlos Mariátegui: An Anthology*. Ed. and trans. Harry E. Vanden and Marc Becker. New York: Monthly Review Press, 2011.

Mariátegui, José Carlos. *Siete ensayos de interpretación de la realidad peruana*. Lima, Peru: Biblioteca Amautu, 1998.

Mariátegui, José Carlos. *Textos básicos*. Ed. Aníbal Quijano. Lima and Mexico, D.F.: Fondo de Cultura Económica, 1991.

Martin, Stewart. "Artistic Communism—A Sketch." *Third Text* 23, no. 4 (2009): 481–94.

Marx, Karl. *Capital*. Vol. 1. London: Penguin, 1976.

Marx, Karl. *Grundrisse: Foundations of the Critique of Political Economy*. New York: Penguin Books, 1973.

May, Todd. *The Political Philosophy of Poststructuralist Anarchism*. University Park: Pennsylvania State University Press, 1994.

Mbembe, Achille. "Necropolitics." Trans. Libby Meintjes. *Public Culture* 15, no. 1 (2003): 11–40.

McLeod, Neal. *Cree Narrative Memory: From Treaties to Contemporary Times*. Saskatoon, Canada: Purich, 2009.

Melitopoulos, Angela, and Maurizio Lazzarato. "Assemblages: Félix Guattari and Machinic Animism." 2012. E-Flux, www.e-flux.com/journal/assemblages-felix-guattari-and-machinic-animism/, accessed Oct. 1, 2014.

Mezzadra, Sandro. "The Topicality of Prehistory: A New Reading of Marx's Analysis of So-Called Primitive Accumulation." *Rethinking Marxism: A Journal of Economics, Culture & Society* 23, no. 3 (2011): 302–21.

Mezzadra, Sandro, and Brett Neilson. *Border as Method, or, the Multiplication of Labor*. Durham, NC: Duke University Press, 2013.

Mezzadra, Sandro, and Brett Neilson. "Extraction, Logistics, Finance. Global Crisis and the Politics of Operations." *Radical Philosophy* 178 (2013): 8–18.

Mignolo, Walter D. "Coloniality at Large: The Western Hemisphere in the Colonial Horizon of Modernity." *New Centennial Review* 1, no. 2 (2001): 19–54. http://muse.jhu.edu/journals/ncr/summary/v001/1.2mignolo.html, accessed Oct. 1, 2014.

Mignolo, Walter D. *The Darker Side of the Renaissance: Literacy, Territoriality and Colonization*. Ann Arbor: University of Michigan Press, 1995.

Mignolo, Walter D. *The Darker Side of Western Modernity: Global Futures, Decolonial Options*. Durham, NC: Duke University Press, 2011.

Mignolo, Walter. "Epistemic Disobedience and the De-colonial Option: A Manifesto." 2007. *Transmodernity*. http://waltermignolo.com/txt/publicaitons/papers lectures/Epistemic_Disobedience_and_the_Decolonial_Option_a_Manifesto.doc, accessed Oct. 1, 2014.

Miller, Robert J. *Reservation "Capitalism": Economic Development in Indian Country*. Santa Barbara, CA: ABC-CLIO, 2012.

More, Thomas. *The Complete Works of St. Thomas More*. Vol. 4. Ed. Edward Surtz and J. H. Hexter. New Haven, CT: Yale University Press, 1965.

Moreiras, Alberto. *Línea de sombra: El no sujeto de lo politico*. Santiago: Palinodia Editores, 2006.

Moyo, Sam, and Paris Yeros, eds. *Reclaiming the Land: the Resurgence of Rural Movements in Africa, Asia and Latin America*. London: Zed Books, 2005.

Muller, Jan-Werner. *A Dangerous Mind: Carl Schmitt in Post-war European Thought*. New Haven, CT: Yale University Press, 2003.

National Institute of Geography and Statistics (INEGI). "Censo General de Población y Vivienda 2000." www.inegi.org.mx/est/contenidos/Proyectos/ccpv/cpv2000/default.aspx, accessed Oct. 1, 2014.

Navarro, Luis Hernández. "The Zapatistas Can Still Change the Rules of Mexican Politics." *Guardian*, December 31, 2012.

Negri, Antonio. *Art and Multitude*. Trans. E. Emery. Cambridge: Polity, 2011.

Negri, Antonio. "The Constitution of Time." In Negri, *Time for Revolution*. Trans. M. Mandarini. London: Continuum, 2003: 21–138.

Negri, Antonio. *Dall'operaio massa all'operaio sociale: Intervista sull'operaismo*. Verona: Ombre Corte, 2007.

Negri, Antonio. "Domination and Sabotage: On the Marxist Method of Social Transformation" [1977]. In Negri, *Books for Burning*, trans. Arianna Bove et al., ed. Timothy S. Murphy. London: Verso, 2005: 231–90.

Negri, Antonio. *The Savage Anomaly*. Trans. Michael Hardt. Minneapolis: University of Minnesota Press, 1999.

Newman, Saul. *From Bakunin to Lacan*. Lexington: Lexington Books, 2001.

Newman, Saul, ed. *Max Stirner*. Critical Explorations in Contemporary Thought series. Basingstoke: Palgrave Macmillan, 2011.

Newman, Saul. *Power and Politics in Poststructuralist Thought: New Theories of the Political*. London: Routledge. 2005.

Nieto, Mauricio. "Historia natural y la apropiación del nuevo mundo en la ilustración española." *études andines* 32, no. 3 (2003): 417–29.

Nietzsche, Friedrich. *The Gay Science*. Trans. Walter Kaufman. New York: Vintage Books, 1974.

Novatore, Renzo. *The Collected Writings of Renzo Novatore*. Trans. Wolfi Landstreicher. Berkeley: Ardent Press, 2012.

Noys, Benjamin. "'Grey in Grey': Change, Crisis, Critique." *Journal of Critical Globalisation Studies* 4 (February 2011): 45–60, www.criticalglobalisation.com/Issue4 /45_60_GREY_IN_GREY_JCGS4.pdf, accessed Oct. 1, 2014.

Noys, Benjamin. *The Persistence of the Negative: A Critique of Contemporary Continental Theory*. Edinburgh: Edinburgh University Press, 2010.

Nunes, Rodrigo. "Politics in the Middle: For a Political Interpretation of the Dualisms in Deleuze and Guattari." In "Deleuze and Political Activism," ed. Marcelo Svirsky, pecial issue, *Deleuze Studies* 4 (2010): 104–26.

O'Brien, Jean M. *Firsting and Lasting: Writing Indians out of Existence in New England*. Minneapolis: University of Minnesota Press, 2010.

Ochao, Todd R. *Society of the Dead: Quita Manaquita and Palo Praise in Cuba*. Berkeley: University of California Press, 2010.

O'Gorman, Edmundo. *La invención de América*. Mexico: Fondo de Cultura Económica, 2006.

Ornelas, Raúl. "La autonomía como eje de la resistencia Zapatista." In *Hegemonias y Emancipaciones en el Siglo XXI*, ed. Ana Esther Ceceña. Buenos Aires: CLASCO, 2004.

"Our Oklahoma. Our Water." YouTube video. Posted by "OK Water," March 16, 2012. www.youtube.com/watch?v=ezj8tZoEFJU, accessed September 9, 2014.

Pagden, Anthony. "Conquest and Settlement." In *Lords of All the World: Ideologies of Empire in Spain, Britain and France c. 1500–c. 1800*. New Haven, CT: Yale University Press, 1998: 63–102.

Pagden, Anthony. *The Fall of Natural Man: The American Indian and the Origins of Comparative Ethnology*. Cambridge: Cambridge University Press, 1982.

Panikkar, Raimón. "The Myth of Pluralism." In Panikkar, *Invisible Harmony*. Minneapolis: Fortress Press, 1995: 52–91.

Parekh, Bhikhu. "Liberalism and Colonialism: A Critique of Locke and Mill." In Jan Nederveen Pieterse and Bhikhu Parekh, eds., *The Decolonization of Imagination: Culture, Knowledge, and Power*. London: Zed Books, 1995: 81–98.

Pastor, Beatriz. "Utopía y conquista: Dinámica utópica e identidad colonial." *Revista de crítica literaria latinoamericana* 19, no. 38 (1993): 105–13.

Peck, Jamie, and Nik Theodore. "Variegated Capitalism." *Progress in Human Geography* 31, no. 6 (2007): 731–72.

Pfeufer, Robbie Kahn. "Women and Time in Childbirth and Lactation." In Frieda Johles Forman and Caoran Sowton, eds., *Taking Our Time: Feminist Perspectives on Temporality*. Oxford: Pergamon Press, 1988: 20–36.

Pickles, John. *A History of Spaces: Cartographic Reason, Mapping, and the Geo-Coded World*. New York: Routledge, 2004.

Pickles, John, Sebastian Cobarrubias, and Maribel Casas-Cortes. "Commons." In Don M. Nonini, ed., *A Companion to Urban Anthropology*. New York: Wiley, 2014: 449–69.

Pickles, John, Sebastian Cobarrubias, and Maribel Casas-Cortes. "Le regard cartographique, les nouvelles cartographies des frontiers, et les responsabilites du cartographe" [The cartographic gaze, new cartographies of the border, and the responsibility of mapping]. In Kantuta Quiros and Aliocha Imhoff, eds., *Géoesthétique*. Paris: B42, 2014: 37–53.

Porto-Gonçalves, Carlos Walter. *Territorialidades y La Lucha Por El Territorio en América Latina* [Territorialities and the struggle for territory in Latin America]. Caracas: Instituto Venezolano de Ciencia y Tecnologia, 2012.

Porto-Gonçalves, Carlos Walter, and Enrique Leff. "Political Ecology in Latin America: The Social Reappropriation of Nature, the Reinvention of Territories and the Construction of an Environmental Rationality." In *Encyclopedia of Life Support Systems (EOLSS)*. Oxford: Eolss, 2013.

Povinelli, Elizabeth A. *Economies of Abandonment: Social Belonging in Late Liberalism*. Durham, NC: Duke University Press, 2011.

Prada, Raúl. "Horizontes del vivir bien." *Revista Praxis en América Latina* 8 (May–June 2012): 4–12. www.praxisenamericalatina.org/4-12/horizontes.html, accessed Oct. 1, 2014.

Prada, Raúl. "Umbrales y horizontes de la descolonización." In Alvaro García Linea, Raúl Prada, Luis Tapia, Oscar Vega Camacho, eds., *El Estado: Campo de lucha*. La Paz: Muela de Diablo and CLACSO, 2010: 43–96.

Pratt, Mary Louise. *Imperial Eyes: Travel Writing and Transculturation*. New York: Routledge, 1992.

Quijano, Aníbal. "América Latina: Hacia un nuevo sentido histórico." In *Sumak Kawsay/Buen Vivir y cambios civilizatorios*, coord. Irene León. Quito, Ecuador: Fedaeps, 2010: 55–72.

Quijano, Aníbal. "Modernity, Identity, and Utopia in Latin America." In ohn Beverley, José Oviedo, and Michael Aronna, eds., *The Postmodernism Debate in Latin America*. Durham, NC: Duke University Press, 1995: 201–16.

Ramírez, Gloria Muñoz. "Interview with Subcomandante Marcos: A Time to Ask, a Time to Demand, and a Time to Act." January 16, 2004. *Americas Program*, www.cipamericas.org/archives/1120, accessed Oct. 1, 2014.

Rasch, William, ed. "World Orders: Confronting Carl Schmitt's *The Nomos of the Earth*." Special issue, *South Atlantic Quarterly* 104, no. 2 (Spring 2005).

Righi, Andrea. *Biopolitics and Social Change in Italy: From Gramsci to Pasolini to Negri*. New York: Palgrave Macmillan, 2011.

Roa, Ivan. "El desborde de la violencia: Raza, capital y grupos armados en la expansion transnacional de la palma aceitera en Nariño y Esmeraldas." Quito: Flacso, 2011.

Rostworowski, Maria. *History of the Inca Realm*. Trans. Harry B. Iceland. Cambridge: Cambridge University Press, 1998.

Sachs, Wolfgang. *The Development Dictionary: A Guide of Knowledge as Power.* London: Zed Books, 1992.

Sakai, Naoki. "Theory and the West." *Transeuropéennes*, 2011. www.transeuropeennes .eu/en/articles/316/Theory_and_the_West, accessed Oct. 1, 2014

Salecl, Renata. *On Anxiety.* New York: Routledge, 2004.

Samaddar, Ranabir, ed. *The Politics of Autonomy: Indian Experiences.* London: Sage, 2005.

Samuel, Raphael. "Mechanization and Hand Labour in Industrial Britain." In Lenard R. Berlanstein, ed., *The Industrial Revolution and Work in Nineteenth-Century Europe.* London: Routledge, 1992: 26–43.

Sánchez, Pérez H., M. Arana Cedeño, and A. Yamin. "Pueblos Excluidos, Comunidades Erosionadas: La Situación del Derecho a la Salud en Chiapas, Mexico." Boston: Physicians for Human Rights and El Colegio de la Frontera Sur, Centro de Capacitación en Ecologia y Salud para Campesino, 2006.

Sanders, C. R. *Customizing the Body: The Art and Culture of Tattooing.* Philadelphia: Temple University Press, 1989.

Sanyal, Kalyan K. *Rethinking Capitalist Development: Primitive Accumulation, Governmentality and the Post-colonial Capitalism.* London: Routledge, 2007.

Sarkar, Saral. *Eco-Socialism or Eco-Capitalism? A Critical Analysis of Humanity's Fundamental Choices.* London: Zed Books, 1999.

Sassen, Saskia. "When Territory Deborders Territoriality." *Territory, Politics, Governance* 1, no. 1 (2013): 21–45.

Schmitt, Carl. *The Nomos of the Earth in the International Law of the Jus Publicum Europaeum.* Trans. G. L. Ulmen. New York: Telos Press, 2003.

Schmitt, Carl. *Political Theology: Four Chapters on the Concept of Sovereignty.* Trans. George D. Schwab. Cambridge, MA: MIT Press, 1985.

Scott, James C. *Two Cheers for Anarchism.* Princeton: Princeton University Press, 2012.

Secretaria de Reforma Agraria, Estados Unidos de Mexico. "Acuerdo por el que se declara el cierre operativo y conclusión de Programa de Certificación de Derechos Ejidales y Titulación de Solares (PROCEDE)." *Diario Oficial*, November 17, 2006.

Seed, Patricia. *Ceremonies of Possession in Europe's Conquest of the New World, 1492–1640.* Cambridge: Cambridge University Press, 1995.

Sepúlveda, J. G. D. *De Regno.* Pozoblanco, Spain: Ayutamiento de Pozoblanco, 2001.

Shanin, Teodor, Gustavo Esteva, and Teodor Shanin. "Pensar todo de nuevo: anti-capitalismos sin socialismo." *Bajo el volcán* 11, no. 18 (March–August 2012): 93–120.

Sharma, Nandita, and Cynthia Wright. "Decolonizing Resistance, Challenging Colonial States." *Social Justice* 35, no. 3 (2008–2009): 93–111.

Shiva, Vandana. *Staying Alive: Women, Ecology and Development.* London: Zed Books, 1989.

da Silva, Denise Ferreira. *Toward a Global Idea of Race.* Minneapolis: University of Minnesota Press, 2007.

Silver, Beverly, and Giovanni Arrighi. "The End of the Long Twentieth Century." In Craig Calhoun and Georgi Derlugian, eds., *Business as Usual: The Roots of the Global Financial Meltdown.* New York: New York University Press, 2011, 53–68.

Simpson, Leanne. *Dancing on Our Turtle's Back: Stories of Nishnaabeg Re-creation, Resurgence and New Emergence.* Winnipeg: Arbeiter Ring, 2011.

Smith, Andrea. "Indigeneity, Settler Colonialism, White Supremacy." In Daniel Martinez HoSang, Oneka LaBennett, and Laura Pulido, eds., *Racial Formation in the Twenty-First Century.* Berkeley: University of California Press, 2012: 66–90.

de Sousa Santos, Boaventura. *La globalización del derecho: Los nuevos caminos de la regulación y la emancipación.* Bogotá: Universidad Nacional de Colombia, 1998.

Speed, Shannon, and Alvaro Reyes. "'In Our Own Defense': Rights and Resistance in Chiapas, Mexico." *Political and Legal Anthropology Review* 25, no. 1 (May 2002): 69–89.

Spivak, Gayatri Chakravorty. *A Critique of Postcolonial Reason: Toward a History of the Vanishing Present.* Cambridge, MA: Harvard University Press, 1999.

Stirner, Max. *The Ego and His Own.* Trans. Steven T. Byington. London: Verso, 1907.

Streeten, Paul. "Strategies for Human Development: Global Poverty and Unemployment." In Streeten, *The Political Economy of Fighting Poverty.* Geneva: ILO, 1995.

Subcomandante Marcos, EZLN. "The Fourth World War." Chiapas, November 20, 1999, *La Jornada,* October 23, 2001.

Subcomandante Marcos. "La Treceava Estela." Pt. 5, July 2003. EZLN, http://palabra .ezln.org.mx, accessed Oct. 1, 2014

Subcomandante Marcos. "La Treceava Estela." Pt. 6, July 2003. EZLN, http://palabra .ezln.org.mx, accessed Oct. 1, 2014

Surin, Kenneth. *Freedom Not Yet: Liberation and the New World Order.* Durham, NC: Duke University Press, 2009.

Surin, Kenneth. "The Sovereign Individual, 'Subalternity,' and Becoming-Other." *Angelaki* 6, no. 1 (2001): 47–63.

Tari, Marcello. *Autonomie! Italie, les années 70.* Paris: Éditions la Fabrique, 2011.

Tarizzo, Davide. "The Untamed Ontology." Trans. Alvise Sforza Tarabochia. *Angelaki* 16, no. 3 (2011): 53–61.

Taussig, Michael. "I'm So Angry I Made a Sign." In W. J. T. Mitchell, Bernard E. Harcourt, and Michael Taussig, *Occupy: Three Inquiries in Disobedience.* Chicago: University of Chicago Press, 2013: 3–43.

Tinker, George. *Spirit and Resistance: Political Theology and American Indian Liberation.* Minneapolis: Fortress Press, 2004.

Tiqqun. *Introduction to Civil War.* Trans. Alexander R. Galloway and Jason E. Smith. Los Angeles: Semiotext(e), 2010.

Tiqqun. *Tout a failli, vive le communisme!* Paris: La Fabrique, 2009.

Toscano, Alberto. "Carl Schmitt in Beijing: Partisanship, Geopolitics, and the Demolition of the Eurocentric World." *Postcolonial Studies* 11, no. 4 (2008): 417–33.

Toscano, Alberto. "Chronicles of Insurrection: Tronti, Negri and the Subject of Antagonism." *Cosmos and History: The Journal of Natural and Social Philosophy* 5, no. 1 (2009): 76–91.

Tronti, Mario. "Our Operaismo." *New Left Review* 73 (January–February 2012): 119–39.

Tuck, Richard. *The Rights of War and Peace: Political Thought and the International Order from Grotius to Kant.* Oxford: Oxford University Press, 1999.

Tully, James. *A Discourse on Property: John Locke and His Adversaries*. Cambridge: Cambridge University Press, 1980.

Tully, James. "Property Disputes." In Tully, *An Approach to Political Philosophy: Locke in Contexts*. Cambridge: Cambridge University Press, 1993: 69–176.

Twiss, Richard. "Richard Twiss: A Theology of Manifest Destiny." YouTube video. Posted by Wicon International, March 7, 2008. www.youtube.com/watch ?v=4mEkMy1KNWo.

Ullrich, Otto. "Technology." In Wolfgang Sachs, ed., *The Development Dictionary: A Guide of Knowledge as Power*. London: Zed Books, 1992: 275–87.

U.S. Census Bureau. "The American Indian and Alaska Native Population: 2010." *2010 Census Briefs*, issued January 2012. www.census.gov/prod/cen2010/briefs /c2010br-10.pdf, accessed Oct. 1, 2014

van der Haar, Gemma. "El movimiento zapatista de Chiapas: Dimensiones de su lucha." 2005. Labour Again Publications, International Institute of Social History, www.iisg.nl/labouragain/ruralmobilisation.php, accessed Oct. 1, 2014.

Vatter, Miguel. "Biopolitics: From Surplus Value to Surplus Life." *Theory & Event* 12, no. 2 (2009). DOI: 10.1353/tae.0.0062.

Virno, Paolo. *Multitude: Between Innovation and Negation*. Trans. Isabella Bertoletti, James Cascaito, and Andrea Casson. New York: Semiotext(e), 2008.

Viveiros de Castro, Eduardo. *From the Enemy's Point of View: Humanity and Divinity in an Amazonian Society*. Trans. Catherine V. Howard. Chicago: Chicago University Press, 1992.

Viveiros de Castro, Eduardo. *The Inconstancy of the Indian Soul*. Trans. Gregory Duff Morton. Chicago: University of Chicago Press, 2011.

Viveiros de Castro, Eduardo. *Métaphysiques Cannibales*. Paris: Presses Universitaires de France, 2009.

Walker, Gavin. "On Marxism's Field of Operation: Badiou and the Critique of Political Economy." *Historical Materialism* 20, no. 2 (2012): 39–74.

Walker, Gavin. "Primitive Accumulation and the Formation of Difference. On Marx and Schmitt." *Rethinking Marxism* 23, no. 3 (2011): 384–404.

Wallerstein, Immanuel. "The Dynamics of (Unresolved) Global Crisis." In Craig Calhoun and Georgi Derlugian, eds., *Business as Usual: The Roots of the Global Financial Meltdown*. New York: NYU Press, 2011, 69–88.

Walsh, Catherine. *Interculturalidad crítica y (de)colonialidad: Ensayos desde Abya Yala*. Quito, Ecuador: Abya-Yala ediciones, 2013.

Walsh, Catherine. *Interculturalidad, Estado, Sociedad: Luchas (de)coloniales de nuestra época*. Quito, Ecuador: Universidad Andina Simón Bolívar/Abya-Yala Ediciones, 2009.

Walsh, Catherine. "Life, Nature, and Gender Otherwise: Reflections and Provocations from the Andes." In Wendy Harcourt and Ingrid Nelson, eds., *Moving Beyond the Green Economy: Connecting Lives, Natures and Genders Otherwise*. London: Zed Books, 2015.

Walsh, Catherine. "The (Re)articulation of Political Subjectivities and Colonial Difference in Ecuador: Reflections on Capitalism and the Geopolitics of Knowledge." *Nepantla: Views from South* 3, no. 1 (2002): 61–97.

Walsh, Catherine, and Juan García. "El pensar del emergente movimiento afroecuatoriano: Reflexiones (des)de un proceso." In *Estudios y otras prácticas intelectuales latinoamericanos en cultura y poder*, coord. Daniel Mato. Buenos Aires, Argentina: Clacso, 2002: 317–26.

Washington, George, to James Duane, September 7, 1783. In *Documents of United States Indian Policy* [1975], ed. Francis Paul Prucha. 3rd ed. Lincoln: University of Nebraska Press, 2000: 1–2.

Weatherford, Jack. *Indian Givers: How the Indians of the Americas Transformed the World*. New York: Fawcett Columbine, 1988.

Weber, Max. "Science as a Vocation." [1918–19]. In H. H. Gerth and C. Wright Mills, eds., *For Max Weber: Essays in Sociology*. New York: Oxford University Press, 1946: 155.

Westerman, Pauline C. *The Disintegration of Natural Law Theory: Aquinas to Finnis*. Leiden: Brill, 1998.

Wilkins, David E., and Tsianina Lomawaima. *Uneven Ground: American Indian Sovereignty and Federal Law*. Norman: University of Oklahoma Press, 2001.

Williams, Leonard, and Brad Thomson. "The Allure of Insurrection." *Anarchist Developments in Cultural Studies* 1 (2011): 226–89. www.anarchist-developments .org/index.php/adcs/article/view/47/54, accessed Oct. 1, 2014.

Williams, Robert A., Jr. *Like a Loaded Weapon: The Rehnquist Court, Indian Rights, and the Legal History of Racism in America*. Minneapolis: University of Minnesota Press, 2005.

Williams, Robert A., Jr. *Savage Anxieties: The Invention of Western Civilization*. New York: Palgrave MacMillan, 2012.

Wood, Ellen Meiksins. *Liberty and Property: A Social History of Western Political Thought from Renaissance to Enlightenment*. New York: Verso, 2012.

Wright, Steve. *Storming Heaven: Class Composition and Struggle in Italian Autonomist Marxism*. London: Pluto, 2002.

Zapatista. Dir. Benjamin Eichert, Richard Rowley, and State Sandberg. Big Noise Films, 2001.

Zapatistas. Fourth Declaration of la Selva de Lacandona. January, 1996.Flag.Blackened.Net, http://flag.blackened.net/revolt/mexico/ezlnco.html, accessed Oct. 1, 2014.

Zibechi, Raúl. "The Art of Governing the Movements." In *Territories of Resistance: A Cartography of Latin American Social Movements*, trans. Ramor Ryan. Oakland: AK Press, 2012: 266–98.

Zibechi, Raúl. "Carta de Raúl Zibechi: Un Nuevo Nacimiento" [Letter from Raúl Zibechi: A rebirth]. Nov. 13, 2012 www.ezln.org.mx /2012/11/13/eco-mundial-en apoyo-de-ls-zapatistas-carta-de-raul-zibechi-un-nuevo-nacimiento/, accessed Oct. 1, 2014.

Zibechi. Raúl. *Dispersar el poder*. Guadalajara, Mexico: La Casa del Mago, 2006.

Zibechi, Raúl. *Territories in Resistance: A Cartography of Latin America's Social Movements*. Translated from the Spanish by Ramor Ryan. Baltimore: AK Press, 2012.

Zinn, Howard. "The Art of Revolution." In Herbert Read, ed., *Anarchy and Order: Essays on Politics*. Boston: Beacon Press, 1954: ix–xxii.k, Slavoj. "How the Non-duped Err." In *Qui Parle* 4, no. 1 (Fall 1990): 1–20.

Žižek, Slavoj. *Less Than Nothing*. London: Verso Books, 2012.

Žižek, Slavoj. *The Parallax View*. Cambridge, MA: MIT Press, 2006.

JOOST DE BLOOIS is Assistant Professor at the University of Amsterdam, Department of Literary Studies and Cultural Analysis, and a member of the Amsterdam School for Cultural Analysis. His publications include "The Last Instance: Deconstruction as General Economy" (2010) and "A Postscript to Transgression: The Gothic in Georges Bataille's Dissident Avant-Gardism" (2007).

JODI A. BYRD is Associate Professor of English and American Indian Studies at the University of Illinois, Urbana-Champaign. She has written numerous articles on Indigenous studies. Her other research interests include indigenous and postcolonial literatures, cultural studies, film, and theory. She is the author of *The Transit of Empire: Indigenous Critique of Colonialism* (2011).

GUSTAVO ESTEVA is the founder of the Universidad de la Tierra in Oaxaca, Mexico. Well known as an advocate of postdevelopment theory, his many publications include *Grassroots Post-Modernism: Remaking the Soil of Cultures* (1998, with Madhu Suri Prakash), and *The Oaxaca Commune and Mexico's Autonomous Movements* (2008).

SILVIA FEDERICI is Professor Emerita of Social Science at Hofstra University. She is also the cofounder of the Committee for Academic Freedom in Africa. Her books include *Caliban and the Witch: Women, the Body and Primitive Accumulation* (2004) and *Revolution at Point Zero: Housework, Reproduction, and Feminist Struggle* (2012).

WILSON KAISER is Assistant Professor of English at Edward Waters College. His publications include "The Micro-politics of Fascism in Carson McCullers's *The Heart Is a Lonely Hunter* and Sinclair Lewis's *It Can't Happen Here*," *Genre* 48, no. 1, and "David Foster Wallace and the Ethical Challenge of Posthumanism," *Mosaic* 47, no. 3. He is currently working on a monograph titled *American Literature and the Politics of Everyday Life*.

MARA KAUFMAN is a postdoctoral Lecturing Fellow in the Thompson Writing Program at Duke University. She holds a Ph.D. in cultural anthropology from Duke University.

FRANS-WILLEM KORSTEN holds joint appointments in literary studies at the University of Leiden and culture and communication at the Erasmus University,

Rotterdam. His research investigates the entanglement of aesthetics and politics in literature. His publications include "Moments of Indecision, Sovereign Possibilities—Notes on the Tableau Vivant" (2009), and "The Irreconcilability of Hypocrisy and Sincerity" in *The Rhetoric of Sincerity* (2008).

FEDERICO LUISETTI is Professor of Italian Studies, comparative literature, and communication studies at the University of North Carolina, Chapel Hill. His research and publications address topics in philosophy and cultural theory and visual and literary studies, with a focus on naturalism and the avant-gardes. He is the author of *Una vita: Pensiero selvaggio e filosofia dell'intensità* (2011); *Estetica dell'immanenza: Saggi sulle parole, le immagini e le macchine* (2008), and *Plus Ultra: Enciclopedismo barocco e modernità* (2001).

SANDRO MEZZADRA studied philosophy and political science at the University of Genoa and the University of Bologna, and received his Ph.D. from the University of Turin in 1993. He has been a research fellow of the Alexander von Humboldt Stiftung and the Max Planck Gesellschaft für Rechtsgeschichte and a visiting researcher at Duke University, Goldsmiths (University of London); between 2006 and 2008 he was Eminent Research Fellow at the Centre for Cultural Research (University of Western Sydney). He is currently Associate Professor of Political Theory in the Department of Politics, Institutions, and History at the University of Bologna.

WALTER D. MIGNOLO is the William H. Wannamaker Professor of Literature at Duke University. His recent books include *The Darker Side of Western Modernity: Global Futures, Decolonial Options; The Idea of Latin America; Capitalismo y geopolítica del conocimiento: El eurocentrismo y la filosofía de la liberación en el debate intelectual contemporanáneo; and Local Histories/Global Designs: Coloniality, Subaltern Knowledges and Border Thinking*.

BENJAMIN NOYS is Reader in English at the University of Chichester. His research interests range over contemporary theory, aesthetics, psychoanalysis, film, literature, and cultural politics. His publications include *The Persistence of the Negative: A Critique of Contemporary Theory* (2010), and he is the editor of the recent volume *Communization and Its Discontents* (2011).

JOHN PICKLES is Phillips Distinguished Professor of International Studies in the Department of Geography at the University of North Carolina, Chapel Hill. An economic geographer trained in political economy and development studies, cultural and social theory, and continental philosophy, he currently focuses his research on European economic and social spaces, particularly postsocialist transformations in central Europe and Euro-Med Neighborhood Policies. His publications include *A History of Spaces: Cartographic Reason, Mapping, and the Geo-coded World* (2005), *Globalization and Regionalization in Post-Socialist Economies: The Common*

Economic Spaces of Europe (2009), and *State and Society in Post-Socialist and Post-Soviet Economies* (2009).

ALVARO REYES is Assistant Professor in the Department of Geography at the University of North Carolina, Chapel Hill. His research focuses on localist politics and black radicalism. He was recently the Special Issue Editor of "Autonomy and Emancipation in Latin America," *South Atlantic Quarterly* (Winter 2012).

CATHERINE E. WALSH is Senior Professor and Director of Latin-American Cultural Studies at the Universidad Andina Simón Bolívar in Quito, Ecuador. Her publications include *Coloniality at Large: Latin America and the Postcolonial Debate* (2008), and *Interculturalidad, Estado, Sociedad: Luchas (de)coloniales de nuestra época* (2009).

GARETH WILLIAMS is Professor of Spanish at the University of Michigan. His research examines Latin American cultural/subaltern studies; populism, cultural hybridity, and consumption. His publications include *The Other Side of the Popular: Neoliberalism and Subalternity in Latin America* (2002), and "The Mexican Exception and the 'Other Campaign,'" special issue, *South Atlantic Quarterly* (2007).

ZAC ZIMMER is Assistant Professor of Foreign Languages and Literature at Virginia Polytechnic Institute and State University, specializing in twentieth-century and contemporary Latin American literature. He is currently preparing a book manuscript titled *Utopia and Commons: Enclosure and Blank Slate in the Americas.*

Note: page numbers followed by "n" refer to endnotes.

hostility to, 183; post-Hegelian insurrectional anarchism, 179–82; vitalism of, 178; workerism as anti-Hegelian, 5

hegemony: Laclau and Mouffe's theory of, 164–70; nation-state and concept of, 163–64

Heidegger, Martin, 172n6

heteronormativity and humanity-nature divide, 115n28

Hobbes, Thomas: *bellum omnium contra omnes*, 36; on Commonwealth, 161, 165; *homo homini lupus*, 32; *Leviathan*, 38; on multitude, 33, 52; Negri on Spinozism and, 34, 35; state of nature, 52–53, 120

Hochschild, Arlie, 201n16

Hoelzl, Michael, 171n171

Holland, Eugene, 198

homo ferus, 125–26

Honig, Bonnie, 224

Hsueh, Vicki, 154n33

hunter-gatherer model and Locke, 144–46

identity: insurrectionalism and, 187; Mariátegui's Incan utopia and problem of, 138, 147, 151–52; tattoos and, 213n25; work and, 209–10

Illich, Ivan, 77, 82, 90

immigrant figure, 224

improvement and enclosure, 142–43, 145

Incas, 146, 147–52

indigenous movements, Andean. *See* Abya-Yalean insurgencies

indigenous perspectivism and savage anthropology, 31–32

indigenous sovereignty: antinomies of empire and, 132–34; background, 119–22; colonialism as commons and antisovereigntism, 128–32; New World *nomos* and, 122–24; settler sovereignty and animalization of the human, 124–28

insurrectional anarchism. *See* savage ontology of life, vitalism, and insurrectional anarchism

interculturality and plurinationalism, 99, 100

International Commission of Integral Agrarian Reform, 75

internationalism and universalism, 216–17, 223

international law. *See* jus publicum Europaeum

Invisible Committee, 184

Italian workerist movement (*operaismo*), 5–7

Jameson, Fredric, 2, 178, 193

Jappe, Anselm, 185

Juntas de Buen Gobierno (Councils of Good Government), 58–59, 61–62, 85

jus publicum Europaeum: decontainment and, 171; *Großräume* and, 123; homogeneous territory of, 55; institutional left and afterlife of, 47; second *nomos* and, ix, 160; sovereignty and, 50–53. *See also nomos*

justa causa (just cause), 141

justus hostis (just enemy), 141

Kant, Immanuel, 4–5, 132, 139–40

katechon: Hobbesian, 165; Laclau and Mouffe's theory of hegemony and, 165–69; Paulist, 161, 171n171; ritualistic-linguistic, 38–39

Keynes, John Maynard, 72

Khatibi, Abdelkebir, 102

Klausen, Jimmy, 154n35

Klein, Naomi, 87–88

knowledge production, new centers of, 77

Kohr, Leopold, 71–72

Kouvelakis, Stathis, 171n171

Koyre, Alexandre, 140

labor, digitalization of, 206–7

Lacan, Jacques, 133, 171n171

Laclau, Ernesto, 161

La Mettrie, Julien Offray de, 206

Lander, Edgardo, 98

land reform, 60, 75, 150

latifundos, 60, 149, 151

Latin American grassroots autonomous experiences: commons, reclaiming, 85–86; eating and food production, 73–75; exchanging, 79; healing and health-care systems, 77–78; learning and education systems, 75–77; living well and good life, 79–82; power vs. no power, 83–85; radical pluralism, 82; reconstitution, 86–91; scale and proportion, 71–72; settling, 78–79; verbs, recovery of, 73. *See also specific movements and places*